BOOK CLUBS

ELIZABETH LONG

BOOK CLUBS

Women and the Uses of Reading
in Everyday Life

THE UNIVERSITY OF CHICAGO PRESS
CHICAGO AND LONDON

Elizabeth Long is associate professor of sociology
at Rice University. She is the author of
The American Dream and the Popular Novel
and the editor of *From Sociology to Cultural Studies.*

The University of Chicago Press, Chicago 60637
The University of Chicago Press, Ltd., London
© 2003 by The University of Chicago
All rights reserved. Published 2003
Printed in the United States of America

12 11 10 09 08 07 06 05 04 03   5 4 3 2 1

ISBN (cloth): 0-226-49261-3
ISBN (paper): 0-226-49262-1

Library of Congress Cataloging-in-Publication Data

Long, Elizabeth, 1944–
    Book clubs : women and the uses of reading in everyday life /
Elizabeth Long.
        p.   cm.
    Includes bibliographical references and index.
    ISBN 0-226-49261-3 (cloth : alk. paper) — ISBN 0-226-49262-1 (pbk :
alk. paper)
        1. Group reading—United States—Case studies.   2. Book clubs—United
States—Case studies.   3. Women—Books and reading—United States—Case
studies.   4. Reading—Social aspects—United States—Case studies.
    I. Title.
    LC6651 .L65   2003
    028′.9′0973—dc21
                                                                    2002153742

FOR

BILL AND DAVID

AND

IN MEMORY OF JANE GREGORY

CONTENTS

PREFACE

When I first began researching book clubs, mention of the topic caused an almost dichotomous reaction. Many women responded with enthusiasm, launching into spirited discussions of their book clubs past or present. Some men responded almost the same way, telling stories about female relatives to whom a book group had meant a great deal. One of the most memorable was the story a colleague at Rice told me about his grandmother. Her mother had been an Irish immigrant who worked as a servant on a large estate in Tuxedo Park, New York. The estate owners took a paternalistic interest in their servants' children and sent the promising ones to college. This particular daughter was very bright, so they packed her off to the State Teacher's College in Albany (now SUNY Albany) to train as a teacher. Later, she married a boy who had grown up under similar circumstances on another estate in Tuxedo Park and who had been similarly sponsored at Yale. He took a job with Bethlehem Steel and rose through the ranks, eventually becoming an executive in Bethlehem, Pennsylvania. My colleague's grandmother, who had taught for a while, soon left her profession to raise a family and participate in social and volunteer activities to advance her husband's career. But being part of the country club set did not mean a great deal to her. According to my colleague, "She lived for the monthly meeting of her AAUW book club. It was her only contact with the life of the mind, and the high point of her month."

This kind of language crops up surprisingly often when women talk about book clubs. Salvation, life raft, saving grace: "You will never know what a difference it made in my life." How extraordinary that a group of women discussing books could mean so much to the participants. Especially when these same book clubs were so invisible to scholars.

It was as if women's reading groups occupied a zone of cultural invisibility. They were not of interest to literature departments, whose major focus is books and authors, not readers. They were not of interest to sociologists or political scientists because women's reading groups do not pursue activities with any obvious relationship to formal political processes. When I began the research, even the activist nineteenth-century groups had aroused no scholarly notice because at that time it was not apparent how much women's organizations had contributed to Progressive reformism (see chap. 2). Scholars of popular culture had not found reading groups interesting because the groups read canonized fiction and did not transform their cultural consumption into a "resistant" subcultural style. Communications departments had not researched them because reading groups were not engaged with the mass media. Leftists were uninterested because book group participants were middle class and clearly not part of proletarian or potentially revolutionary culture.

Reading groups had slipped through disciplinary cracks to find themselves in a scholarly no-man's-land. In itself, this was enormously interesting. The fact that such groups were *not* interesting to academics became part of what I needed to understand, part of their fascination.

In particular, reading groups seemed not interesting to men both inside and outside of the university, unless like my colleague they had a female relative who had been in one or they had participated themselves. Women could often understand that a gathering of women to discuss books and their lives might hold some intrinsic value. I take this, in part, as a legacy of the consciousness-raising movement. It is also symptomatic of the enduring fact that the sex-gender system often appears to women—and more often to men—as something just personal rather than a structural issue of general social concern. Amazingly, it can still be said that "the personal is political" for much of what women find problematic about their lives: how we should feel, what we should look like, how much we should care for others, how we should manage the division of labor at home, what we should be as parents, why our careers can be difficult to manage alongside families, how to find an effective voice in public.

I often felt that male academic colleagues could not understand why an intelligent person might consider women's reading groups a serious topic for investigation.[1] This so irritated me that I researched the history of reading groups in response. I reasoned that men found the topic unworthy because they could not understand how it related to more legitimate (read important) issues such as modernization, inequality, or social change. There was no clear link between these small culture groups and large-scale social phenomena. As a rejoinder to that dismissal, I made the case that reading groups were important because they were more closely related to what the academy recognizes as things of importance than scholars had previously thought. This both deepened the project and made me aware of limitations in the traditional academic hierarchy of values. In this sense, to take reading groups seriously had the potential, like much feminist scholarship, to destabilize received notions in social thought.

This issue of Not a Good Topic continued to plague me throughout the writing of the book. I remember a photography class whose professor lectured us on how to make a wonderful photograph. According to him, this wasn't just an issue of proper technique; one must find a compelling subject. Later, one of the students proposed photographing people in lines for his class project. Our professor was dubious: Lines . . . hmm . . . well, maybe you can find something there, but on the whole, Not an Interesting Subject. In fact, the portfolio was fascinating. Frank had recognized that lines are a fundamental characteristic of life in a bureaucratic society, though differentially experienced by rich and poor, young and old, minorities and whites. His photographs took waiting in lines seriously as a form of social behavior; his images were funny, sad, gritty, satiric, lyrical—a slice of the human condition in the late twentieth century.

I hope this topic also serves to bring to light a significant realm of experience. One of the hallmarks of life as we know it is that people construct themselves with materials culled from a vast cultural storehouse. These cultural materials come to us as commodities to be sure, but they are what we use (and are used by) as we imagine our futures and create our lives. Reading groups are part of this process for the women and the smaller numbers of men who participate in them. They are examples of one of the defining ways we make ourselves today.

Researching Houston's Reading Groups

This volume is an exploratory case study of white women's reading groups in Houston, Texas. Although it draws on historical sources to describe Houston's nineteenth-century book clubs, it is based mainly on fieldwork, interviews, and a small survey conducted among contemporary groups. The social world of these reading groups is described in chapter 4. In this preface, I describe methodological choices made during the research, because they determined the book's scope and approach.

At the beginning of the research, I estimated there would be approximately a dozen reading groups in Houston, a figure slightly higher than an estimate of six to eight made by the book editor of the *Houston Chronicle* when, in the late 1980s, we discussed a story about reading groups. As I mobilized informal networks of acquaintances to discover other groups and then began to lecture about the project at Rice and in the community, it became obvious that the phenomenon of reading groups was both dramatically more widespread than expected and of very positive importance to many participants. I found myself driving hundreds of miles around the city to wealthy mansions, transient-feeling apartments, library meeting rooms, and anonymous condominium developments, sharing refreshments from gourmet brunches to store-bought cookies, and sitting in on groups discussing an equally wide range of books. Lectures in the community yielded growing piles of scribbled leads to more groups, while a small notice in the

Rice alumni magazine *The Sallyport* brought responses from thirty alumni across the country—responses that often included enthusiastic descriptions of their reading groups and literary choices.

At that point, I decided to pursue the research on a case study basis, focusing on Houston and Harris County. The grounds for this decision were several. First, as a sociologist, I was eager to determine where this cultural form was located socially: who belonged, and from which social strata and subgroups did members come? Given the surprising number of reading groups, taking a nationwide census of them was clearly impractical, but by concentrating on one large city I might locate through systematic efforts all the reading groups in the city, including those not discoverable by informal networking. This procedure could be invaluable for discovering social and literary variability that might otherwise elude the researcher.

Systematic outreach seemed especially important because most reading groups are informal gatherings of acquaintances, making them a grassroots phenomenon that, despite its respectability, is as thoroughly underground as are many socially stigmatized or even illegal activities. Meeting for the most part in people's homes, such groups are documented only by lists of phone numbers and addresses for other members, and although some groups do keep lists of titles they have read, these too very rarely circulate beyond the membership. Only book discussion groups that have links to more formal institutions—such as the Rice Faculty Women's Book Club, the University of Texas Alumni Book Club, or the reading group advertised in *Leisure Learning Unlimited*—leave traces in the public record, and those are in the minority among reading groups. As a consequence, reading groups are almost inaccessible to the outside investigator, except through informal networks or through voluntary responses to more formal methods of outreach. This means that demographic knowledge—about how many reading groups there are even in this one city and who, exactly, comprise their population—is unavoidably more shaky than it is for more formally organized and more public associations.

Especially under such conditions, the breadth of knowledge that might come from researching reading groups I could easily discover around the United States would be compromised by the fact that these might only be the kinds of groups someone like myself could easily find. On the other hand, a case study of one city promised to yield more accuracy or depth, in the form of an accounting of types of groups that might only be discoverable through intensive and systematic effort. In a sense, this is the promise of methodological care in social research: to produce knowledge that can go beyond the positional or ideational limitations of the researcher.

Plans for systematic outreach into the world of Houston's reading groups were furthered by my acquaintance with a reading group member who became interested in the project. JG had free time to provide volunteer help. She was also considering applying to graduate school and was intrigued at the prospect of conducting social research. Becoming an unpaid research coordinator during much of 1990 and 1991, she not only helped conceptualize, organize, and record the investigation but also gathered together a support team of other volunteers, mainly from her reading group.

This cadre of researchers sent out two massive mailings of flyers and letters to schools and other institutions of learning, libraries, bookstores, and religious organizations as well as to women's groups, writers' groups, businesses, unions, and numerous other community, professional, and service organizations. A Rice student followed up the mailings with telephone calls. Using responses to these mailings and earlier leads gleaned informally, we attempted to complete short interviews on all old and new contacts, carefully checking for overlaps and groups that had disbanded.

The Team, as we called ourselves, worked with tremendous enthusiasm and dedication. We consciously mobilized women's volunteer culture for the effort: aside from three students, all the workers were reading group members with long histories of leadership in civic volunteer work and (during the actual mailings) whatever friends or relatives they could persuade to assist with the work. Throughout this effort, my assistants on the project were demonstrating, often with pointed amusement about my own organizational shortcomings, the kind of intelligence and organizational effectiveness that had enabled their predecessors in the nineteenth-century women's club movement to make such a mark on community life not just in Houston but across the country.

In all, we found 121 book discussion groups in Houston and Harris County. We classified them on two major dimensions. The first was whether or not they were affiliated with more formal organizations (our headings for affiliated groups were AAUW, Education, Great Books, Religious, Sororities, Foreign Culture, and Miscellaneous). Among the unaffiliated groups, we also indicated those that had special interests and those that read only genre books.

We also classified the groups by gender. A total of 77 of all the reading groups (or 64 percent) were women's groups, 4 (or 3 percent) were men's groups, and 40 (or 33 percent) included both men and women. These figures, in fact, were very similar to the percentages by gender that I had gleaned in my much less systematic efforts at outreach.

Here was a research conundrum. Systematic research had confirmed the more qualitative research efforts. Both this census and a small-scale survey administered to a dozen groups leant credence to what I had already learned about book groups through informal networking or convenience sampling, as well as through the ethnographic or (as it is usually called in sociology) field research I had been conducting since I first brought a tape recorder to a reading group. On the one hand, this was reassuring.

On the other hand, even these careful efforts did not yield an exhaustive accounting of reading groups in Houston. An anecdote: late in the summer of 1991, when data from our outreach were gradually filling a drawer of files and had already generated an elegantly compartmentalized master list in a three-ring binder, I went to the basement of Rice's Fondren Library to request some books from Interlibrary Loan. In chitchat about the books and the broader project, it emerged that the librarian herself belonged to not just one but two reading groups—and that we did not have a record of either one of them. Stunned, I asked whether she had received any of my mailings to the Rice faculty and staff. Well, yes. . . . And she had thought it was all very interesting, but she had never called us back.

Clearly, voluntary self-reporting meant that we missed any groups that did not come forward to be questioned. So, unless some called in with fabricated groups, we had an undercount of Houston's reading groups, and by what amount it was hard to estimate. Similarly, it was impossible to know what kinds of groups did *not* call in and whether they differed from the groups that did in any significant way aside from the fact that they did not call.

Given the fact that the population of reading groups proved impossible to count reliably, I focused my energies on the interviews and observations of groups that had always been at the heart of the project. In defense of this qualitative approach, I argue, first, that the study features several overlapping methods, each of which yielded information that generally accorded with information collected by other means. Second, the information I acquired about Houston's reading groups looks very much like that garnered by other people, whether journalists or book group experts, who are working the world of reading groups across the United States. Third, my central questions are about why people choose to participate in this activity and what happens to them in their engagement with literature and with each other. Such questions are most fully responsive to open-ended interviewing and direct observation.

At around the same time, I made two other significant research decisions. The first was to concentrate the research on women's reading groups. The numbers alone indicated that this was a cultural forum largely populated by women. Over half the groups in Houston were women's groups, and only a very small percentage were for men only. What I was learning about the history of American book groups also suggested that women's reading groups had a genealogy stretching back over a hundred years, so historically as well as numerically this was an important forum for women. By concentrating only on women's reading groups, the research lost a comparative edge; it could not speak to the differences between mixed-sex or all-male reading groups and those composed only of women. I have tried to compensate for this lack by including examples from such groups where they are relevant. On the other hand, concentrating on women's reading groups focused the research on the cultural constituency most clearly attached to book discussion groups. This seemed particularly compelling because both nineteenth-century and contemporary women's reading groups have used their groups to consider issues of identity and the nature of womanhood. If not precisely "woman's culture," women's reading groups seemed an especially apt venue for learning how literature contributed to the negotiation of women's identity and why this kind of deliberative space might be especially important to women.

Second, after preliminary investigations into the distinguished history of African American book clubs, in the end I focused the research on white women's reading groups. Again, there were several reasons for this. First, there were practical difficulties finding African American or Latina groups. Informal networking among colleagues of color did not yield the kinds of leads I was able to generate among the white community. The Amistad Bookstore, which people said might be a good contact point for black women's reading groups, closed just as I was beginning the research.[2] I interviewed the founder of the one African American group that responded to outreach in 1991 and ended up discussing with her book group the life and times of Lulu B. White, a civil rights activist whose Chat-an-Hour Literary and Social Club was active in Houston's black community in the 1950s and 1960s.[3] The fact that they did not ask me to sit in on the group as an observer but invited me as an outside lecturer raised another set of issues.

The color line was still pervasive in Houston's reading groups, mainly because the informal networks from which groups arise were still not racially integrated. My racial similarity to members of white reading groups made my presence relatively invisible to them, which meant that over time observation had less distorting effects on the "natural" interaction of the groups I sat in on. This was not the case with the African American group I attended, where my racial difference from group members was visible. As a result, my social characteristics as a field researcher were responsible for my playing a very different role in black and white groups. This had political, epistemological, and methodological ramifications.

I did not want to engage in research of the kind that had marked early stages of feminist inquiry in history, sociology, literature, or theory, when black women's experiences were assimilated to the white "norm." In these fields, research has proceeded by recognizing the depth of historical and cultural differences between black and white women, and by developing an understanding that different categories of analysis may be necessary for comprehending these groups in their particularity. I did not want to make an inadequate or tokenist comparison between black and white women's reading groups, or appropriate the experiences of African American women within categories of knowledge that worked for white women. As I continued the research, I gradually became aware that my racial difference from members of black women's groups encouraged the posing of different research questions than were posed in my work with white women's groups. As others have shown, these questions led in many different directions, and in the end I decided that it was beyond the scope of this research to deal with the political, epistemological, and methodological complexities introduced by the issue of racial difference. As is the case with men's and coed groups, I include references to black women's reading groups where appropriate. I also attend to exclusion and the cultural construction of race within white groups, attempting to bring a critical eye to the boundary work (Lamont 1992, 2) that marks racial cleavages among groups of women readers. Much such work remains to be done, although other scholars (Gere and Robbins 1996; Gere 1997; McHenry 1999, 2002) have already made important contributions.

Organization of the Book

In the chapters that follow, I use the case study of women's reading groups in Houston to argue that what has traditionally been thought of as a passive and receptive activity is in fact integral to the constitution of both social identity and the sociocultural order. Understanding the practices of reading groups contributes to an understanding of how people create meaning and to ensuing orientations toward action from the meanings and experiential frames with which their culture surrounds them.

To perceive people's uses of culture in this fashion requires questioning a series of oppositions that we have taken for granted as ordering relations between the categories of the personal and the social—or public and private. Traditionally, academics have treated large-scale social processes, such as globalization or modernization, as solidified, naturalized, and public. Such processes are usually associated with the realms of technology, economics, or the polity, and therefore with men. Most scholars also conceptualize them as determining other "softer" or cultural activities that are characterized as private or merely subjective, and generally the province of women. If we can begin to understand cultural practices, such as reading group formation and the activities that ensue, as creative behaviors that bring people into new relationships with themselves, each other, and the environing social world, then perhaps we will achieve a more balanced appraisal of the relationship between individuals and their society.

Clearing the ground for this reappraisal, I argue in chapter 1 for the need to understand reading as a social practice. The argument begins with an analysis of the ideology of the solitary reader as expressed in visual representations of reading in European and American art. Claiming that this understanding of reading has obscured its social dimensions, I discuss the social infrastructure of literary production, distribution, and evaluation as well as the social contexts in which reading is taught and the habit is nurtured. Next, I examine the ways in which American popular culture marks leisure reading by both class and gender, showing its social valence. Finally, I discuss how the sociological analysis of associations and culture and some recent conceptualizations of reading can be extended to better understand the nature of reading in society.

In chapter 2, I introduce a historical dimension by first briefly recounting the importance of small groups of readers for the transformations of modernity in Europe. I devote most of the chapter to an analysis of the white women's reading group movement that followed the Civil War, detailing the organizational, ideological, literary, and "sisterly" practices that gave these women the skills and self-confidence to re-imagine themselves both individually and collectively. I also describe how this literary movement became a broader movement for social reform, a development that the women involved attributed directly to the influence of the books they studied as well as to the ways that self-organization acquainted them with the skills of the public sphere. Although noting the club movement's exclusivity along class and racial lines, the discussion highlights their accomplishments. The major contribution of this account is its focus on Texas, and Houston in particular. To illustrate how the national movement played out in the frontier state of Texas, I describe the Houston Ladies Reading Club as it studied American literature, hosted suffragists on a national tour, and persuaded the Houston city council to help finance a library.

In the third chapter I contextualize and re-introduce Houston's contemporary reading groups by tracing first the similarities and then the differences between them and their precursors. Salient differences include a college-educated membership as well as a shift toward much more informal organization and discussion, and the disappearance of the nineteenth-century sense of collective mission. I argue that these differences can be attributed primarily to immense changes in middle-class women's lives and secondarily to changes in the literary field.

Contemporary white women's reading groups, the heart of the book, provide the focus for the next three chapters. In chapter 4 I discuss the social dimension of book groups, including a brief discussion of the setting in Houston and some of the social dimensions along which groups vary. I analyze how groups begin and why people decide to found or join them, which points up some of the ways that women feel at odds with present-day social arrangements. This chapter also covers leadership, rules, and differences in selection practices.

In chapter 5 I take up issues of group identity, including differences in group tone and the different underlying literary and social assumptions that inform each group. This chapter also describes members who feel isolated or marginalized because they do not "fit" the parameters of the group's identity, including those who leave groups. Book selection as it relates to how the group understands itself and its relationship to literary authority is an important aspect of group identity. I analyze such processes, which often involve complex negotiations with the literary universe and other group members.

In chapter 6, the analysis centers on the groups' literary discussion and related conversation. In this chapter I argue that if books become the language through which people narrate their own experience and understand the experience of other group members, conversation can show considerable insight and innovative understanding. Empathy and complex patterns of identification seem crucial to this process, which appears to use literature, in Kenneth Burke's phrase, as "equipment for living." For instance, a nuanced identification can lead group members to personal insights and encourage groups toward critical appraisals of the social order. In this chapter I also detail conversations that enabled women to work through troublesome disjunctures between social strictures and their own experiences or ideals. In sections on the classics and on race, I argue that book discussions can—but do not always—lead group members toward creative and expansive appraisals of social "others" as well as of their own historical situation and life choices.

In chapter 7 I use the interviews as well as documentary research to provide a preliminary description and analysis of three developments that have affected present-day communal reading practices. These are the rise of chain bookstores and in-house discussion groups, Oprah Winfrey's Book Club, and on-line book discussion groups. All have engaged women in larger numbers than men. All also point toward possible changes in the literary hierarchy of value as well as in the relationship between readers and various incarnations of literary authority. Yet they show how tenacious the practice of gathering to discuss books remains, despite important changes in the universe of communication.

In the conclusion, I revisit some of my initial theoretical concerns with the meaning of reading, culture and the constitution of subjectivity, and women's relationship to the public sphere.

ACKNOWLEDGMENTS

It is a pleasure, indeed a celebration, to acknowledge the institutions and people who have supported me in the long and often arduous journey to the completion of this book.

I received generous support from three institutions. The National Endowment for the Humanities awarded me a Fellowship for College Teachers in 1989–90, which gave me a year of freedom from academic duties. I am very grateful for their support. At Rice University, the Center for Cultural Studies made it possible for me to begin this work as a Cultural Studies Fellow and provided an audience for its first presentation. The Feminist Reading Group provided me with other opportunities to discuss the ongoing research, and several of its members gave generously of their time and expertise at every stage. Members of Rice's sociology department provided a collegial, encouraging atmosphere and extremely helpful readings. In the spring of 1986, I spent a sabbatical at the American studies department at the University of Pennsylvania. I especially thank Janice Radway, Drew Faust, and Charles and Jessica Rosenberg for their warm and intellectually stimulating hospitality.

I have also relied on the support of informal networks and communities. I am particularly grateful to "The Team" of reading group volunteers that undertook major outreach efforts to locate and interview Houston reading groups in 1990–91. (I have withheld their names to protect their privacy.) Warm thanks also to Anne Klein, Gudrun Klein, Kathryn Milun, Sharon Traweek, and Angela Valenzuela of the Women's Reading/Writing Group at Rice University. Their reading of my writing provided very special feedback.

As I begin to thank individuals, I would again like to celebrate the warm intellectual and personal relationships that have marked the writing of the book. And if I have inadvertently omitted any names, please forgive my memory: it has been a long project. First, I mention those who read the manuscript for the University of Chicago Press: Michele Lamont at an early stage, and later, Janice Radway and Andrea Press. They all made themselves known to me, and both Radway and Press helped me extensively with revisions. Lynne Huffer, Bronwen Lichtenstein, Helena Michie, and Carol Quillen also critiqued the manuscript in its entirety and fielded sometimes demanding questions about their invariably perspicacious comments. Others critiqued parts of the manuscript: Jon Cruz, Sharon Farmer, Michele Farrell, Michael Fischer, Sharon Hayes, Dorinne Kondo, George Lipsitz, Susan Lurie, George Marcus, Chandra Mukerji, Michael Schudson, Barbara Sicherman, Katherine Stone, and Diana Strassmann. Many of these colleagues also helped me over rough spots and blockages in the writing process.

Everyone at Rice University is fortunate to work with wonderful students. I have been fortunate also in having their help on this project. I mention in particular Kelly Bolen, Amy Chang, Zeynep Iber, Helen Kim, Rachel Orkand, and Uma Thirugnanasampanthan. Julie Roach and Cynthia Guadalupe deserve special thanks. Julie dedicated most of a semester after graduation and before medical school to providing unpaid research assistance to me and another professor. Her research was invaluable, her supportive companionship even more so. In the final stages of the project Cynthia Guadalupe, my son's tutor during the school year, dedicated her time to final manuscript preparation and extended child care. Her help was crucial and generously given.

I also thank a very supportive group of friends and family members—you know who you are!—for helping with the personal side of this project and, like my academic friends and colleagues, for making the journey itself worthwhile. Also a word of appreciation for our wonderful cat Fred. The book is dedicated to my husband Bill and my son David, who have filled my life with love and adventure.

Finally, I express great gratitude for all of the reading group participants who allowed me to sit in on their groups and to survey and interview them—and even to participate in some of their discussions; they fed me both literally and figuratively. Knowing these people has not only enriched my life but made this book a reality. My Book Group, especially, accepted me for years as a member who was also a researcher; they showed great generosity of spirit and an amazing capacity to forgive the presence of a bulky recording apparatus. The dedication of this book also remembers a very special reading group friend.

This book is my creation in one sense, but in another very important way it belongs to everyone who helped bring it into being.

ONE

On the Social Nature of Reading

In her provocative book *Academic Writing as Social Practice* (1987), Linda Brodkey explores and assails what she calls the image of "the writer who writes alone." According to Brodkey,

> When we picture writing we see a solitary writer. We may see the writer alone in a cold garret, working into the small hours of the morning by thin candlelight. The shutters are closed. Or perhaps we see the writer alone in a well-appointed study, seated at a desk, fingers poised over the keys of a typewriter (or microcomputer). The drapes are drawn. . . . Whether the scene of writing is poetic or prosaic . . . it is the same picture—the writer writes alone. . . . And because such a picture prevails as the reigning trope for writing, we find it difficult to remember that the solitary scribbler tells only one story about writers and writing. In this story, writers are sentenced to solitary confinement, imprisoned by language. . . . We know this story well, for there are moments when the solitude overwhelms us, when we do not understand the words we are writing, and when we cannot recall our reasons for doing so. (54–55)

Brodkey claims that the image of the solitary scribbler is "taken from the album of modernism" and that it presents a dominant and partial vision of writing by representing only one moment of the writing process—the timeless freeze-frame of isolation and alienation. This "official story," according to her account, is replicated both in formalist literary criticism and in academic studies of "composition" as a purely individualistic and cognitive affair (1987, 57–70). I think modernism provides just one version of the writer who writes alone, a version that puts the spin of romantically alienated genius on a far older story (visually represented by some of the early images of solitary writers assembled here). Nonetheless, I agree with Brodkey that the image of the solitary scribbler interferes with an accurate understanding of the writing process because it overprivileges the moment of isolation. It also suppresses the social aspects of writing: reading other writers, discussing ideas with other people, and writing to and for others in a language whose very grammar, genres, and figures of speech encode collectivity. As Raymond Williams puts it in "The Tenses of the Imagination" (1983, 261): "I am in fact physically alone when I am writing, and I do not believe, taking it all in all, that my work has been less individual, in that defining and valuing sense, than that of others. Yet whenever I write I am aware of a society and of a language which I know are vastly larger than myself: not simply 'out there,' in a world of others, but here, in what I am engaged in doing: composing and relating."

The Solitary Reader

A similarly powerful and similarly partial picture of the solitary reader governs our understanding of reading. This is not surprising, given that before the advent of books printed in the vernacular most readers were also writers. In reader response theory, this isolated individual appears in several guises: the phenomenological reader of Roman Ingarden and the early Wolfgang Iser, the subjective or psychoanalytic reader of David Bleich and Norman Holland, the "ideal reader" spun out of academic readings of texts, and even, to a certain degree, the "resisting reader" who is a woman, although there at least the individual reader brings a social identity to her encounter with the text (Ingarden 1973; Iser 1978, 1989, 1993; Bleich 1975, 1978, 1988; Holland 1968, 1975, 1991; Fetterley 1978).[1]

The solitary reader also has a complex visual history, and I summon it up briefly as indicative of some of the lenses through which we have envisioned reading as a cultural practice—lenses that have not always clarified the object of inquiry. The first set of images represents a tradition that begins in early Christian art and continues through the nineteenth century. Here the reader, like the writer who writes alone, is withdrawn from the world and suspended from human community and human action (fig. 1). He is a scholar, surrounded by the symbolic attributes of serious research. Or he considers the book and his own mortality—whose grim aspect can be transcended through the word, which links each reader to another man in a genealogy of immortal ideas and, in its most serious and holy aspect, harks back to that original author, the transcendent patriarchal God who was, in the beginning, the word. These images represent the sacred aura of reading in a period of severely limited and, among Christians, mostly clerical literacy. The boundaries between reading and writing are blurred because both are privileges of scriptural authority. Yet such authority exacts its price: the scholar-anchorite is allowed at most a distant view of the sensuous delights of earthly intercourse.

These images not only oppose reading to sociability and the *vita activa*

1. Antonello Da Messina, *Saint Jerome in His Study*. Reproduced by courtesy of the Trustees, The National Gallery, London.

but also privilege a certain kind of reading: erudite, analytic, and as morally and intellectually weighty as the tomes that inhabit these cells and are inhabited by their solitary readers (figs. 2 and 3). This is the visual representation of the serious reader. Although his lineage has been severely diluted by secularization, democracy, and mass education, most academics and all modern readers who aspire to "the serious" are his heirs.[2]

2. Johannes Vermeer, *The Astronomer.* The Louvre. Copyright Photo R.M.N.

The initial perturbations of these vast social transformations—which brought literacy to new constituencies of class and gender—were recorded in late medieval images of the Virgin Mary and the Magdalene reading (fig. 4). These illustrations began to appear in the psalters and books of hours destined for aristocratic and often female readers.

As the secular and private sphere of leisure expanded, images of women reading proliferated. Seventeenth-century Holland, whose commercial expansion fueled an artistic revolution that elevated the bourgeois interior as subject and "domestic realism" as genre, was a particularly fruitful site for early modern representations of the figure of the female reader. In such pictures, the solitary woman reads, encompassed by an interior that is no less timeless than the scholarly study but profoundly domestic. Her reading is inscribed within the family circle, and, as in *The Letter* by Gabriel Metsu (fig. 5), her "serious" reading is interruptible.

Usually, in fact, she reads a note, so her reading is ephemeral and circumscribed by the ties of personal relationships. If the scholar transcends the world, she is firmly positioned in the mundane. In Jan Vermeer's painting *Woman in Blue Reading a Letter* (fig. 6), the map of the world pulls us toward the distant horizon of Dutch mercantile adventures, while the woman preserves the heart of the home. But the letter seems to mediate between the two, bringing the outer world inside and enabling the woman to go beyond a purely interior life through her reading.

By the eighteenth and nineteenth centuries, many images of women reading alone complement those of the serious male reader/writer. Domesticity continues to frame these readers, but now it is less serene than sensuous, frilled, and frivolous. The pictures celebrate the sheen and softness of the feminine sphere; they are as decorative as are the women. The books—grown tiny now—serve as the cultural decorations of a literacy at once leisurely and trivialized (fig. 7). The women themselves are less contempla-

3. Edgar Degas, *Edmond Duranty in His Study.* Collection of Mr. and Mrs. Julian Eisenstein

4. Vittore Carpaccio, *The Virgin Reading*. National Gallery of Art, Washington. Samuel H. Kress Collection

tive than languorous, narcissistically absorbed in imaginative literature that helps them while away the hours (fig. 8).

Although upper class or solidly bourgeois, these readers provide the pictorial ancestry for our modern conceptualizations of escapist readers of mass-market genres (Radway 1984).[3] Such women read not to write but to passively consume—but consume what? Perhaps the novels whose moral effects were so debated 150 years ago. When these women do write, it is not books but letters, as is so delicately portrayed in *The Letter* by Mary Cassatt. Thus the solitary woman reader/writer finds her ideological place in a binary opposition that associates authoritative men with the production and dissemination of serious or high culture and even privileged women with the consumption and "creation" of ephemeral or questionable culture.[4]

Important distortions of either pole of real literacy are wrought by this gendered opposition of images of reading. The solitary male represents a simplistic image of even high cultural literacy, whereas the image of the self-absorbed female devalues women even as it trivializes the notion of culture as soft and inconsequential. Moreover, their visual absence shows that the access of certain class and racial groups to representations of reading has been even more circumscribed than their access to literacy itself. But rather than exploring such issues, I concentrate instead on some consequences of construing reading as a fundamentally solitary practice. All involve suppression of the collective or social nature of reading. The latter part of this book focuses in detail on one sociocultural form—the group of readers—that

5. Gabriel Metsu, *The Letter.* Courtesy of The Putnam Foundation, Timkin Museum of Art, San Diego, California

6. Johannes Vermeer, *Woman in Blue Reading a Letter.* Courtesy of the Rijksmuseum, Amsterdam

has been rendered all but invisible to academic analysis. In this chapter I point out some other theoretical and empirical repressions that are accomplished by the cultural hegemony of the solitary reader.

Like Brodkey in her discussion of writing, I do not mean to deny the immensely private qualities of reading—only the idea that they are the whole story. Understanding reading as a purely solitary activity neglects two crucial aspects of its social nature. The first is the social infrastructure that is necessary, at the most concrete level, for enabling literacy and encouraging the habit of reading.

By the "social infrastructure of reading" I mean two things. Foundationally, reading must be taught, and socialization into reading always takes place within specific social relationships. Early images show mothers teaching children how to read, which substitutes a relational maternal lineage of literacy for the abstract paternal genealogy of books and ideas that assumes both adulthood and prior reading competence. Familial reading is both a form of cultural capital and one of the most important determinants of adherence to reading in later life.

Classrooms provide a more formal, public context for teaching and learning reading, one that varies immensely depending on who the parties to the relationship are. This partially explains why reading does not attract certain groups of students. As Daniel and Lauren Resnick explain in their essay "Varieties of Literacy," books and reading can be profoundly trans-

7. Jean-Honoré Fragonard, *A Young Girl Reading*. National Gallery of Art, Washington. Gift of Mrs. Mellon Bruce in memory of her father, Andrew W. Mellon

8. Jean-Baptiste-Camille Corot, *The Magdalene Reading.* The Louvre.
Copyright Photo R.M.N.

formed in the school setting: "A test, as in school literature courses, for example, can change the context for even the best of literary texts from plea-
sure-giving literacy to functional literacy" (1989, 188). At its best, this social
relationship can open up new ways of reading (symbols, structure, attention
to intertextuality); at its worst, it can produce "the dismal sacred word"
(White 1993, 122–34) and a sense of thralldom to a deadening educational
process. This thralldom can so alienate poor students that they never feel the
pleasure of the text, and it leads even good students to invent ways, such as
reading ahead of the class, to reclaim the autonomy of their reading from
scholastic authority.

Even beyond formal socialization into reading, the habit of reading
is profoundly social. As mid-twentieth-century American empirical studies
of adult reading show, social isolation depresses readership, and social involvement encourages it. Most readers need the support of talk with other
readers, the participation in a social milieu in which books are "in the air"
(Berelson and Asheim 1949; Ennis 1965; Matthews 1973; McElroy 1968a,
1968b; Yankelovich, Skelly, and White 1978).

Reading thus requires, in the second sense of the term, an infrastructure as social base, in much the same way as modern transportation requires
a physical infrastructure of highways, airports, and fuel supplies. The multi-

volume *History of the Book in America* (Amory and Hall 2000) is a wonderful example of what it means to fully understand the social and technological infrastructure needed to support a country's literary culture.[5] Articles on book distribution and marketing, reading instruction in nineteenth-century schoolrooms, book serialization in newspapers, the growth of the library system, censorship, and copyright laws and intellectual property disputes—or publishing everything from literary, scientific, and technical books to inspirational pamphlets or gift books—make it clear how complex the institutional support for individual reading has come to be.

The hegemonic picture of reading as a solitary activity also suppresses the ways in which reading is socially framed (Goffman 1974, 1959; Gans 1975; Bourdieu 1996a, 1993, 1984; Rose 2001; Lemert and Branaman 1997). By this I mean that groups of people (literary critics, publishers, or English professors, for example) and institutional processes, from standardized testing to censorship, shape reading practices by authoritatively defining what is worth reading and how to read it. This authoritative framing affects what kinds of books are published, reviewed, and kept in circulation in libraries, classrooms, and the marketplace, while legitimating only certain kinds of literary values and certain modes of reading (see Radway 1997).

Academics tend to repress consideration of variety in reading practices because of our assumption that everyone reads (or ought to) as we do professionally, which usually involves a cognitive and analytic approach to texts. Recognizing the importance of the collective processes that determine the availability of books, privilege some styles of reading while dismissing others, and either legitimate or devalue certain books inevitably brings into view both the commercial underside of literature and the scholar's position of authority within the world of reading. Both raise questions about the politics of culture, including the role of the academy itself. This may partially explain resistance to scholarship that discusses issues of literary value in relation to historically contingent social relationships within the academy and questions of power and authority among the various elites and constituencies that make up the literary field.[6]

The ideology of the solitary reader, then, suppresses recognition of the infrastructure of literacy and the social or institutional determinants of what is available to read, what is "worth reading," and how to read it. It has helped to frame our understanding of the cultural world so that the importance—historically and in the present—of groups of readers and how or why they read books has been nearly invisible to scholarship. This lacuna also seems linked to the prevailing analytic distinctions between "culture" and "society" and to the related tendency to seek the sources of social development either in an idealist conception of "great men of ideas" (the writer who writes alone) or in a materialist frame that locates innovation in abstracted forces of technological determinism.

Excavating the Social in Popular Images of Reading

As is so often the case, popular understandings of the social world of reading can be a useful complement to scholarly analysis. This next section uses two cartoons as a springboard into the connotative aura that situates reading practices in our cultural imagination. Both gender and class are at play here, despite their tendency to disappear in academic analyses of reading.

Women Who Read Too Much

On my office door is a cartoon from the *New Yorker* showing a woman with glasses reading in an armchair (fig. 9). Her book is titled *Women Who Read Too Much,* a spin on the mid-1980s personal growth best-seller *Women Who Love Too Much.* I thought it was funny when I clipped it, but the humor resonates with several of the issues that this book explores—layers of meaning about gender, culture, and the act of reading that have had tremendous influence in my life and that of others, both readers and nonreaders.

First, it is *women* who read too much. (What would a man who read too much look like? I imagine a corporate desk with a busy executive sneaking time to read a novel concealed like pornography behind the sober pages of a stock report.) Despite the vast changes in women's lives since the

9. *The New Yorker* cartoon, 4 April 1988. © The New Yorker Collection 1988 Mick Stevens from cartoonbank.com. All rights reserved.

nineteenth century, reading for pleasure still lingers, in connotation at least, in a realm of leisured bourgeois private time that is female and domestic. This gendered vision is freighted with nostalgia for an idealized home in which genteel women passed their hours in soft and inconsequential activities involving needlework, flowers, and books. Leo Tolstoy recorded that vision in *Childhood, Boyhood, Youth* when he recalled the women of his friend Dimitri's family reading in the gallery near the avenue of birch trees one golden evening at Kuntsevo. No matter that Tolstoy, a man, wrote the vision; reading is womanly and genteel, a receptive pleasure (Tolstoy 1964 [1857], 238–52).

Reading, too, is a self-induced pleasure. One does not have to refer to Roland Barthes (1975) on the pleasure of the text to know the almost auto-erotic quality of reading's joys. It can be serious, but more often it belongs to the world of compensatory or predictable satisfactions. One of my own fears (the Protestant ethic's feminine nightmare) is that I will turn into the kind of woman who spends her hours lying on a chaise longue, eating bonbons, and reading. This "reading" (always nonserious, for eating junk is associated with reading trash) links to women in two slightly different inflections.

First, spinsters are purported to read rather than to be involved in the world of adult heterosexuality and family living. Indeed, the woman in the cartoon not only has glasses (a bluestocking? ruined her eyes with too much reading?) but is angular and homely, with an old-fashioned hairdo, a frumpy dress, and a chinless face of "a certain age." In this way of thinking, reading, chocolate, and cats or lap dogs deflect the unfortunate spinster from normalcy, while providing a (perhaps) harmless escape for her empty hours. Yet the escape is not entirely harmless, for it is *too much:* it keeps her from engaging in the busy mainstream of life.

On the other hand, housewives are also suspected of reading *too much.* Addicted to romances, the literary equivalent of soap operas, they neglect their family responsibilities and fritter away their time. In this connotative universe, reading requires social control lest it take over from more worthy pursuits. Americans have long been characterized by their ambivalent attitude toward reading: it is good up to a point, but then it is too much and should be supplemented by healthy outdoor play. It is too much especially for women—so the issues of social control of leisure have a gendered inflection. Like female sexuality, and unpaid female work outside the marketplace ("What did you *do* all day?"), female reading requires surveillance. It is especially dangerous, perhaps, because it is about consumption and pleasure, and often about sexuality and romance, which women "should" be getting inside the socially legitimated structures of the family and the real world. Women's reading, both as activity and as content (fiction, stereotypically romance fiction), threatens because it represents escape and holds forth at least the possibility of subverting the structures that discipline our lives.

Great Books at Billie Jo's

A second cartoon on my office door plays with the issues of social stratification and cultural value that reading raises by its position within our social world (fig. 10). Analyses that conceptualize reading simply as a skill (something like tying one's shoelaces) or even as a medium of communication, rather than as a set of activities and attitudes that involves some members of society and excludes others, fail to take this kind of relationship into account.[7] In such analyses, reading tends to be conceptualized formally, as if it had certain essential properties that were always and everywhere the same. From this perspective, reading often figures as a singular and unmitigated good rather than as a host of variable and socially informed cultural practices. But George Price nails this on the head. His cartoon shows a man on the street passing Billie Jo's, a lower-middle-class bar. The round-windowed door of the bar signifies an old-fashioned working-class aesthetic that is making an ironically sophisticated reappearance in "retro" films and postmodern cafés. The passerby notes with surprise a sign in the storefront, next to a spindly plant, announcing "Great Books 5:00–6:00."

The humor comes from unexpected juxtaposition. It relies on the fact that we "know" who reads and where they do it, which is certainly not at Billy Jo's. In particular, Great Books groups bespeak an affiliation with high culture and with serious, even weighty, conversation. This kind of literary sociability is light years removed from the working-class bar scene that I imagine is inferred by the readers of the *New Yorker*. Billy Jo's looks like the kind of place where tired hardhats and service workers drop by after a long day's work. If Great Books brings to mind good wine and classical music, Billie Joe's stands for beer and the sports channel on the big-screen TV. Billie Joe's is the twentieth-century descendant of the bars that the nineteenth-century temperance activists invaded both by tract and in person, in an attempt to convert patrons to the ideology of domesticated Protestant asceticism. Conversely, the Great Books movement is one descendant of the desire for moral uplift and self-improvement through culture that characterized those same middle-class reformers.

It is partly because reading as an institution—from publishing to elementary school teaching—is in the hands of just such middle-class or upper-middle-class people that it so often doesn't "take" among Americans who are not middle class. In America, reading is often presented as part of a whole package of values and behaviors that arouse the kinds of truncated and self-contradictory resistance Paul Willis (1977) analyzed in his study of British working-class young men's attitudes toward school. This resistance is hard for middle-class people to understand, because it is obvious to them that reading has large payoffs in terms of both occupational success and its more intrinsic pleasures. Reading meshes well with the delayed gratifica-

10. *The New Yorker* cartoon, 1 September 1986. © The New Yorker Collection 1988 Mick Stevens from cartoonbank.com. All rights reserved.

tion of extended schooling or budgeting of time and money. But such payoffs are less clear for people who approach reading and schooling without the other financial and cultural resources of the middle class. For them, allegiance to middle-class values means more often accepting positions as inferiors within a stratified society than achieving large leaps in social status. Moreover, adherence to middle-class behavior patterns and values—even when possible—almost inevitably means forsaking other lifeways and cultural values that have remarkable sustaining power for individuals, families, and wider collectivities (see, for example, Whyte 1943; Stack 1974; Sennett and Cobb 1973). Thus, there is a deeply contradictory field of meanings and strategies clustered about literacy in our society.

On the one hand, privileged, well-intentioned reformers address literacy as a moral or social problem and in much the same terms as they address the drug problem—generating posters and campaigns with a similar tone of hectoring misaddress. On the other hand, non–middle-class constituencies push for the kinds of material reforms that would enable literacy to become part of a broad strategy of empowerment (more money for inner-city schools, more books, more lunches, better teacher training, and, by implication, better social-welfare and employment opportunities), reforms that spread beyond literacy per se and become part of a struggle for changes in the distribution of wealth and power, pitting them against some wings of the privileged classes. Somewhere in between stand those educators who are trying to develop and implement policies or techniques that will, in fact, help all children learn how to read.

The cartoon reminds us that literacy and the practices of reading it produces in our society can never be divorced from questions of power, privilege, exclusion, and social distinction. Not only is literacy always taught and practiced by real people in concrete social situations, but, perhaps less obviously, reading lies in the shadow of the institutional order. It is subject both to the dictates of the state—in the public school system most obviously but also in laws of copyright and censorship—and to looser systems of cultural authority. Except perhaps as a regulative ideal, reading is never disembodied or unsituated, even when readers turn their reading to unorthodox or subversive purposes. On the other hand, reading feels so deeply private that the ideology of the solitary reader speaks profoundly to what people experience when they read. This paradox is what gives the image of the solitary reader its imaginative power. And how, indeed, can we approach the paradox? One avenue comes with the sociological insight that we are thoroughly and unavoidably social creatures even within what we perceive as our most individuated and singular moments of being. To paraphrase Raymond Williams (1983, 261), whenever we read, we must be aware of a society and of a language that we know are vastly larger than ourselves: not simply "out there," in a world of others, but here, in what we are engaged in doing—making sense of the words on a page and reading.

Theoretical Discussion

Understanding reading as a wholly solitary activity locates it securely in the realm of private life. This is problematic because of pervasive assumptions in social science that there exists a strict opposition between public and private life and that significant social development occurs mainly within the public realm. Such views privilege the level of large formal institutions and "macro-social" processes, whose development has, it is assumed, characterized the emerging contours of the modern world and similarly shaped the contours of social identity. This conceptual frame also presumes that the most important source of social change is large and organized aggregates of people, so here, too, the public realm is paramount.

When practices such as reading and other forms of cultural consumption are forced into the "private" side of this Procrustean classification system, scholars tend to understand them as epiphenomenal, marginal, or inconsequential. Theorists assume such activities to be determined by "macro" processes rather than being, at least in part, constitutive of social identity and the sociocultural order.[8] There is an important self-alienated irony in this view of culture. Most intellectuals are moved to write not only by instrumental imperatives but by the conviction that our ideas may matter to those who read them, a conviction that calls into question at least some of the above distinctions and assumptions.

Once the ideology of the solitary reader is unsettled, various prospects, linkages, and relationships within the sociocultural world can become visible. For example, cultural consumption appears less a private and passive affair than one source of social as well as individual identity. Writing, reading, and the academy (and its writing and reading practices) do not seem located in some transcendent sphere outside the web of social relationships or even cultural politics. More broadly, the "doing" of culture appears more integrally implicated in the "doing" of gender, class, race, and social development in general than theorists often assume.

In this section, I lay out some of the conceptual implications of inquiring sociologically into what happens within groups of white women when they read and discuss books together. This is an exploratory case study of a sociocultural phenomenon that has not been much investigated, so on one level it is a work of recovery. Until very recently, the small scale, informality, mainly female constituency, and cultural concerns of reading groups have exiled them to the margins of scholarship. They don't fit established traditions of inquiry, whether into the nature of reading or into the nature of voluntary associations. Like much work about women and gender, this study is also interdisciplinary, drawing from and opening out toward several scholarly fields but again fitting comfortably into none. I begin here with some questions about the role of culture in group association and civil society, and then move to issues clustered around cultural reception and reading, although in the empirical chapters that follow they are inextricably bound together.

Questions about Groups and Associations

The study of reading groups calls into question some recent thinking about the associational life of Americans. This has been the focus of much recent scholarship, whether inquiring about the traditions that inform civil society, critiquing the excesses of American individualism in the name of "communitarianism," or expressing concern that the social ties that bind Americans into a vibrant and democratic polity are loosening.[9] The most widely read representative of such books is Robert Putnam's *Bowling Alone,* published in 2000 to much acclaim. I examine his take on reading groups as exemplifying certain larger problems that vex his project and other related scholarly initiatives.

Beginning with a series of provocative articles in the mid-1990s and continuing in his best-selling book, Putnam advances the thesis that America's social capital has been eroding since the 1970s.[10] By *social capital* he means the multifarious ties that bind people together in associations, small groups, and even personal networks of friends and acquaintances. Concerned not just by the sharp drop in voter participation since the 1960s but by general indices that show a loss of social trust among Americans, he looks to trends in organizational participation and even private sociability to understand what he thinks is a process that is undermining both democracy and civil society.

One of his most compelling ideas, developed in a comparative study of political engagement in different regions of Italy (1993), is that participation in even nonpolitical groups (e.g., village singing societies) enhances civic participation and political involvement in general. This makes his work sensitive to small-scale and not explicitly political groups, such as those described in the following chapters or the bowling leagues whose decline his title refers to.

Putnam uses reading groups as one example of his thesis that there has been a trajectory of decline in civic engagement. He chronicles the rise in socially activist post–Civil War literary clubs among women, noting their contribution to Progressive Era reforms. (Chapter 2 of this book shows how some of these same cultural developments played out among women in Texas.) He then surmises, on the basis of survey data, that there has been a relative decline in reading groups in recent years.

There are several reasons to doubt both Putnam's empirical claims and the conclusions he draws from them. First is his almost exclusive reliance on surveys. Arguing from surveys that were gathered for other purposes, he claims that the number of women's reading groups did not rise in the late twentieth century. Yet these "secondary" data may not be a good research tool for this argument. The surveys he cites show no rise in the numbers of people belonging to "literary, artistic, or discussion groups" (150). This may be a term more evocative of traditional reading groups, which were larger and more formal than the book groups of today. If so—and it is hard to delve deeply enough into this from his presentation—women responding to the surveys may not have answered in a way that could give him accurate information. My evidence suggests, contrary to Putnam, that there has been an almost explosive growth in the number of women participating in informal reading groups since the 1980s. Certainly, everyone involved in the book business as well as journalists, cultural commentators, and educated women in general would claim that this is the case.

Second, he makes shaky inferences from general population trends. He claims that reading groups find members predominantly among single, college-educated women and that because this cohort has grown in proportion to the population as a whole, whereas the number of reading groups has supposedly remained flat, this represents a relative decline in book groups. As he says, "The proportion of single female college graduates who belong to a literary, artistic, study, or discussion group actually fell from one in three in 1974 to one in four in 1994" (149). Again, this argument is problematic. There is no question that more women are college educated now than in the 1960s; in fact, that may be one reason reading groups are on the rise. But most of the women in the reading groups I have found or heard of more impressionistically are married. So one of his basic assumptions about who joins women's reading groups is almost certainly false, and the inference of relative decline is doubly problematic.

Third, Putnam says that membership in the Great Books program has fallen by about half since its height in the 1960s. Putting all these sources of information together enables him to claim that reading groups are actually in decline and to use them as one more nail in the coffin of American civic engagement (2000, 281). The decline in Great Books groups is real, as is the case with many of the older organizations whose decline he maps in the book. But the Great Books groups are centrally organized and coeducational, and their reading programs, even instructions for discussing books, also come from a central source. Their decline has little relevance to the universe of locally organized women's reading groups I study. Indeed, the fact that these grassroots groups are thriving at a time when the Great Books program holds less interest for people may indicate that new forms of sociability and associational life are pushing aside older groups and organizations. This would provide evidence for a profound shift in associational behavior among Americans rather than for its decline.

Similar criticisms—both of Putnam's excessive reliance on survey data to the exclusion of more nuanced histories and case studies and of his tendency to downplay new forms of sociability and association among Americans—have been made by some of his readers. This makes it less likely that the case of women's reading groups, which is only one among many social phenomena he considers, is just one oversight in his larger argument and more likely that, in this and other cases, his scholarship will spark a debate that revises some of his conclusions.

Putnam's focus on formal groups may make it difficult for him to see or understand new forms of civic engagement, new ways that our social situations generate social capital. There is an important gender component here, for Putnam grants that traditionally men have been more involved in formal civic associations and public life, whereas women have been more responsible for generating and maintaining informal social connections (93–94). He makes a persuasive case for the decline of many formal organizations, such as civic clubs, fraternal organizations, and the PTA, but he also claims that the more informal ways Americans connect with each other—from dinner parties at home to card games—are on the decline as well. (He finds some exceptions, such as self-help groups, but he discounts them because involvement in such groups does not "spill over" into other forms of organizational involvement.)

I worry that this aspect of his argument relies on categories and research instruments that do not capture some of the important shifts in women's everyday lives. For example, many of the formal groups that have involved women do not address the needs and schedules of the growing numbers of working women. The PTA, for example, is often structured so that only stay-at-home mothers have the time for intense involvement. Auxiliary organizations for wives suffer the same problem. When I came to Rice University there was a faculty wives organization of the kind common at many colleges and universities. As more and more faculty wives became employed and the university recruited more women faculty and staff, the organization changed its name to Rice Faculty Women, but the activities still took place during the working day or over long lunchtime meetings. Now the organization is in danger of dying out because the constituency it once served no longer exists and the group has been unable to develop a schedule congenial to working women or a mission of interest to women who are no longer united as "faculty wives." In cases like this, it seems obvious that less formal groups, such as reading groups, or informal school-related child-care groups, will do a better job of reaching working women, so the decline in larger organizations is only part of the story. Yet informal groups are a part of the story that does not seem to register well on Putnam's radar.

Similar issues suffuse Putnam's writing about informal sociability patterns. He argues that in the past fifty years there has been a general decline in the informal connections between friends and neighbors, whether over card games and dinner parties or during participation in sports. Yet he does not seem to capture or approve of those forms of sociability that may be on the rise. He cites a decline in greeting cards but does not mention the explosion of e-mail cards and forwarded jokes. He is similarly dismissive of the burgeoning universe of online groups discussing everything from books to environmentalism, birthing to bureaucracy. He downplays work-related friendships because of their instrumentality—although he waxes nostalgic about work buddies gathering at bars—but has not carefully observed or discussed such friendships at work with the people (for example, working women) who may find them a real source of community. Reading groups are relevant here as well, for they may be the kind of informal group adaptation to new circumstances that is springing up as bridge games decline, but Putnam's methods make that sort of invention difficult for him to discern.

Putnam's limited historical perspective also weakens his discussion.[11] He acknowledges that there are cycles of civic engagement and celebrates the Progressive Era as one of them, but the twentieth century structures most of his narrative. It fits his argument well, showing rising involvement in both formally organized and informal groups, then a decline on many indices since the 1950s, 1960s, or 1970s. Yet the Progressive Era witnessed organizational innovations in the wake of earlier civic disengagement. Informal groups may have been responsible for beginning that wave of innovation. Nineteenth-century women's reading groups, for example, challenge some of Putnam's assumptions. He denigrates contemporary "self-help" groups, yet post–Civil War women's reading groups engaged women because they offered self-cultivation rather than the "true, womanly" altruism that had characterized earlier women's associations. As women learned to hold and defend opinions and to be more confident of their abilities, they moved onto a wider stage of action. Some of the same open-ended development may characterize our era. Older organizational forms have become less attractive as the rhythms of people's lives have changed, but new kinds of associations may be forming in ways that are difficult for us all to perceive at this point. It is true that busyness and a rampant materialism have invaded our private lives, while bureaucracy and a lack of political responsiveness characterize the public sphere. Yet there is some hope to be found in groups of women forging a creative deliberative space in their reading groups to reflect on the normative issues that riddle our culture and to consider the disjuncture between their desires and the socially mandated identity for "woman."

Reading and Cultural Reception

Janice Radway (2001, 7) has argued that the conceptual model common to much academic thinking about reading is linear, establishing "a spatial starting point and a temporal moment of origin" centered on the writer—still our locus of culturally valued creativity—and what he or she has written in the text. The reader is then conceptualized "as coming after, as subsequent to, and therefore usually as subordinate to the author as well." Understanding reading as a transfer of information from this point of origin to another point of reception "may unwittingly function to structure our understanding of the social process (of reading) as necessarily hierarchical . . . as the registering of the impact of one subject upon a less powerful or at least less active other."

Beginning with readers and inquiring about what they are doing with books stand this model on its head. A reader-centered model focuses our attention on reading as one kind of cultural practice, a form of behavior that performs complex personal and social functions for those who engage in it. For example, when groups of women get together to discuss books, they are often searching for intellectual companionship they cannot find in other areas of their lives. They may be extending their knowledge of literature or of literary interpretation. They may also be distinguishing themselves as especially cultured and literary people. Most interestingly, as they read and talk, they are supporting each other in a collective working-out of their relationship to the contemporary historical moment and the particular social conditions that characterize it. This activity is quite literally productive in that it enables women not merely to reflect on identities they already have but also to bring new aspects of subjectivity into being. By looking at women's reading groups, as this book does, one can see people in the process of creating new connections, new meanings, and new relationships— to the characters in books or their authors, to themselves, to the other members of the group, to the society and culture in which they live. In other words, they are in the process of remaking themselves in dialogue with others and with literary texts.

This process is the least understood aspect of what Wendy Griswold (1994, 14–17) calls "the cultural diamond," which is her analytical device for investigating connections among cultural objects, cultural creators, cultural receivers, and the social world. Perhaps it is so difficult to understand because, like other thinkers, sociologists tend to be drawn to the level of structures and firmly demarcated "objects," whereas the reading process is a complex, messy commingling of subjects: that of the author as encoded in writing and that of the reader, whose own subjectivity is opened to change by encountering the book.

This tension between structure and process underlies the masterful opus of Pierre Bourdieu, the French sociologist of culture whose work has shown most systematically how deeply implicated culture is in the reproduction of social inequality. His work on education (1979; Bourdieu and Passeron 1977) was the first to enter the American scene. In it, he showed that middle- and upper-class children's informal acquisition of cultural capital (for example, knowledge of art or high culture, even knowledge about sophisticated food, or the experience of other cultures gained through travel) undercuts the mission of formal schooling to "level the playing field" and equalize opportunities. Bourdieu (1988, 1996b; Bourdieu, Passeron, and Saint Martin 1994) has also generated a penetrating critique of elite education and the professoriat as they relate to the preservation of bureaucracy and state power. But his contribution is much broader.

Linking his theoretical interests to empirical studies of cultural phenomena—ranging from museum attendance and the "midlevel" art of photography to language, literature, and social suffering (1990a, 1990b, 1991, 1993, 1996a, 1999)—Bourdieu has explored culture in both its meanings: as artistic products and as "a whole way of life." Most impressively, he details how people's cultural judgment of everything from music and the arts to home decorating, styles of entertainment—even what makes a "proper" meal—both expresses and solidifies their position within our stratified social order. As he says in *Distinction* (1984, 6), "Taste classifies, and it classifies the classifier." Another of his analytic contributions, the idea of "habitus," points to the ways that our early experiences are ingrained in our intuitive, even bodily, dispositions to feel comfortable in certain cultural milieus and ill at ease in others, to feel superior to some people and intimidated by others. This "structuring structure" shapes people's life trajectories, he argues, as much as their differential relationships to the economy (169–225). In fact, he claims that an equally objective field of cultural stratification accompanies the system of economic stratification, leading to splits among social groups along both dimensions. For example, he locates most intellectuals within the "dominated" fraction of the dominant classes (260–317). They maintain their superiority on the basis of their cultural authority, whereas members of the "dominant" fraction of the dominant classes may have less refined taste and less articulated positions about deconstruction or the decline of European humanism, but they control by virtue of their economic power.

Bourdieu himself wants to strike a balance between structural determinism and more "subjectivist" views of society as the creation of individuals. His work—an analysis of what he calls the subjective side of the objective social order—is one approach to that problem. But his fascination with objective sociocultural fields and structures leads to an important gap in his work. He analyzes how people acquire the competencies and the dispositions to be involved with certain kinds of culture and how they both perceive and judge a broad array of cultural objects. But he does not spend much time conceptualizing their *engagement* with culture beyond that level. In other words, he glosses over the process by which people allow themselves to subjectively inhabit a cultural product, such as a novel, to become involved with its characters or the voice of its author, to connect with it on levels that may not be apparent to them until much later in their lives, perhaps even to be changed by that process and to embody those changes in different ways of understanding and acting in the world.

This absence is surely one reason that Bourdieu's work has been so much better at explaining social reproduction than at explaining social change. Without grasping, in contradistinction to his formulation, the objectivity of the subjective practices of cultural life, it is difficult to perceive the subtle and elusive ways that we not only are shaped by culture but also take it up and with it forge new meanings and new possibilities for our lives. This book begins to fill in this gap, thereby contributing to an understanding of how people's engagement with culture helps them to negotiate personal identity and social change. By showing how women have read and reflected on books in nineteenth- and late-twentieth-century Texas reading groups, it restores to view the practices through which particular socially situated actors actively construct for themselves a particular take on, and relationship to, the social conditions of their lives. Reading, especially when combined with communal reflection and discussion, provides the occasion for this activity, resources for reflection, and, in some cases, motivation for taking individual or collective action beyond the world of books. In this sense, beginning not with authors or books but with groups of readers, and then exploring the complexity of what their actual *reading* entails, reveals the fluidity and creativity that are as essential to "the social" as are structures, institutions, and other more graspable social objects.

The nature of the encounter that engages readers with books has recently drawn the attention of Wayne Booth (1988), Adam Zachary Newton (1995), and Martha Nussbaum (1990, 1995). Each is working the borders of literature and philosophy to discuss the ethical relationship that ensues when readers take up a book. Their writing is fascinating in part because it explores the very territory that Bourdieu leaves on the margins of his elaborate maps of cultural consumption. They also begin from a position that this book describes ethnographically. Each is moved by a conviction that reading can be transformative. I am in sympathy with their projects and with their descriptions of reading as an activity. Yet they all tend to hierarchize the relationship between book and reader in quite traditional ways that curtail the potential their work might have if it were more reader-centered and less formalist.

Nussbaum turns to reading as one aspect of a broader argument about what an adequate moral philosophy ought to entail. Ever since her work *The Fragility of Goodness* (1986), she has asserted that systems of ethical rules or "a watertight procedure of calculation" cannot settle moral dilemmas "before the fact." In the spirit of Aristotle, she argues that the content of any abstract outline of ethics "must be given by experience" and that its claims can be elucidated "only by appeal to life and to works of literature" (1990, 141). To specify what a good life is, or morally to assess another's life, moral philosophy must be able to illuminate ethical problems as they arise in their concrete particularity, because our moral lives are in a sense "stories" themselves, "in which mystery and risk play a central and valuable role" (142).

Complementing Nussbaum's insistence that ethics must confront the lived particularity of individual lives is her claim that an ethical response is complete only if it includes emotion as well as abstract reason. She argues that emotions such as love or fear are intelligent in that they are based on our (admittedly imperfect) understanding of the situations and relationships that elicit an emotional response. To exclude intuition, imagination, and emotion from our moral deliberation, then, does not purify reason but rather cripples it.

Reading fiction (and Nussbaum concentrates almost entirely on nineteenth- and twentieth-century "classic" novels) is a particularly valuable endeavor for cultivating an ethical sensibility because it embodies moral issues in the life stories of particular characters to which readers respond on many levels. As she says about Henry James's *The Golden Bowl*, but also more generally:

> To work through these sentences and these chapters is to become involved in an activity of exploration and unraveling that uses abilities, especially abilities of emotion and imagination, rarely tapped by philosophical texts. . . . If traditional philosophical texts do not record this whole adventure, call upon all of the abilities that are engaged in it, this would be a good reason to think that a Socratic enterprise requires texts like this one for completion. (1990, 143)

Nussbaum explores the limitations of traditional moral philosophy through reflections on individual books. She also argues, through the analysis of novels such as Dickens's *Hard Times,* that utilitarianism and conceptual systems from rational-choice theory to certain schools of development economics are profoundly flawed because they reject the diverse particulars of human experiences and human needs in favor of quasi-mathematical modeling (1995, esp. 13–52). Reading novels can be morally educative because they confront a reader with individual lives often quite different from the reader's own and demand an empathic yet reflective response to those lives, a "judicious spectatorship" as she calls it (72–78). In this sense, "novels can be a school for the moral sentiments, distancing us from blinding personal passions and cultivating those that are more conducive to community" (1990, 240).

Like Nussbaum, Booth, in *The Company We Keep* (1988), characterizes the encounter between reader and book (he too concentrates on novels) as a relationship that develops during the reader's experience with the author, implied author, and characters of a novel. In his view, this encounter, like friendship, has the capacity to form the reader's character. Hence the title. But Booth is looking to reform not philosophy but literary criticism. He describes the origin of his project during a discussion among faculty members about whether or not to include *Huckleberry Finn* in an introductory humanities course. Paul Moses, the one black member of the staff, burst out in protest that he found the portrayal of Jim offensive and Twain's views of race so distorted that the book was bad education.

At that moment Booth, like the other white faculty members present, was appalled at the eruption of an overt ethical appraisal into literary judgment, but twenty-five years later he makes a powerful claim for its legitimacy. One way of understanding his current position is to see it as a response to two developments that have affected literary criticism in recent decades. First, more diverse populations have entered the field of criticism and, in the process, have made claims that the traditional Anglo-American literary canon should be expanded and that the classics should be reexamined with regard to their representation of women, minorities, and other cultures. Moses questioned Mark Twain on that basis. Second, deconstructionists and others of their ilk have conceptualized books as referring not to the world but only to other texts, thus elaborating a formalist and textually bounded universe of theoretical discourse. Embracing the first of these currents in criticism while rejecting the second leads Booth to rehabilitate "our commonsense inclination to talk about stories in ethical terms, treating the characters in them and their makers as more like people than labyrinths, enigmas, or textual puzzles to be deciphered" (x).

Asking himself, "What kind of company are we keeping as we read or listen?" he explores the "ethical quality of the experience of narrative in itself" (10). Likening readers' experiences with narratives to other personal relationships, Booth suggests that we arrive at our sense of value in both "by *experiencing* them in an immeasurably rich context of others that are both like and unlike them" (70). To differentiate this learning process from either induction or deduction, he names it "coduction," emphasizing the comparative process by which we unavoidably perceive and judge any person or story against a backdrop of all other people and stories we have known. This process involves both a surrender to the experience of an author's offering and a refusal to surrender to its errors, failings, or excesses (136). Booth, then, has both rehumanized literary criticism and begun to think quite explicitly about the processes (for him, character formation is particularly important) that link books to lives as readers move back and forth between the literary company they keep and the other contexts within which their own lives take shape.

Newton (1995, 7, 9) rejects Nussbaum's and Booth's views about the ethics of reading because he sees them both as dealing with a second-order discussion either of the meanings to be found in a narrative or of the narrative's capacity to induce compassion and pity or to train a reader's ethical sensibility. In the wake of post-structuralism, these appear to him as manifestations of a limited humanism. For him, a prior ethical demand imbues the encounter between reader and text.

As he says, "One faces a text as one might face a person, having to confront the claims raised by that very immediacy, an immediacy of contact, not of meaning" (11). Drawing on the philosopher Levinas, he argues that an ethical summons proceeds from any intersubjective encounter, that the very face or presence of each singular, concrete Other exercises a binding moral claim on the self that "precedes both decision and understanding" (12). Despite obvious differences, encounters with texts are similar to encounters with other people in that "narrative situations create an immediacy and force, framing relations of provocation, call, and response that bind narrator and listener, author and character, or reader and text" (13). Such a narrative ethics is enacted as one reads and responds to a book, so it involves understanding narrative structure and form themselves as an ethical relation, rather than moving outside the interpretive act to apply some kind of moral "lessons for life" (26).

I find it unclear what Newton's narrative ethics entails, beyond a demand that the reader take up whatever burden of responsibility comes from being in some sense answerable (45) to the book. This responsibility seems to involve remaining as cognizant of or as open to whatever "armature of intersubjective relation" the book's structure entails (7). Thus Newton eschews the idea of a merger between readers and the characters or narratives they read, but rather he proposes that we must "think the infinite, the transcendent, the Stranger." He clarifies this best when he asserts that the theory of narrative ethics "entails the perhaps peculiar notion that characters' fates take place in the presence of readers" (292). Here, he is proposing the reader as witness: one who is awake to the moral weight of a story and who remains ethically responsive to it as to the fate of another person.

All three of these analyses show the cultural dynamism of reading as an activity. They recognize it as an intersubjective encounter with moral dimensions and an open-ended quality that can have repercussions in reflection and conversation long after the reader has closed the book. But from a sociological perspective, none of them goes far enough.

First, they accept too readily a book-centered or formalist view of the reading process, which leads them to downplay the possible variety of readers, readings, and uses of literature. This tendency varies with each writer. For example, Newton (1995, 12) refers to the "ethical summons which proceeds from intersubjective encounter," as if both parties laid claim on each other. Yet in his analysis, all of the meaningful summonses, the "framing relations of provocation, call, and response" that bind reader and text, appear to come from the book. The reader is the self, while the text's narrative structure and form are the Other that confronts him (13). Newton's tendency to explore narrative ethics through his analysis of individual narratives also signals that, for him, the "armature of intersubjective relation" is seemingly internal to the form of the books themselves (7).

Booth and Nussbaum are more open to the fact that readers also "call" the books they read, and perhaps for different purposes. Nussbaum (1995), for instance, seems particularly sensitive to protomanagerial readers (e.g., law students at the University of Chicago) who may need the salutary influence of narratives to appreciate the full individuality of the poor, the marginalized, and the oppressed. Booth (1988) recognizes that readers do not always seek the same *kind* of company from books, sometimes needing the escape of a mystery, sometimes the heroic intensity of Tolstoy. He also realizes that cultural frames can change profoundly the nature of reading. In one offhand moment, for example, he comments that if a novel appears as required reading, much of the pleasure of reading it can disappear. Yet again, both analyze individual books as if their own readings could stand for those of other readers, and all three assert that the very structure and form of each narrative condition the encounter between reader and book.

As a sociologist, I am less interested than are these three thinkers in a singular and formalist portrait of *the* encounter between book and reader and am more curious about the reading practices of ordinary readers. In that context, it is dubious that even the same narrative leads to an encounter with readers that has the same features every time it is enacted, because the readers who are themselves "calling" the book encounter it with such richly differentiated previous experiences. Attention to the socially situated nature of readers, as well as to what they are looking for in each reading experience and what aspects of a book's "face" or presence they attend to, demands an understanding that readings of even the same book can be profoundly different.

This is particularly obvious when one considers large scales of social difference. For example, Barbara Sicherman's work (1995) on readers of Louisa May Alcott's *Little Women* shows how important that book was for young Jewish immigrants who wanted to learn how to be "real" American girls. Jonathan Rose's *The Intellectual Life of the British Working Classes* (2001) mines working-class autobiographies that show the centrality of reading in the struggles of nineteenth-century workers to remake their lives. From books they discovered new horizons, a new set of competencies and desires (a broader and more varied "cultural toolkit" in Anne Swidler's terms [1986]), and dreams that empowered them to forge innovative lives individually and collectively. Many of them read the classics, yet they fashioned readings and uses of literature different from those that middle-class audiences gleaned from the same books.

In a more recent example, the critic Raymond Williams (1973) recalls reading Robert Herrick's poem *A Thanksgiving*. To Williams, a working-class boy from Welsh mining country, Herrick's description of the "little house" whose "humble Roof" sheltered him in exile during Cromwell's reign elicited this response: "I first read this poem, as a child, under a roof and a porch probably lower than Herrick's, and I could then neither get the lines out of my mind nor feel other than angry about them" (72). This one moment helped Williams formulate the understanding of disjunctures in class experience that underlies all of his theoretical work on culture and society.

The weight of the lives readers bring to their encounters with books is apparent even when examining a population of college-educated white women, as does this book. Consider the young girls of my generation who delighted in Marjorie Morningstar's ambitions to become a New York actress and forgot that in the end Herman Wouk consigned her to marriage with a suburban dentist. Or the woman who, reading Thackeray as a young girl in a small Texas town, discovered a desire to live among people who had witty conversation at dinner and became a witty urban intellectual herself. Consider also the romance readers who found affirmation for the worth not just of women but also of the "womanly" values of love and relationship. And the group of women who, discussing a novel about a father-son relationship, found in it the grounds for a careful examination of their relationships with their own mothers and daughters.

All these "reading relationships" speak to a second limitation in the work of Newton, Booth, and Nussbaum. Concerned to establish the importance of ethics to literary criticism or, conversely, the importance of literature to moral philosophy, they elaborate only one dimension of intersubjectivity in reading. They are right insofar as the kind of ethical comparison between literature and personal experience that narratives encourage in their readers (Booth's "coduction") involves a transitive movement both into and beyond books. Most readers value this "oscillation," as Certeau (1984, 173) describes it, and it is one of the things that sets their engagement with books apart from much academic literary criticism. This reflection involves issues of moral value, so here, too, these three critics have it right. But these examples suggest that only a very broad definition of ethics can do justice to the ways the women readers described in this book responded to the books they read and discussed.

One reason for this limitation is that Nussbaum, Booth, and even the post-structuralist Newton are humanistic defenders of legitimate culture. As reformers, their goal is the amelioration of a tradition whose core is its canon of literary texts. They are invested in the view that such books are inherently educative, in the Latin sense of "leading out" or "bringing up." At its most extreme, such assumptions can lead to the notion that educated people who read good books will necessarily be good people, a notion that ignores Bourdieu's insights about the role legitimate culture plays in perpetuating social inequality. Specifying that these good books must be read in a certain way may seem to loose the hold of such notions. But insofar as theorists stipulate what constitutes a "proper" reading, they remain embroiled in a form of cultural control, not just in education but also in the "refinement, policing, and evaluation of particular ways of reading and writing" (Radway 2001, 6).

Dramatizing the way this approach attempts to restrict the plurality of readings to a single "right way," Certeau (1984) refers to it in territorial terms. In his most famous metaphor, elite "official" interpreters "make of the text their 'private hunting reserve'" (171). Readers must then snatch what they need from the grounds of legitimate culture, "like nomads poaching their way across fields they did not write, despoiling the wealth of Egypt to enjoy it themselves" (174). Janice Radway (2001), too, points to the subversive nature of "wayward" readings: "Readers and readings may always go awry. . . . They may wander off into uncharted, fantastic, unprecedented territory. They may take up a relationship to certain literary personages, whether authorial or textual, who are normally prohibited to them as subjects for admiration, identification, emulation, or desire" (26). The open-ended multiplicity of actual readers' readings is especially alarming to scholars invested in a tradition of Great Books, because it threatens to destabilize the very textual building blocks of their authority. If an individual book can provoke such divergent experiences among readers, and if it has meaning only through its readers, then does it not somehow change every time it is drawn into a new reading relationship? Even worse, may readers not find something worthwhile in even a "bad" book?

A view that privileges legitimate culture and legitimates only certain readings must be unseated in order for us to ask some basic social questions about actual readers and their diverse yet never random readings. If readings are relationships, then what is going on in these relationships? How do they matter for the subjects engaged in such relationships among all the other relationships that populate their lives? How does the fluid commingling of selves that takes place in people's reading experience affect their enactment of their individual and social identity? It is to these questions that I turn in the following chapters.

TWO

Nineteenth-Century White Women's Reading Groups: Literary Inspiration and Social Reform

Historically, reading has been social in a quite specific sense different from that discussed in chapter 1. In Europe, since medieval times, and especially since the advent of printing and the rise of vernacular literature, reading has drawn people together in groups that meet to talk about books. The history of such reading groups has been difficult for scholars to perceive, a singular exception being the French salon movement, which has lodged itself in the collective memory as a spectacular combination of aristocratic and literary brilliance. Most reading groups have been much less socially distinguished and much less visible to their contemporaries, and they have left only obscure historical traces in their wake.

The historical invisibility of reading groups is partly the result of the plain fact that reconstructing the past of grassroots groups is a daunting research problem. Such groups may also be hard to see because they do not easily fit the binary oppositions that shape our categories of thought, or if they do, they fall on the wrong side of these distinctions. For example, they are leisure-time groups, so by definition they are not part of the "serious" world of politics, religion, or work. For the past two hundred years, reading groups have also been predominantly women's groups, and ordinary women's activities have only recently drawn historical attention. Reading groups also fall between even Jürgen Habermas's expanded version (1989) of the public sphere (which includes, along with the state, the coffeehouse, the press, and other occasions and institutions that foster public opinion) and our taken-for-granted notion that "private life" is more or less equivalent to the notion of family life. And they are small groups, so they have neither the fascination of individual genius and its products nor the obvious importance of the large-scale social transformations (industrialization, modernization, and globalization) that shape our individual lives.

Yet reading in groups may heighten the empowerment that literacy often brings in its wake. Certainly, from the time of the sixteenth-century Protestant reading groups, the eighteenth-century salons, or the Chartist

31

correspondence societies of early-nineteenth-century England, such book-oriented associations have played an important role in the cultural politics of class, religion, and gender in Europe. Cultural and social historians, whose work promises to undermine some of the constraining conceptual frames mentioned above, have recently shown how important were groups of readers for the social changes that brought modernity to Europe.

My story centers on America, but it is worth reviewing their findings briefly if only because Americans carried some of these traditions with them when they came from Europe. Americans also referred back to earlier groups of readers in a conscious attempt to find or invent traditions (Hobsbawm and Ranger 1983) for their own quite innovative nineteenth-century reading groups.

Brian Stock (1983) has found evidence of what he calls "textual communities"—groups of readers in close communication with each other through books—as early as the twelfth century. According to him, this form of association not only empowered people but also helped to create community, sustain collective memory, generate knowledge, and challenge tradition.[1] Somewhat later, according to remarkable work by Elizabeth Eisenstein (1979) and Adrian Johns (1998), printing encouraged a myriad of book-based associations—both intimate and far flung—to emerge with stunning speed and profound effects on knowledge and people's sense of themselves and their world. Benedict Anderson (1991) claims, in fact, that what he calls print-capitalism and print-languages were crucial in furthering modern nationalist consciousness, which relies on a sense of belonging to what he calls imagined communities.

"Printing and the People," Natalie Davis's important essay (1975) on sixteenth-century France, both grounds and extends the work of Eisenstein and Johns in that particular historical context. Davis discusses the ways that groups of readers made newly available printed material their own. In this fashion, reading groups become not merely vehicles for the dissemination of ideas but cultural innovators as well, sometimes by progressing from reading to writing and publication of their ideas. Evening gatherings within peasant communities began to feature readings from the vernacular Bible, which allowed them to reflect on its message without the help of a priest, and from the very popular book *Le roman de la rose,* which brought new ideas about women and love. Craftsmen, too, read in groups—instructional books as well as the Bible—and, especially if they were printers, occasionally built up reputations as scholars and authors themselves. The most "modern" reading groups were probably the secret Protestant assemblies, because "they brought together men and women who were not necessarily in the same family or craft or even neighborhood" (Davis 1975, 214).

Reading in such contexts, can, in Davis's words, "provide people with new ways to relate their doings to authority, new and old" (214). Groups of readers clearly gave sixteenth-century French women a new sense of their own competence, for Davis's work traces women authors to earlier participation in humanist literary discussion circles. This experience apparently empowered them to write in some numbers on subjects from poetry to midwifery, the latter an explicit challenge to male-dominated and non-empirical traditions of medical scholarship. Attention to such groups of readers enables the analyst to generate a newly complex and gender-balanced picture of the cultural shifts of early modernity.

Although Robert Darnton (1974, 1979, 1982, 1984) is less interested in small groups of readers as audiences and agents of social change than is Davis, his multifaceted study of the Enlightenment in France represents perhaps the best example of what it means to take seriously the social dimensions of a literary movement. The Enlightenment has been remembered as a constellation of philosophical giants whose ideas, through abstracted processes of dissemination, set in motion the avalanche of social revolution and cultural modernity. In a series of books and articles, Darnton anatomizes the complex web of commerce, law, literary patronage, and idiosyncratically responsive readers who, in fact, constituted the literary culture of the Enlightenment. In his analysis, mercenary Swiss typesetters and monopolistic Parisian publishers, corrupt censors, ill-paid peddlers, and cunning book smugglers working provincial byways and local fairs were the circulatory system that gave life to the Enlightenment.

More subtly, he argues that the content of the Enlightenment itself was much more complex and closely linked to popular forms and audiences than its representation in the twentieth-century academy indicates. He brings to life a host of would-be philosophers, literary hacks, and readers who ordered erotica or scurrilous antiauthoritarian political pamphlets much more commonly than they ordered Diderot or Rousseau, or who, if they ordered Rousseau, read him as a manual for how to raise their children. Such people—the bastards of literacy—created the political ferment and shift in moral sensibility whose development we have enshrined in a legitimate genealogy of great thinkers and the intellectual heirs who read them. These historical accounts demand reconsideration not just of reading itself but of the ways we conceptualize culture and its impact on social change.

Enlightenment ideals of equality and reason proved a powerful social force to constituencies of readers outside the bourgeois world of male citizenship. The work of several historians shows how women across Europe imported what they took to be the form and substance of the French literary salon in order to educate themselves and claim intellectual and moral authority.[2] E. P. Thompson's account (1972) of working-class radicalism in England, which is focused on the Chartist movement for universal suffrage, discusses a similar process across the borders of social class. He shows that craftsmen's study groups and correspondence societies in nineteenth-century Britain played a crucial role not only in the ideological ferment of reformism but in the stitching together of isolated groups of working men into a powerful social movement. All of this work demonstrates that the social and intellectual empowerment engendered by this form of cultural association has had consequences in the realm of social action as well as ideas. Indeed, it constitutes a de facto demand to reframe the action/idea dichotomy by paying attention to culture less as a group of static and abstracted values than as ideas articulated and sustained within concrete social practices. It also shows that reading groups historically offered forums for critical reflection that were crucial for helping people define the moral and ideological dimensions of their social identity (Long 1986, 1988). So, reading groups were not simply influenced by the social transformations of modernity; they also helped to shape the present we are still negotiating.

American history, too, provides evidence of the transformative potential of discussing books in association with other people. In the rest of this chapter, I explore a particularly dramatic example of this process: the literary club movement that spread with astonishing rapidity among white women after the Civil War. Nineteenth-century literary clubs engaged women, first, in the then-revolutionary activity of "self-culture" and, second—on the heels of regional and national organization—in a broad spectrum of Progressive Era reforms. Their accomplishments are especially impressive because at that time women could not vote. From our viewpoint, these women left an ambiguous political legacy, but their successes played a large part in shaping a social world with expanded opportunities for women. This new environment has proven hospitable for the rather different kind of women's reading group that flourishes today.

Origins of the White Women's Literary Club Movement

After the Civil War, white women's book clubs spread from the urban centers of the Northeast across the American continent to the West almost as fast as did the frontier. (The Shakespeare Literary Club of Clarendon, Texas, was begun a scant seven years after initial white settlement [Seaholm 1988, 212].) For the thousands of women who took up the torch, these were not merely local literary gatherings but a broad-based social movement, inspiring tremendous dedication, enthusiasm, and devotion.

Although the idea and even the form of the literary association were indebted to late-eighteenth-century white women's reading groups and the scattered legacy of free African American women's literary groups dating back to the 1830s, post–Civil War groups' myths of origin referred mainly to a more distant and glamorized past.[3] They looked back to medieval women's religious associations, Anne Hutchinson's circle, or the French *salonières*. But in the main, like most Americans of their day, book club members looked forward. The literary club movement meant progress and, in the words of clubwoman Mary Livermore, "a necessary step in the evolution of women" (Seaholm 1988, 92).

To accomplish this step, these literary women drew on organizational structures developed in a host of charitable and reform associations that had involved thousands of women from the 1830s on and in women's associations that had sprung up to provide support for both Northern and Southern war efforts during the Civil War. They also drew on their experiences in popular educational associations—the Chautauqua movement and local lyceums, for example—that had generally been led by men but involved women as audience members.

In Texas, as in other frontier states, women emigrating from other areas and women in touch with distant kinfolk or friends who were already in a group brought with them both the idea and the format for book clubs. The New England Women's Club and the notable New York literary group Sorosis (both established in 1868) provided inspiration for dozens of literary clubs across the nation, through the press and through tireless lecturing on the part of such stalwarts as educator and reformer Julia Ward Howe, who presented her talk "How Can Women Best Associate?" to gatherings from New York to San Francisco.

The flavor and fervor of early Texas groups are exemplified by an account of the beginnings of the Ladies Reading Club of Houston, generally regarded as the first literary club in Texas. It was born in Adele Briscoe Looscan's drawing room in 1885.[4] As Mrs. Looscan recalled the occasion in 1921:

> It was on a day early in February, 1885, that she [Mrs. Carrie Ennis Lombardi, the first president] called upon me, and in her sweet, modest fashion opened a subject very near her heart. It so happened that her dominant thought had also been my thought for months, only awaiting an opportunity to broach it to her, and to a few others of our friends. The idea we wished to develop was the formation of a circle or club, who would be interested in meeting . . . for the purpose of intellectual and social culture.

Together, they set out by carriage across the brick and dirt streets of Houston (then a city of 23,000) to call upon "such intimate friends as we agreed ought to be interested" and enrolled nine members at the first meeting. April "witnessed a more regular organization" (Looscan 1921), and by the end of the year the group numbered twenty-four, with a slate of officers, a formal agenda, and careful minutes of each meeting. Patterning itself after the Ladies Literary Club of Grand Rapids, Michigan (one of the founders had connections there), the Texas group began by studying the history, science, art, and literature of a specific country. For their first year's program they chose Egypt, "as at the time it was attracting the attention of the civilized world on account of the conflict in the Soudan [*sic*] and the tragic fate of the gallant Gordon" (Looscan n.d., 39).[5]

Why did the reading group become lodged as the "dominant idea" in the hearts of these two Texas ladies and of thousands of other like-minded ladies from Maine to Kansas and California in the years after the Civil War? Several factors appear, from this vantage point, as important.

First, a cluster of structural developments had led to a shift in middle-class women's lives, which simultaneously gave them more leisure time, narrowed their traditional sphere of domesticity, and widened the gap between their daily lives and the rapidly expanding worlds of their menfolk. By the late nineteenth century, many American women of the growing middle- and upper-middle classes were no longer the economic partners of their husbands in enterprises that were both home and workplace (Cowan 1983). With industrialization, women became the managers and ornaments of a home rigidly separated in both ideology and practice from the myriad settings in which the work of the larger world took place under predominantly masculine control (Stearns 1979). Pundits and poets celebrated the piety, refinement, and morality of the "true woman" nestled in her "haven from the heartless world" (Lasch 1977), but women's horizons were less expansive than were those of the men who took the helm in the hurly-burly age of invention and manifest destiny. Literary clubs offered such women a chance of becoming experientially part of a broader world. As Megan Seaholm (1988, 206) says, the literary club "added a dimension to 'true womanhood.'"

Second, during the latter nineteenth century, education was becoming crucial for middle-class Americans, yet women of the middle orders stood in a tenuous relationship to the institutions of learning. If they received any education outside the home, it usually ended at the eighth grade. With rare exceptions, young ladies' seminaries or academies (there were approximately two hundred of these at the height of their influence) provided only enough substantive instruction to make bright young women hungry for more.[6] The situation was even bleaker in the South. In 1850, almost 25 percent of adult white Southern women were illiterate, and many schools for young women closed during the Civil War (Seaholm 1988, 42–43).

Higher education for women improved in the late nineteenth century, but in 1870 only about 750 B.A. degrees were granted to American women.[7] As one graduate put it, "A college woman was . . . a curio" (Martin 1987, 43). For the large numbers of middle-class women who could not attend college, the literary club offered the possibility of lifelong learning. A member of the Dubuque, Iowa, Conversation Club said, "Our university must be in our homes. This country is too large to go to a place or a professor. The learned, inspiring minds must come to us."[8]

Third, when higher education for women was just beginning its tantalizingly slow expansion, two other arenas that had satisfied women's need for culture and activity outside the home had begun to disappear. The popular lyceum movement (which had involved members of the Ladies Reading Club of Houston not only as audience members but also as librarians) began to wither as formal education grew. Similarly, the Civil War, like more recent wars, fostered self-reliance and tremendous organizational activity among women. Especially noteworthy was the Union's United States Sanitary Commission, staffed entirely by women, which raised $30 million for the war effort and provided a whole gamut of support services for soldiers and their families.[9] The New England Women's Club, founded a month before Sorosis in 1868, claimed as members several women who had been leaders in "The Sanitary" (Martin 1987, 60). In the aftermath of the conflict, an endeavor that offered association with other women "for literary, scientific, and artistic purposes" (in the words of the New England Women's Club) promised a relatively apolitical continuation of the independent activity encouraged by the war. In the words of Katherine Nobles, a southern commentator, the reading or culture club offered a "middle way" that appealed to women in her region who would never have espoused suffrage (Seaholm 1988, 104).

Finally, women turned to culture with such moral and aesthetic fervor because in the late nineteenth century, high culture—whose appreciation, preservation, and transmission already seemed the special province of the fair sex—had itself taken on an almost sacred aura. American adulation of individual literary genius reached an almost frenzied pitch. Contemporary British authors such as Dickens and the Brownings acquired an unprecedented glamour in the American cultural imaginary, becoming one model for creative individualism, while past literary masters such as Shakespeare took on the patina of sacred cultural icons.

During this same period, as Lawrence Levine (1988) and Paul DiMaggio (1982a, 1982b) have convincingly shown, the American urban upper classes poured money into an ambitious program of cultural construction. Not only did they erect the massive museums, theaters, and concert halls that brought Culture to American cities, but in so doing they instantiated a version of high art that stripped cultural forms such as the opera or Shakespeare's plays of their populist thrust. This material and ideological effort imbued legitimate culture with an intimidating seriousness. By making it more exclusively the property of the wealthy and well educated, this construction of high culture gave it more power to legitimate the established social hierarchy. Educators also conceptualized literary culture as a foundation of American citizenship and a tool for Americanization that might mitigate threats of immigration and class conflict, turning it into a pillar of what Robert Bellah (1991) calls America's "civil religion," which both defines and makes sacred the national purpose.

Yet, as is so often the case, such initiatives had unintended consequences. Educators may have understood "good books" as agents of moral
uplift and social control, but their efforts helped broaden literacy and literary circulation. If critically approved literary works and the arts in general
took on a quasi-sacred aura during this period, they perforce also became a
cultural resource for people to use for their own ends. The construction of
late-nineteenth-century high culture that served nationalism, individualism, and the cultural authority of the upper classes also provided an opportunity for women to build on their supposedly "instinctual" affinity with
the aesthetic realm. By appropriating high culture with the systematic discipline and seriousness that it required of its acolytes, they could also appropriate its cultural authority.

The Literary Club Movement and Its
Effects on Members

Ideology: Self-Culture for Enlightenment

The women who founded literary clubs were aflame with the then revolutionary desire for education and self-development, which they called self-
culture. This was an exhilarating challenge to the norms of altruistic service
that had underwritten earlier nineteenth-century women's associations and
their considerable range of benevolent and reform activities. For example,
in Texas, the Denton Woman's Shakespeare Club motto was "Step by step,
we gain the heights," and the Chautauqua Literary and Scientific Circle of
Waxahachie urged its members to "Neglect not the gift that is in thee" (Seaholm 1988, 2, 184). Similar sentiments suffused the mottoes of clubs across
the country.

Its leaders often characterized the literary club movement as a bold
and innovative step. According to Jane Croly, New York City journalist and
founder of Sorosis and later the General Federation of Women's Clubs:
"The cry of women emerging from a darkened past was 'light, more light,'
and light was breaking. Gradually came the demand and the opportunity
for education; for intellectual freedom; for cultivation of gifts and faculties"
(Martin 1987, 39).

Accounts of early literary clubs often include evidence that male authorities, from pastors to husbands, perceived these activities as a threat to
domestic order. For instance, a 1938 description of the Dallas Shakespeare
Club (founded in 1886 and distinguished as one of the first Shakespeare
clubs in the United States) says of its early years: "Its members read Shakespeare for pure enjoyment and then hurried home to reach the fireside before the arrival of their husbands, most of whom had a very decided dislike
for any kind of club. Later the club read Shakespeare more slowly and criti-

cally, the husbands still fumed, and some members, so the stories go, dropped out to keep peace in the family" (Seaholm 1988, 209). Husbands of members of the Rhode Island Woman's Club nicknamed it the Society for the Prevention of Home Industry, and one New York journalist quipped: "Woman has laid down the broomstick to pick up the club" (Blair 1980, 24). Authors satirized women's literary clubs, and cartoonists caricatured them.

Other local club leaders, and probably the majority of rank-and-file members of women's clubs, may have been more conservative than Croly. The following view, from Mary I. Wood's article "The Woman's Club Movement," probably represents that of many members of literary clubs: "Women are not creators: they are not discoverers. . . But [the] high calling of conserver and preserver has belonged almost exclusively to woman. It is upon this fundamentally true basis that the Woman's Club movement is founded: there was no great scheme of distinct and separate work laid down by founders of the club movement" (1910, 15).[10]

True—and pleasingly nonthreatening—as this statement may be, it is equally true that women's association for self-development through literary education empowered its participants, changed their identity both individually and collectively, and nurtured a strong sense of social mission. These literary and associational practices led those groups of readers to try their hand at rewriting womanhood, as I trace in the next sections, with special emphasis on Texas readers.

Organization: Signaling Seriousness

The literary group's major activity was the discussion of one or several books, which was initiated by a report from a member (or sometimes a guest) on a book or topic that the entire group or a committee had selected, often as part of an annual program. This kind of reading club still lingers on, often among the most elite circles, some members of which have kept these traditions for a century or more.

Literary clubwomen signaled the seriousness of their endeavor by meticulous attention to organization and parliamentary procedure and by their stated purposes and their programs of study. Although each group was different, they bore a strong family resemblance to each other. Most groups had a constitution and by-laws in place after only a few meetings.[11] These usually featured the club's purpose, membership requirements, officers, and election procedures. Leadership most commonly rotated among all the members by self-conscious design, so that everyone would be exposed to growth in confidence and skills. This also accorded well with women's supposedly noncompetitive nature and may have represented a conscious attempt to build a "womanly" organizational form. By-laws established dues, meeting times and procedures, and penalties or fines for absences or lateness. The Austin Pathfinders, for example, passed resolutions that rain and muddy streets were not an excuse for absence, that there would be no whispering during recitations, and that refreshment would be served only on special occasions (Seaholm 1988, 222).

Parliamentary procedure also signaled the solemnity of these literary endeavors and separated their work from more informal women's social groups. Some clubs appointed a parliamentarian, many held parliamentary "drills," and most conducted their meetings according to *Robert's Rules of Order* or Mrs. Shattuck's *Woman's Manual of the Parliamentary Law.*

The club year tended to run from fall to spring, following the school year, and a committee usually set out an entire year's program, which was often printed up in a yearbook for members. Individual meetings followed an exacting format. The section titled "Order of Business" in the 1917–18 yearbook of the Axson Club of Houston provides a typical example: the items on the agenda are Minutes of Last Meeting, Report of Corresponding Secretary, Treasurer's Report, Report of Committees, Unfinished Business, New Business, Critic's Report (the critic raised procedural questions), Program, Adjournment (*Axson Club* 1918, 7).

All these efforts imparted gravity to an activity that, in its early years, was not yet wholly defined; they also proclaimed legitimacy in the terms of the public sphere (Seaholm 1988, 221–23; Martin 1987, 65; Blair 1980, 69). This was a bold message for members, for other women, and also for the men who watched this cultural innovation from the sidelines. As an account of the first annual meeting of the Texas Federation of Women's Literary Clubs in 1898 records, "At the regular proceedings the following days, gentlemen were in attendance, manifesting a quizzical interest, and on the *qui vive* for parliamentary blunders, which were furnished, to their evident amusement, but the ready tact and wit of the president saved the day" (Christian 1919, 23).

Literary clubwomen announced their purpose in flowery prose that has a slightly naive ring in our more jaded age. Adele Briscoe Looscan of Houston's Ladies Reading Club said they had formed so that "each may cultivate a taste, which thus far has been wanting for her mental development; that new avenues may be opened, new chambers unlocked for the intelligent mind, which must find in all of them something to interest, something to elevate" (1890). Her sentiments were echoed by ladies from Massachusetts to Georgia, as recorded by the list of statements of purpose in Jane Croly's massive *History of the Women's Club Movement in America* (1898).

Because they were pursuing their own self-development, women generally barred men from membership, feeling that they might be silenced by the men's presence. For much the same reason, the mainstay of their programs were reports prepared by the members themselves, followed by questions and discussion, although clubs did have guest speakers. Women put a tremendous amount of effort into their reading and whatever written composition was entailed. About her second report, one clubwoman said: "Never before had I spent so much labor in the preparation of anything, nor, I presume, shall I ever do so again" (Martin 1987, 91).

Reading

Literary club programs varied tremendously in depth and sophistication but evidence a certain commonality of focus. Usually, they concentrated on those branches of knowledge that could be construed as at least potentially within women's sphere of interest and could be studied without recourse to specialized instruction or rare books, for most clubs met in towns or cities without libraries.

Book acquisition was a particular problem for groups in Texas and other frontier states, which often lacked not only libraries but even the means of easily transporting books from the nearest ports. (Books were usually shipped from publishing centers in the Northeast, so books for Texas arrived via New Orleans or, later in the period, from Galveston.) In 1870, Texas could claim only 711 miles of railroad tracks, and even Austin, the state capital, was not connected to the railroad until 1877. Houston—meeting place of thirteen railroads, according to one early booster publication—was fortunate by comparison. By 1890, the situation in Texas had improved dramatically, with eight thousand miles of track added in twenty years (Metzger 1984, 59). This rail network was crucial not only for book circulation but for commerce in general, because at that time there was no other means of cheap, efficient transportation in the state.

When one reads accounts of the early book trade in Texas, it is a puzzle how literary clubs managed to find the books to discuss at all. Philip Metzger's careful study (1984, 126) of publishing and the book trade in Austin says of the period between 1870 and 1900: "Fifteen or sixteen separate booksellers began business during the period; most lasted only two or three years." Only one of those booksellers boasted a circulating library. Penn's library stocked fifteen hundred titles, and an annual subscription cost between $7 (if one checked out one volume at a time) and $22, for which relatively princely sum the customer could check out up to four volumes at once. Most of those books were novels, and most were English novels published between the 1840s and the 1860s. Works by Charles Dickens and Sir Walter Scott were by far the most popular selections, with volumes by James Fenimore Cooper and E. D. E. N. Southworth tying for seventh place on the list. Metzger also mentions *Little Women, Little Men,* and *Uncle Tom's Cabin* as available American titles (81–83).

Metzger says of Austin: "Most of the booksellers of the period, probably nearly all, sold other merchandise besides books" (1984, 127). This was also true for Houston. Of the six booksellers listed in the *Houston City Directory, 1895–1896,* none sold books alone. B. P. Bailey and Co. is listed as an agent for the Remington typewriter, George T. Lathrop as a printer and rubber stamp manufacturer, and Miss Lizzie I. Moody as a seller of not only books but also jewelry, hair goods, toys, bric-a-brac, and Butterick patterns. All of them sold stationery, newspapers, and periodicals as well. George W. Baldwin is also listed as the proprietor of the Houston City Library, which may indicate a circulating library like Penn's in Austin (*Houston City Directory* 1895–96, 371, 87, 88, 100, 180, 227, 256). The establishment most closely resembling a city library during the period was the Houston Lyceum Library, whose holdings, thanks to the work of the Ladies Reading Club, later became the basis for the Houston Public Library. In 1888–89, when the Lyceum Library was open for 237 days, 1,471 people availed themselves of its services, but there is no accounting of the number of books in its collection or the titles checked out. By 1904, when the doors of the Houston Public Library opened, it held about ten thousand volumes and more than four thousand government documents (Hatch 1963, 60, 75).

By the end of the century, libraries were under construction throughout the state, in many cases the result of the efforts of women's literary clubs. The book trade in Texas, as in other frontier states, was also becoming more closely linked to national channels of distribution. Changes in the pattern of book distribution helped connect local booksellers to the national trade, and *Publishers' Weekly* (established in 1872) became, in Metzger's words (1984, 127), "a major form of communications in the book industry. Its columns offered, among other things, news of the latest books and complete ordering information." Apparently, the publication was used by at least a few of Austin's booksellers, whose advertisements of out-of-print books and books for sale in *Publishers' Weekly*'s pages provided "clear evidence that they were interested in tapping into regular national markets."

One can assume that by the early 1900s it was relatively easy for Texas women's literary clubs to acquire even recently published or specialized books. Earlier in the period, and especially in smaller, more remote municipalities, it must have been very hard. Women most likely relied on the personal libraries of family and friends as well as on whatever semipublic collections existed in their hometowns. They also probably circulated books among members of their clubs, a pattern that Anne Ruggles Gere (1997, 186) mentions as characteristic of less wealthy book clubs elsewhere in the country. The difficulty in acquiring books probably also constrained early Texas book clubs to select reading material that was widely available. This would have pushed them toward literary classics (Shakespeare, Wordsworth, Browning) or the kinds of worthy *and* popular fare, such as Dickens and Scott, that did well among patrons of the circulating libraries of the day. Material constraints, in other words, probably worked to reinforce the canonical (or critically approved) and Anglophile thrust of the period's high literary culture.

The majority of literary club programs centered on literature, history, or the fine arts, often organized—as was the case with the Ladies' Reading Club program mentioned previously—by cultural geography. There was usually a leavening of issues of the day (including socialism, suffrage, and, increasingly, social reform) and some discussion of "home economics," the rubric under which Catherine Beecher was professionalizing women's domestic concerns.[12] The Ladies Reading Club minutes record a meeting in February 1888, for instance, that covered Vinegar, Yeast, and Dust. Looscan analyzed the latter "and again demonstrated her ability to find 'sermons in stone' " (Ladies Reading Club 1888). Of the sciences, botany appeared with some regularity, but most women had only an elementary knowledge of mathematics or classical languages, and that necessarily limited their fare, although some groups heard lectures on evolution or astronomy, and psychology appears to have been of general interest.

Within this limited compass, programs were very ambitious. Women's untrammeled hunger for knowledge, in fact, often gave the early programs of individual clubs a dilettantish and scattered quality. El Paso's Current Events Club, for example, studied Roman history one year, interspersed with papers titled "Women as Rulers" and "Can Criminals Be Reclaimed?" (Cunningham 1978, 19). Most groups quickly shed a miscellaneous approach to knowledge and settled into quite systematic and serious programs of study. A typical example comes from the first yearbook of the Houston Ladies Reading Club, from the 1901–2 club year. American literature was the topic. The outline covers the Colonial Period, 1607–1764 (subdivided into early and late), the Revolutionary Period, 1765–87, and the Constitutional Period, 1787–1820. Meeting almost every week, the club began in October with meetings on Captain John Smith, John Rolfe, William Bradford, and Edward Winslow and ended in May with Daniel Webster and John Calhoun. After the reports and readings, programs featured less formal "table talks" and "discussions"—usually but not always related to the writer under consideration.

The progression from a potpourri in 1888, which featured yeast one month and Henry James the next, to this kind of program in 1901 was quite typical for book clubs across the country, although some—such as Austin's Pathfinders Club—gained reputations as "brainy" from their inception (Seaholm 1988, 213).[13] Most women had been "trained to silence," and little in their daily lives gave them the confidence to embark upon even a somewhat rigorous program of education and oral presentation or discussion in front of a group of peers.

Book clubs consciously fostered women's ability to express themselves. Groups initiated the "roll call"—which required some response from all present on a given topic, sometimes related to literature, sometimes to current events or an aspect of domestic experience—to ensure that everyone would speak. They assigned reports to every member for the same reason, and as clubs began to organize within states and across the nation, they disseminated program outlines, papers from other clubs, and even pamphlets on how to approach an author and his works to help new clubs and untrained members (Gere 1997).

Over time, standards for literary analysis began to improve both within and across clubs. Where secondhand reports had once served, clubs began to expect more original compositions and more polished presentations. In the Mosaic Club of Bloomington, Illinois, when someone read directly rather than referring to notes, other members would ostentatiously yawn or look out the window (Martin 1987, 96). Some clubs introduced debates. Others began to emphasize literary production, becoming forums for sharing members' essays, poems, or short stories as well as for book discussion (Gere 1997). Some clubwomen were so much in demand as writers and speakers that they made club lecturing and writing their lifework, even their careers.

Analysts such as Blair (1980) claim that these literary groups were engaged in a passive activity—as consumers of culture—and that most did not produce scholars or career women. But such a perspective neglects the important abilities and competencies that literary clubs fostered. This "mild form of compulsory education" (Scott 1991, 118) not only exposed women to the discipline of learning but also brought them into the world of intellectual analysis, opinions held and defended, and confident self-expression.

The content of their discussions helped them in this self-transformation while circumscribing its parameters as well. When they studied history or cultural geography, many women were for the first time looking beyond very limited personal horizons. Their aspiration to *general* knowledge—what Jane Croly (1898, 12) called "knowledge of the history and development of races and peoples and of the laws and principles that underlie this development"—was itself a challenge to the ideology of pure domesticity. Most clubs actually functioned within fairly constrained historical boundaries: they oriented themselves almost entirely toward Europe, especially England, as the source of American traditions. If they ventured as far as Asia or Latin America, it was with the pleasing sense of undertaking an exotic voyage (one Houston club's yearbook features a geisha on the cover for the year they studied Japan) or of journeying as companions to such colonializing figures as "the gallant Gordon," whose "tragic fate" brought the Ladies Reading Club to their initial focus on Egypt.

When it came to women's issues, however, even relatively conservative reading clubs were apt to entertain positions critical of the status quo. Blair (1980, 69–70) cites groups giving papers on such topics as "Margaret Fuller," "New York State Laws Affecting Women," and "Women's Suffrage" and quotes at length a paper titled "Women in History," by Syracuse club-woman Sarah Sumner Teall, which argued for reconceptualizing the meaning of history itself: "A celebrated teacher of History once said to me, 'When women do anything worthy of record, they will get due recognition,' and I wondered if he had had a mother. . . What has history been in the past? Men's story of men's triumphs and trials; his victories and defeats. . . It has not been considered by the ordinary historian . . . that woman's work, sufferings, achievements, were worth recognizing and recording."

Like their study of history, reading clubs' literary studies seem from our perspective constraining as well as enabling. As might be expected, popular culture was almost entirely absent from clubs' programs; the same was true of almost all avant-garde literature. Their basic curriculum centered on the classics of imaginative literature, and their canon was overwhelmingly Anglophile. Browning, the Brontës, Dickens, and George Eliot were among the most popular authors, but all were overshadowed by the immortal presence of the Bard. Seaholm (1988, 233) calculates that Shakespeare accounted for more than half of the programs of Texas reading groups in 1902–3. But numbers alone cannot convey the enormity of his influence nor the awe his work inspired. Here are the words of the chronicler of Houston's Ladies Reading Club for 1888, who turned to Shakespeare for one of the last meetings of that year:

> That the last shall be *first* and the *first,* last! After having been under the . . . spell and . . . witchery of the great minds of America and Great Britain, right here, just as our . . . current year is drawing to a close, this afternoon, March 6th, 1888, we knelt humbly, hesitatingly, with most womanly reluctance, before the shrine of the inimitable, the incomparable, the greatest, the mightiest of all, William Shakespeare, poet by the grace of God. As in the ancient days, Solomon's mines must have startled the minds and dazzled the eyes of those who crept near enough to gaze upon the wondrous plenitude of its fabled riches, so on this, our initial Shakespeare meeting, when quotations were called for, the depth of the mine opened was so great, the jewels so inexhaustible, so rare . . . that our ladies bring their tribute just a trifle timidly. (Ladies Reading Club 1888)

Timid or not, the group dove into Shakespeare—although exactly what they read is unclear from their notes—and also presented some secondary literature about him, including Emerson's famous essay. My point is this: If this audience approached Shakespeare with the reverential awe befitting an immortal and godlike figure—and such was clearly the attitude of many reading groups—they were not merely succumbing to the orgasmic bliss of cultural consumption but also appropriating the very aura of his godhead for themselves. Reading Shakespeare—however hesitatingly and reluctantly—brought them forth from the serried ranks of passionate devotees into the elite status of initiates, the act of textual communion allowing them to incorporate some of the transcendent cultural sanctity he represented for them.

The quasi-religious significance of Shakespeare and lesser literary immortals thus served to authorize a certain kind of reading for book clubs as well as conferred a more generalized cultural authority on their members. For if such books were (in varying degrees) sacred, then, like the Bible, they could become the textual ground for considering the most crucial ethical dilemmas, for debating the nature of human nature, and for defining identity.

Reading clubs found the latter issue particularly fascinating, especially in regard to women. According to Seaholm, almost every Texas club that studied Shakespeare discussed "Women in Shakespeare" or more specific topics such as "Shakespeare's Mothers" or "Women's Friendships in Shakespeare." They also carefully scrutinized almost every one of his female characters. *The Taming of the Shrew* inspired debates on "Was Katherine a Womanly Woman?" and "Katherine's Obedience." The Standard Club of Colorado City, Texas, claimed that "Shakespeare's women were for the most part, true, noble, and womanly." Nonetheless, Seaholm finds more discussions about Lady Macbeth than any other female character in Shakespeare. Such discussions usually condemned her but demonstrated a fascination with the complexities of female power. Seemingly, although Texas clubwomen interpreted Shakespeare's female characters as "true women" and appropriate role models for their own lives, their processes of identification were as complex as those of reading group members negotiating womanhood in the twentieth century.[14]

Like Lady Macbeth, Ibsen's heroines seemed especially fascinating to Texas women's clubs, who used them to discuss "Wifehood," "Woman's Duty to Herself," and the "Woman Question." Although most used their reflections about Ibsen to reinforce relatively conservative views, they were clearly interested in debating "the rights and responsibilities of woman and the meaning of modern womanhood" (Seaholm 1988, 236–37, 240). As Seaholm says, this was "education for identity," and literary clubs' desire to learn was driven by a hunger to elucidate woman's nature and proper or potential place in the larger world.

Literature not only gave women cultural authority and a projective screen on which to discern their identity but also inspired them to embrace a broad mission of social betterment that transcended their own self-development. If literature represented the highest accomplishments and the noblest ideals of the human spirit, then it demanded similarly noble efforts from the elect among its followers. For clubwomen, this was a direct and obvious connection. "The Club women who used to study Shakespeare have been looking around them upon life's Stage," said Mrs. A. O. Granger of Georgia (1906, 253). Kate Cassatt MacKnight (1906, 293–94) extended this line of thought:

> The literary and self-culture club is, as a rule, the beginning and sup-
> port of all those important elements which . . . develop the interests
> of women in the forward movement of humanity. For after spending
> months studying the idealism of Tennyson, or the scathing arraign-
> ment of all that is sordid, found in Browning . . . then, at last coming
> to John Ruskin, with his appeal for more simple and spiritual living
> . . . one naturally begins to open one's eyes, to look about, and to in-
> quire if we have any right to continue to live amid hideous sur-
> roundings; or to permit children of our "land of the free" to be
> destroyed by drudgery, or vicious environment; or to stand idly by
> while the grandest and most beautiful . . . scenery in our country is
> destroyed by the blind greed of grasping commercialism.

Sisterhood and the Transformation of Identity

Literary clubs clearly enabled women to gain organizational skills, the ability to participate in serious, orderly, and rational discussion, the self-confidence of cultural authority, and, coupled with all of these, the knowledge—
both factual and ethical—to form opinions about the wider world and
their own place within it. All this is the stuff that most theorists of the public sphere and modern social movements would point to as necessary con-
stituents of collective social action. It is equally clear that these groups also
gave their members a deeply felt sense of solidarity. The ways this solidarity and concomitant program of social reform took shape cannot be fully
explained by models of either rational disputation or rational self-interest.

The community of women in reading groups was bound together
and inspired to action by "love and ritual" as well as by the powers of textual
analysis (Smith-Rosenberg 1985). This was crucial for their ability to
revalue not only themselves as individual actors but also the meaning of
womanhood collectively. In turn, this enabled them to formulate a critical
appraisal of the status quo and a visionary program to reform it—both in
the interests of the literature, arts, and education they held so dear and in
broader but still "womanly" arenas. For many of these readers, their book
clubs became a site for developing not only literary skills but also strong and
nurturing ties with other women that fostered a genuine feeling of sisterhood and an exhilarating sense of the powers and possibilities of Woman.

Meetings became a cherished event that brought women out of the narrow round of their domestic concerns. For example, the Dallas Pierian Club observed its scheduled meetings even when they fell on Christmas Eve or New Year's Eve: "December 24, 1903, found the Pierians studying Japan and the Yoritamas feudal system."[15] Rituals and traditions were a central part of club life. Yearbooks feature club colors, flowers, and mottoes along with the literary programs, and club minutes express the joy women felt at the beginning of each club year in passionate perorations that celebrate their beloved clubs and their strong feelings for fellow members. As one Dallas woman said, "'Tis not alone as students that we boast, but of harmony that has ever prevailed and the great love for one another that is ever a true Pierian characteristic" (*Dallas Clubwoman,* August 19, 1908, 1). Almost every club held at least one special meeting during the club year to celebrate the fellowship of the reading club itself. Often these were anniversary celebrations, a yearly Gentlemen's Night, or—as for the Ladies Reading Club of Houston—an annual "pic-nic" held at the end of the club year.

Similarly, even though many clubs forbade extensive refreshments, and some banned them altogether, clubwomen often mention the importance of conversations "over the tea cups" for developing their self-confidence. Stella Christian (1919, 42), historian of the Texas women's club movement, defends the generous hospitality that marked the first meetings of the Texas Federation of Women's Clubs, "because, upon these occasions, clubwomen met face to face, with the leisure to go deeper into their problems, receiving practical aid and counsel from each other. Many of the notable achievements of the Federation had their inception in the heart-to-heart talks between the clubwomen over the 'cup o' tea,' when denizens of city and country hamlet communed together and exchanged ideas." Traditionally loath to speak in public, women found in literary clubs a welcoming environment that enabled them to find and value their own voices.

Association also brought these women, often for the first time, out of the restricted circles of kin, neighbors, and those who shared political and religious sympathies and into egalitarian forms of contact with other women rather different from themselves. One clubwoman called her reading group "a democracy of brains" (Seaholm 1988, 98) because status had so little meaning in their discussions, and many others claimed they experienced an increased sense of fellow feeling with and for different kinds of women because of participating in book clubs. For example, a member of the Dubuque (Iowa) Ladies' Literary Association noted a "constantly growing fellowship [and] the disappearance of the class spirit" (Martin 1987, 459). Their aspirations for sisterhood were sincere, and the "mixing" of local cliques—of society women and career women, of women from different denominations (even across the Protestant-Catholic or Jewish-Christian divide), and of single and married women—was not an illusion

(Seaholm 1988, 98). From the historian's viewpoint, however, the groups are more notable for their homogeneity than for their diversity.

Almost all book clubs, for instance, drew members from the "middling classes." Clubs were limited by racial as well as class boundaries. African American women of extraordinary achievement sometimes belonged to a white club, but both state and national federations prohibited African American clubs from joining their organizations. So African American women's book clubs led a separate existence and organized nationally in 1896 as part of the National Association of Colored Women.[16]

Reading club members were likely to be mature women. Many joined only after their children were grown. Generally there was relative homogeneity of age as well as of race and class within individual clubs, unless they developed into the large "department clubs" that might boast upward of two hundred members. Most reading clubs, however, stayed small enough so that they could meet in each other's homes.

Book clubs often shared a common background of some sort: education, religion, neighborhood, or their husbands' occupations. Consequently, a social hierarchy of clubs prevailed in most large communities. Blair (1980, 64–66) describes the club hierarchy in Providence, Rhode Island, which ranged from the prestigious and overwhelmingly Yankee Rhode Island Woman's Club to a club dominated by single women—clerks, teachers, bookkeepers, and dressmakers—that met in the evenings because so many members worked. This kind of homogeneity may have made it easier for women to speak in their book clubs. It also contributed to the limitations of the ideology that emerged from them. Limited though the social compass of many groups was, however, they allowed many women their first exposure to other women who differed from them to some degree, so association in these book clubs encouraged women to develop an identity that was—again, to some degree—different from that of wife, mother, and homemaker.

The "semipublic" identity that developed among women in book clubs required a diminution of what one clubwoman called a "tedious selfhood" limited to purely "self-inclusive" thinking about subjects such as dress, family, neighbors, or the fads of the day (White 1903, 620; Howe 1874, 6). Association and discussion could "dispel prejudices and broaden . . . insight," leading to tolerance, a measure of objectivity, a sense of cooperation, and the ability to work together. As one woman wrote of her literary club, "Sorosis afforded me an atmosphere so genial, an appreciation so prompt, a faith so generous, that every possibility of my nature seemed intensified, and all its latent powers quickened into life" (Martin 1987, 131).

Accounts of club life consistently celebrate the new cooperation among women and, with it, the members' newly heightened sense of their abilities and value as a sex that came from work in culture clubs. Nancy Phayre, the heroine of Helen Winslow's novel (1906, 46) about club life, *The*

President of Quex, discovers as a newly elected president that "she must lay aside her likes and dislikes in the club" to harness the energy of her main rival for an important project. Texas clubwomen deliberately shared the power and responsibilities of state office to nurture less established clubs and to spread the club idea into communities in which it had not yet taken root. As Christian's Texas history (1919, 41) reports: "Many ladies of strong clubs waived nominations that would doubtless have given them election, in order that the offices might be scattered, geographically speaking, or given to weaker clubs that they felt needed the educative results of responsibility. All action was harmonious."

"Harmony" is a word that surfaces often in these accounts. It encapsulates several qualities nurtured by club life: cooperation, loyalty, support for other women, and the ability to work in concert for worthy goals without pettiness or self-seeking. It is a word, too, that signifies a union of head and heart. It highlights the emotional qualities of empathy, altruism, and what one woman called the sisterly pride and affection—in short, the womanliness—of this new collective identity. As one Texas clubwoman said:

> Long ago it was held up to women that they had little of the feeling of comradeship which is common among men . . . and that they could never accomplish anything of magnitude as a class, because they could not work together peaceably and effectively. Nearly all women will admit that this was true. The result was a lack of harmony until this club idea began to take root, and what a glorious boon it has been to women, as the use and beauty of organized work came to be known. (Seaholm 1988, 92)

The spirit of generosity, sympathy, and fellow feeling that prevailed in literary culture clubs empowered their individual members and gave them an unprecedented sense of their own capabilities.

Sisterhood and pride in their sex—fostered by rational and substantive literary discussion and by the cooperation that membership in literary clubs inculcated—enabled these women to reframe the very category of "woman" itself. From the wellsprings of this new collective identity came the desire to move from the book club to broader levels of organization.

State and National Federation: From Shakespeare to Social Reform

Organization and New Ambitions

Like the idea of the literary club, the idea of gathering individual clubs together into a broader federation of clubs spread quickly across the country.[17] Once women had begun to see themselves as capable of organizing to act in harmonious and united purpose in small literary groups, further horizons of organization and novel collective ambitions suggested themselves. This process of cultural leavening involved a complex interchange between local groups and the national scene.

The "woman movement"—a loose conglomeration of groups that held in common the assumption that women had something special to offer society—was gathering strength.[18] Its representatives wrote prolifically in the national media and, like Julia Ward Howe, tirelessly crisscrossed America on the lecture circuit.

Local literary groups often organized at least in part in response to these national currents, and once they organized, the groups were even more open to the currents' influence. For example, a local group might subscribe to a national reading group service and then, like at least three Texas groups that sent representatives to Boston to the national meetings of the Anna Tichnor Society to Encourage Studies at Home, find itself linked in close communication with women from all over the country (Seaholm 1988, 8, 229). Similarly, local groups became natural contacts for speakers on the national lecture circuit who were attempting to find audiences for their messages.

In just such a fashion, Adele Looscan and the Houston Ladies' Reading Club became hostesses for a meeting with two famous suffragist sisters—Victoria Claflin Woodhull and Tennessee Claflin. As a journalist in a Houston newspaper recounted many years later, when he was a boy one elderly club member had tipped him the extravagant sum of five dollars to escort her and her daughter to the meeting. In his words, "No grown-up man wanted to attend the 'hen party' as it was called in those days." His account gives a fascinating glimpse into what was a consciousness-raising event for him and probably for some of the women: "It was the first time he had heard the ladies lambaste the male element good and planty [sic] and they called 'a spade a spade.' Victoria Woodhull got up and asked why all this mock modesty today, in calling a 'leg of the table a limb of a table'? In those days when a leg was mentioned in the presence of the fair sex, it created blushes from all sides" (Ziegler n.d.).

Events of this kind, repeated over and over (how many times, one wonders, did Victoria Woodhull ask local audiences about legs and limbs?), were a catalyst that brought local women into touch with ideas and personalities that helped to further the sense of empowerment and mission already begun in their own groups. The effects of that process were no less powerful for being marginal to formal politics. While the Ladies Reading Club of Houston was not in the forefront of the fight for votes, they and others like them began to undertake activist tasks of their own once they began to federate, and this broader organizational scope seemed to call for a larger collective purpose. As one chronicler put it, "Literary culture was the *raison d'être* of the . . . club, but it was felt that such an organization of women as the State Federation must stand for some united effort for social advancement in Texas" (Seaholm 1988, 344).

Rewriting Womanhood, Reforming Society

The General Federation of Women's Clubs—which began both nationally and in Texas as an association of literary and culture clubs—became an important agent of Progressive Era reform.[19] By the late 1890s, the "pure" study club had begun to seem anachronistic, as clubs took up reformist work at every point in the social order at which women felt they had particular concerns or special authority.[20] As they defined it, this was a large territory. As one movement ideologist explained it: "Women's place is in the home. . . . But Home is not contained within the four walls of an individual home. Home is the community. The city full of people is the Family. The public school is the real Nursery. And badly do the Home and the Family and the Nursery need their mother" (Skocpol 1992, 331).

Modern historians have characterized this position as maternalist. On the one hand, this means that the ideology of clubwomen's social and political programs built on the special nature, roles, and competencies that had been attributed to women throughout the nineteenth century. *Maternalism* can thus mean motherhood writ large: a selfless, if imperialist, maternal impulse bursting the shackles of domesticity to domesticate the public realm—indeed, all of social life. As one Texas spokeswoman put it, "The zealous club woman begins with her home and pauses not till she has reached the seats of the mighty" (Texas Federation of Women's Clubs 1904–5, 52).

On the other hand, parallels to *paternalism* give the term ironic overtones. Both are ideologies and practices that imply not only protection or care but authority, social control, and clear relationships of domination and subordination. In this sense, *maternalism* refers to white middle-class women's assumption of the right to enforce their vision of social betterment on populations divided from them by race and class, as well as on all children and (insofar as possible) on all masculine activities that lay outside of war and commerce.

The early work of women's clubs centered on education and culture: they established almost 75 percent of the public libraries in the nation—and according to Seaholm (1988, 272), more than 85 percent of those in Texas—began kindergartens, pushed for vocational education and other curricular reforms, founded college scholarships and dormitories for women, and campaigned for universal compulsory education.

In Texas, for example, clubwomen financed college scholarships for women, led the fight to establish a women's dormitory at the University of Texas at Austin, and were—in cooperation with the Women's Christian Temperance Union (WCTU)—instrumental in founding what is today Texas Women's University, the state's most important all-women's institution for higher education. The enabling legislation, passed in 1901, created the Texas Industrial Institute and College for the Education of White Girls in Texas (Seaholm 1988, 358). The Texas Federation of Women's Clubs (TFWC) also played an important supportive role in establishing compulsory education, kindergartens, and vocational education. Responding to the difficulty they themselves experienced obtaining books, they also sponsored up to fifty-three traveling libraries and a traveling art exhibit (278). And in a move that, like the charter for the Texas Industrial Institute, demonstrated white-supremacist as well as pro-educational politics, the TFWC supported the poll tax, whose revenues went toward a common school fund while disfranchising most black voters (Seaholm 1988, 364–65).

Expanding the definition of education, they addressed issues of welfare and crime prevention for young people. Texas clubwomen concentrated their efforts in three areas: the parks and playground movement, campaigns against child labor, and work toward a juvenile justice and "reeducation" system. The Parks and Play Grounds committee of the TFWC was in place before 1907 and had already garnered enthusiastic support from many local clubs before its foundation. Because parks and playgrounds combined aesthetic, health, and child-welfare concerns (not to mention social control: well-supervised outdoor play was thought to combat hooliganism), they were a very popular local project.[21]

If playgrounds and parks were to nurture strong and educable children, these children must at the very least be free to attend school. So Texas clubwomen, like their sisters across the nation, agitated for anti-child-labor laws. In Texas, the cause apparently caught fire in 1903, after members of the Fifth District visited the Cuero cotton mills and witnessed the horrors of child labor for themselves.[22] They also fought for early closing hours and helped to enact protective labor legislation for women.

Texas clubwomen were very active in the arena of juvenile delinquency. They were instrumental not only in convincing legislators to pass the a law creating the state's first juvenile court in 1907 but also in establishing corrective educational institutions for boys (1909) and girls (1913). On the local level, clubs often urged city councils to appropriate funds for juvenile probation officers, and in Dallas, clubwomen paid the first officer's salary (Seaholm 1988, 296–98, 372–80).

In Texas, these women were often initiating programmatic efforts to bring amenities to their villages and towns for the first time. Perhaps the most significant efforts of Texas clubwomen in this regard lay in the realm of pure food and water. They began by a statewide campaign (both informational and educational in nature) to investigate existing conditions and to publicize successful models of laws and procedures already in place elsewhere. Then they moved to intense lobbying of the state legislature and local city councils. Their most important victory was the passage of the Pure Food Act of 1907, which established state standards and appointed a state commissioner to enforce them (Seaholm 1988, 310).

The activism of the TFWC was inflected differently than were other state federations because Texas was so rural. The Industrial and Social Conditions Committee, in many states the spearhead for industrial reform efforts directed at women, never found a major role. Conversely, the Rural Life Committee was very active. Their most popular project was the establishment of rest rooms for farmers' wives on market days in town. For example, the Gainesville, Texas, XLI Club procured a room from the county commissioners and then staffed and maintained it, providing magazines and books as well as child care on First Mondays and entertainment on Trades Day (Seaholm 1988, 412–13).

Clubwomen felt that there was a direct connection between the hours they spent studying literary classics, the parliamentary seriousness of their meetings, and their ability to become effective (if nonvoting) citizens. From this vantage point, the connection seems no less direct but less entirely positive. First, the literary club was an act not only of empowerment but also of discrimination or distinction. Clubwomen were proud to be different from those women who did not so organize themselves, and they accepted a doctrine of natural difference that separated them from men. Just as they did not question the elevated status of high culture, they usually did not question either capitalism or their own privileged place within it. They tended toward reformist initiatives that softened the harsh effects of an inequitable social order without attempting to dismantle either the existing social hierarchy or its underlying causes.

This is especially clear in regard to race and class. As noted earlier, the "General" Federation of Women's Clubs refused to allow black women's clubs into the organization, and clubs supported educational reforms that had racist effects, such as the poll tax and the foundation of a segregated women's college in Texas. The Texas libraries they founded were for white patrons only. Curricular reforms such as vocational education were also intended to better the lives of the less privileged without granting them equal opportunity. Even on the issue of gender, clubwomen proved relatively conservative. Individual clubs included suffragists among their members, and almost all of them discussed women's issues. Yet most clubs refused to let politics, especially suffrage, become an explicit part of their mission. The General Federation of Women's Clubs did not officially support woman suffrage until 1915. It is true that many feminists, professional women, and women who served in government in the 1920s and 1930s gained organizational skills and formed networks within the women's club movement that were of immense value to their later efforts. It is equally true that the vocation most clearly legitimized by club work was that of the professional volunteer—a way of life limited to the educated and affluent (Seaholm 1988, iv).

A similar ambiguity pervades all middle-class reformism of the Progressive Era. The borders between social betterment and social control are often difficult to discover in Progressive initiatives, whether in battles against municipal corruption or in the parks and playground movement. "Science" and "expertise," the supposedly disinterested watchwords of Progressivism, legitimated the status claims of a rising professional elite. Clubwomen were no less interested parties. Despite their limitations, however, their gender may have given them more distance on the status quo than their menfolk had, if only because the "womanhood" they stood for was the ideological receptacle for social and cultural values banished from the center stage of nineteenth-century America.

Why Did We Forget Them?

Resolutely nonsectarian, nonpartisan, and (formally) apolitical, the General Federation of Women's Clubs, as Theda Skocpol (1992, 631) says in her important work on state-building at the turn of the twentieth century, "devised ways of making political demands felt outside of party meetings, or elections, or standing bureaucracies." They accomplished a great deal by relying only on the indirect influence of nonvoters and the suasion of moral authority. Yet because they worked outside of formal political processes and handed successful programs over to more public (male) authorities, their successful initiatives disappeared from view as they were incorporated into governmental administration.

Skocpol calls their modus operandi "moral education." Their own motto was Educate, Agitate, Legislate! Education linked clubwomen's "outside work" with the literary "self-culture" that had gone before. In fact, their first step was self-education. Clubwomen immersed themselves in the study of social conditions with the same dedication they had devoted to the classics. They toured schools and prisons, refuse-ridden alleys, sewage systems, and sweatshops. They constituted fact-finding bodies. They wrote exposés and inquiries. State and national officers urged them to "take up" certain topics in their individual clubs. More specific instructions were also common. In 1916, after Texas had established a special rural school fund, the state federation instructed clubs not only to study the state's school laws but also to survey rural schools in their own county (Seaholm 1988, 476–77).

Once informed, they ventured forth to educate the public. As one speaker declaimed: "Men make laws. Women, just such women as you, are all the time writing the greater higher law . . . the law of Public Opinion. . . . Get information as to the truth of conditions and then spread abroad the knowledge you have gained. . . . Here within the sound of my voice is influence enough to overturn or build up a kingdom" (Skocpol 1992, 362).

The strategy of education and agitation spoke to the heart as well as the head, attempting to arouse the public conscience through moral suasion. Movement strategists recommended beginning this work close to home. As Terrell's "Succinct History" (1903, 17) records, once the TFWC leaders understood that "the husbands, fathers, brothers, and sweethearts of club women were men of influence in the affairs of State," the president issued circular letters to each club, "asking that in the home and social circles the influence of each member should be used, with voters who could directly influence legislation. Thus was created a great, silent force for the enactment of good laws." Sometimes Texas clubwomen formulated more specific goals along this line; for example, in 1902 the Austin American History Club decided that each member would try to convince three men to vote for the constitutional amendment to increase school taxes.[23]

I first became aware of clubwomen's tactics when researching how the Ladies Reading Club established a free public library in Houston. Since 1847, there had been a lyceum with a library for members. As was the case in many cities, the institution's popularity had dwindled by the latter years of the century.[24] Gradually the women of the Ladies Reading Club worked their way into the organization, first as members, then as donors of books and sponsors of a "lady librarian" (Hatch 1965, 20, 38, 40–42). At this point, their dedication had made them crucial players in the development of the library.

At the next stage, they took the lead. First, they persuaded the city fathers to appropriate public funds for their cause. They did so by inviting the mayor and his aldermen to lunch with them at the lyceum. In the minutes of the club, the moment is preserved thus: "Oh for a kodac [sic], for an immortal picture, of the seven men in evidence when the door was finally opened to them. They looked startled, wordless, and were in a moment motionless, hat in hand, facing the Reading Club!" When the ladies greeted them, "they grasped as do drowning men—at a straw" (Hatch 1965, 43).

Mrs. H. F. Ring continued the story in a paper delivered to the State Federation in 1924:

> I shall never forget the faces of our city officials as they came into our
> rooms. They wore a kind of shamed look, as though they had let

themselves in for "a piece of women's foolishness" and would gladly
bolt at the last minute. But the wiles of the women were laid too
deep for that. Every door was closed, but the front and that well
guarded. After being shown our books and circulation lists they were
bountifully served [the ladies had prepared a luncheon of chicken
salad, hot biscuits, and coffee], and then the needs of the library were
presented to them in a way that commanded their respectful attention.

The funds were forthcoming, to the tune of $2,500 annually. Next, the City
Federation of Women's Clubs wrote to Andrew Carnegie, who agreed to
pay the costs of a new building if the city would promise an annual appropriation of $4,000. This also being forthcoming, the library was launched.

Yet ironically, once the Houston Public Library became just one
among many civic institutions, the role of the Ladies Reading Club van-
ished into that institution's prehistory. In a similar fashion, clubwomen's
substantial accomplishments across the nation were easy to forget because
the programs or initiatives that proved successful became incorporated into
the masculine domain of formal politics and public institutions.

There is another more heartening reason for our amnesia. Clubwomen's attempt to expand and raise the status of women's sphere contributed to a deep transformation of our society. Important foundations of
the welfare state were built by the "maternalist" programs clubwomen initiated, although bureaucracy has grown to obscure their influence. Similarly, middle-class white women's lives today are quite different from those
of early-twentieth-century women, in part because of the effort of nineteenth-century activists, who reimagined and then rewrote womanhood in
a way that significantly expanded opportunities for their daughters and
granddaughters. Women's education, marriage, and childbearing patterns
and their participation in work or politics all show the influence of these
foremothers, but the very transformations they helped to effect make it hard
for us to have any organic memory of them.

When I was researching the Ladies Reading Club in the Houston
Metropolitan Archives, I used to muse on the forgetting. I would sit with a
few other researchers, quietly scribbling notes in the serene backwater of
the Texas room in the Julia Ideson building. The original Carnegie Library
building was long ago sacrificed to commercial development in the grand
Houston tradition. The Ideson building is a graceful 1920s Spanish revival
building that narrowly escaped the same fate. It is named after the first
Houston librarian, a single professional woman who served her city, and its
women's clubs, for forty years. Few people understand that connection. Just
as few know that the nearby Looscan Branch Library memorializes a

founder of the Ladies Reading Club. In the slanting sunlight of the Ideson building's spacious corridor stands a reproduction of the Venus de Milo, now yellowed, peeling, and altogether scabrous looking, which had been donated to the Carnegie Library by the Houston Art League. Sometimes, as I walked by that statue, I felt that the other librarians and I—all, quite clearly, a little eccentric—were the only ones in the building who could walk through these layers of time as layers, also, of meaning.

THREE

Between Past and Present: Introductory Reflections on the Changing Nature of Women's Reading Groups

Nineteenth-century white women's reading groups provided their members with knowledge, solidarity, and skills in self-expression and group organization that empowered them to reimagine themselves both individually and collectively and then to embark upon a series of substantial social reforms. Despite many similarities between nineteenth-century groups and those of today, current reading groups differ in both subtle and more obvious ways from their precursors. In general, contemporary reading groups are much less meticulously organized, no longer require written reports, and, most dramatically, are not geared toward collective social action or politics. Such differences are mainly the result of the social and cultural factors that have wrought tremendous changes in middle-class women's lives over the past century. To a lesser degree, transformations in what Bourdieu calls "the literary field," especially the professionalization of literary studies in the academy, can also account for some changes in the cultural meaning of reading that may affect the mission of contemporary women's reading groups.

Similarities between Present-Day Book Clubs and Their Predecessors

Nineteenth-century white women's reading groups had many characteristics that current groups would immediately find familiar. In terms of their literary practices, for example, modern women might not recognize some individual titles but would see a kinship in literary choices that balanced classics with "good" mainstream fiction, while tending to avoid the literary avant-garde or popular culture. They would also identify with their predecessors' fascinated attention to women characters. Also both historically and in the present, women's reading groups have chosen nonfiction books that would elucidate historical or scientific developments for the general reader, that would illuminate the issues of the day, or that would inform them about the lives of others, especially women.

Present-day women could probably also relate to the social processes by which earlier reading groups formed, especially their precipitation out of informal social networks that brought together somewhat different yet broadly similar kinds of middle-class to upper-middle-class women for literary discussion with like-minded peers. Twenty-first-century women are, however, linked to a wider variety of formal organizations (including the workplace, alumnae groups or sororities, and a host of specialized women's organizations) from which book groups also form. Both then and now, women have usually been drawn to reading groups as adults, often adults with children, and have frequently stayed in their groups for many years, experiencing the changes of adult life in the company of these companions. Some socially elite groups are well over a century old, quite literally tying the nineteenth century to the present. Even mother-daughter groups, recently quite popular, existed in the nineteenth century.

The emotional closeness that such groups can foster, and the concomitant sense of solidarity, has also been a constant over time. In fact, the rituals of solidarity that reading groups celebrate have remained uncannily similar. Like nineteenth-century groups, present-day women's reading groups have "pic-nics" together, attend cultural events together, hold annual Men's Nights, or set aside a special evening every year that is dedicated to honoring their warm feelings for each other and the group that brings them together. I imagine that nineteenth-century clubs witnessed the conflicts that also mark book group interactions today, but evidence of conflict is difficult to unearth from the flowery language of harmony that characterized their public self-descriptions. Despite such conflicts, many contemporary reading groups, like those of the past, provide a special kind of closeness that is a degree apart from ordinary friendships. This provides a strongly supportive, even empowering, environment for participants—much as was the case a century ago.

What one might call the "cultural work" that women's reading groups perform has also remained very similar along at least three dimensions. Both historically and in the present, book discussion groups have given women different ways to "narrate the self," that is, to understand their lives or vicariously to live through other choices, other ways of being in the world. This kind of imaginative experience, enabled both by encountering literature and also by hearing what other women bring to and carry away from their reading, contributes—although not in any simplistic way—to identity formation, development, even change.

In C. Wright Mills's (1959, 5) terminology, reading groups have also provided a space for women to think about how their inner lives and external careers relate to "the larger historical scene." In reading groups, women have found themselves considering the place of women in relation to men or individual lives in relation to some of the values and categories (religion, race, family, sexuality, nation, the public sphere) that structure the narratives we read and the lives we lead. Again, I posit that this reflection is creative, not simply reactive, for it has led and continues to lead to cultural invention.

Finally, these groups have always enacted an interesting tension between equality and cultural or social distinction. Ideally, women's reading groups are gatherings of equals, and many groups, past or present, have described and experienced themselves in this fashion. Yet by constituting themselves as reading groups and differentiating themselves from social groups that "just chat," they have ideologically constituted themselves as hewing to a higher purpose than many other women's groups.

Whether in the nineteenth or in the twenty-first century, they have also pragmatically drawn a boundary around themselves that excludes women who do not find literary discussion an easy or pleasurable activity. Nonreaders (even occasional readers!) need not apply. Practically as well as conceptually, the "boundary work" of reading groups has separated them from other women whose educational or social backgrounds would make them uncomfortable discussing books. Literature becomes a cultural marker for distinction. As such, it may provide part of the cultural, even moral, undergirding for the almost utopian feeling of specialness that has tended to pervade reading groups, a counterpoint to the liberatory experience of discussing books among peers, which also makes them special occasions.

Social distinction has also appeared among reading groups both historically and in the present. This is most obvious in the case of the racial divide that has separated black and white women's reading groups. Hierarchical relations between groups have also existed along class lines, in part because reading groups have tended to draw members from preconstituted informal social networks. Thus the social hierarchy of reading groups in large communities, whether in nineteenth-century Providence or twenty-first-century Houston. Internally as well, reading groups can leave some members marginalized because of social differences or differences in literary taste and cultural orientation. I do not mean to imply that reading groups were or are *really* hierarchical despite pretensions to equality. Rather, they make both gestures—toward inclusion and exclusion—simultaneously. It is the tension between the two, I think, that has made them such fruitful sites for the reproduction and reworking of the cultural hierarchy.

Differences between Contemporary and Nineteenth-Century Groups

Most differences between historical and contemporary white women's reading groups result from the ways middle-class women's lives have changed during the past century. Today, for example, almost all reading group members have completed a college education and many have attained master's or Ph.D. degrees. It is a rare group that includes even one participant who has not attended college. Higher education for women, once a reform that reading groups supported by fund-raising for scholarships and other social agitation, is now commonplace. In fact, since 1982 women have graduated from college at an even higher rate than have men (U.S. Department of Commerce 2001, table 284, 175), which makes contemporary women's reading groups seem like an endeavor in continuing or lifelong education rather than a compensatory activity.

This is just one instance of a more general process in which twentieth-century white middle-class women can be situated historically, from the perspective of concrete changes in their lives. An account of these changes can both illuminate why women continue to be more involved with reading groups than are middle-class men and explain some of the differences between present-day women's book clubs and their nineteenth-century counterparts. This context is also useful for considering what kinds of "identity work" women might be accomplishing in contemporary reading groups, which the next three chapters address.

Why Reading Groups Now?
And Why Are Most Participants Women?

In the twentieth century, middle-class white women's lives changed dramatically. Like all Americans, they were affected by the great events of the century, from the Depression to the two world wars, the Cold War, and more recent limited conflicts, as well as by the spectrum of modern movements for social justice and ecological awareness. Women felt the impact of consumerism and the mass media, the rise of an increasingly urban service- and information-based economy, and the gradual emergence of a global world order. They experienced the growth of therapeutic discourse, the rise of New Age spirituality, and the recrudescence of religious fundamentalism. They witnessed the rise of ethnic and religious diversity in the United States, and they lived through a rising tide of divorce and threats to the family from drugs to school violence. Yet the transformations of middle-class women's lives have also been inflected differently than have those of their male counterparts in both substance and timing.

For example, American women did not achieve full, voting citizenship until 1920, and it was not until the 1960s that formal barriers to educational equality for women crumbled. In the nineteenth century, large numbers of men entered the marketplace as wage earners in the industrializing economy. Yet it was the twentieth century that witnessed women's massive entrance into a pattern of paid employment that more and more resembled men's.[1] As sociologist Arlie Hochschild (1989, 11–12) says, "It is women who are being drawn into wage work, and women who are undergoing changes in their way of life and identity. Women are departing more from their mothers' and grandmothers' way of life, men are doing so less."

Demographic changes affected the sexes differently as well. American women shared with men the benefits of longer, healthier lives, but the decrease in family size, coupled with a longer average lifespan, had far more impact on women, giving them many more years without the responsibilities of child rearing. Women's increased control over their own reproduction also had immense implications for women's sexuality as well as for family planning. And although this issue is still under debate, some analysts claim that even divorce affects women more than men, whether emotionally or financially.

It can be argued that middle-class women's lives changed more during the twentieth century than did those of their male counterparts. Hochschild's work implies that this is the case. And Theodore Caplow's 1970s restudy of Muncie, Indiana, the famous "Middletown" of Robert and Helen Lynd's pioneering 1920s community study, provides some fascinating support for this notion. For example, in the 1920s almost no middle-class women worked in Middletown, and working-class women worked only when their husbands were unemployed. "By 1978," Caplow reports, "this situation had changed out of all recognition" (Caplow and Chadwick 1979, 376). Almost half the middle-class women worked (the same proportion as working-class women), and a husband's unemployment was no longer an important motivation.

Among Middletown youth, although high school boys' patterns of independence from home (as measured by nights out per week) shifted little between 1924 and 1977, high school girls' patterns showed that they stayed home much more in 1924 but that by 1977 they were away from home as much as boys. Similarly, by 1977, high school girls, who fifty years before were four times as likely to be dependent on their families for money as were boys, were earning and managing their own money at the same rates as boys. And in terms of what they valued from parents, in 1924 adolescents listed "spending time with their children" as the most desirable quality of a father but "being a good cook and housekeeper" as most desirable in a mother. By 1977, adolescents claimed that the most desirable quality of both mothers and fathers was "spending time with their children and respecting their opinions" (Bahr 1980, 39–41, 48).

Culturally, as well, the consensus about how middle-class men ought to live their lives has been relatively stable and strong over the course of the past one hundred years, continuing to privilege a primary dedication to work complemented by a secondary involvement with the family. Yet during that same period, women have faced the fracturing of what historian Barbara Welter (1966) has called "the cult of true womanhood," the nineteenth-century ideology that assumed women should be domestic, pious, pure, and submissive. Now there are several competing ideals about women's nature and proper place. Liberal ideology highlights women's similarity to men. New traditionalists raise the banner of difference and a revival of domesticity. Radical matriarchalists also claim large differences between the sexes, sometimes harking back to a goddess-inspired spirituality. Contemporary women have a considerably larger array of life choices than did their predecessors, and their lives are not only very different from those of their mothers and grandmothers but also very different from each other.

Yet all of these choices are matters of public and private contention. It seems that whether a woman has or does not have children, whether she works for wages or works at home, whether she stays in a marriage, gets a divorce, or comes out as a lesbian—let alone when and how she does any of these things—some scholarly study or social group can find fault with her choice. And because women are more involved with the family than are most men, even if women are happy with their chosen path, their lives usually involve sharper transitions than do men's. For example, college-educated women learn habits of discipline, efficiency, goal-directedness, and career-directed ambition, but raising young children also requires a very different set of emotional and intellectual sensitivities. At the other end of the parenting years or upon the occasion of divorce, women more often than men move from a family-centered life into full-time paid employment, another demanding disjuncture.

In the recent past and present, then, women have had to negotiate many issues in order to fashion a life for themselves. This process is more open-ended than is the case for many middle-class men because of women's newly expanded range of choices and a lack of clear-cut templates. It can also be more compelling because women, more often than men, are in the grip of conflicting expectations both from the environing culture and from their own internal sense of what a woman ought to be. This could explain why women, more than men—and despite what social analysts measure as significantly less leisure time for women than for men—choose to engage in collective reflection and dialogue between texts and lives. Reading groups serve a much-needed function for contemporary women, for whom the "social construction of identity" is less an academic theory than a pressing personal question.

Further, women's new relation to the world outside the home has continued to be vexed by gender issues. In part because women reformers of the nineteenth century never really tackled what they saw as the "masculine" public sphere of business and government, during the twentieth century women have been accepted into the public world on its own pre-existing terms. Women have gained rights as university students, citizens, and workers by inclusion into these social categories as if the categories themselves were not already gendered. Yet higher education, the state, and the world of work have had—and even now continue to have—a masculine "bent." For example, women's legal status assumed dependency on a man until very recently, and the courts still treat women differently than they do men.

By the same token, higher education in America has, until quite recently, been very different for women than for men. This is most obviously related to heavily normative expectations about what women's lives will be like after college. These expectations have changed during the twentieth century, but certain commonalities have continued to mark women's experience of higher education with remarkable persistence.

Most obvious were the formal barriers to educational equality, such as women's exclusion from colleges and universities or postgraduate programs and professional schools. The second wave of feminism and the federal government's passage of Title IX were responsible for lowering those barriers to educational equity. Less formal barriers—from disparities in funding or sexual harassment to differential parental expectations, differences in tracking and counseling, or peer cultures that pit educational attainment (especially in certain subjects) against feminine popularity—have been harder to erase.

In this regard, it should be noted that women college students have been disproportionally represented among the humanities and social sciences. This may be because of barriers discouraging women from entrance into the sciences or engineering, or because of the perception that there is a less instrumental link between women's university education and careers than there need be for their male counterparts. Given their differential participation in the labor force, college-educated women may have also maintained some links to the nineteenth-century ideal of the accomplished and cultured woman, which would account for the fact that female undergraduates have been overrepresented in academic majors involving the appreciation of art and literature. This kind of experience during college may contribute to the fact that reading groups attract more women than men even now.

As for work, the very success of nineteenth-century women's attempts to broaden their sphere of action—first, in reading groups and, later, in agitation for social reform—contributed to dramatic transformations in women's participation in the world of paid employment. Once confined to a severely limited domestic sphere, middle-class women today face so many conflicting demands on their time and energy that it is less surprising that their reading group activity has changed than that it has not disappeared altogether. The twentieth century has witnessed a revolution in middle-class women's work life, both at home and in the marketplace. Yet this has failed to integrate women equitably into the marketplace, while leaving them with a bewildering array of life choices and few, if any, clear models to follow.

At the turn of the twentieth century, married women's experience of work was very different from that of their husbands. Many middle-class women never worked outside the home. And although their work was demanding, it was confined to a domestic sphere that most men and women considered to be separate from and almost antithetical to the capitalist marketplace.

The twentieth century witnessed vast changes in this pattern of employment for women, so that by 2001 women comprised 46.6 percent of the paid workforce, and even among mothers with children under three, more than 50 percent are employed.[2] Various factors have contributed to this shift. The Depression caused women to search for employment, either as a supplement to their husbands' earnings or as sole wage earners for their families. World War II also disrupted traditional patterns of employment. During the late 1940s, both ideological forces (a revived cult of domesticity was one pillar of the postwar "return to normalcy") and institutional pressures (the closure of federally financed day-care centers) pushed women into the home. Yet the 1950s actually witnessed a rise in married women's employment. The women's movement of the 1960s, fomented in part by educated but unemployed married women (suffering the "problem that has no name," according to Betty Friedan's influential book *The Feminine Mystique* (1974 [1963], 11–17), validated women's paid employment, raised consciousness about barriers to women's entry into a variety of jobs and careers, and urged social supports such as child care that would make the workplace more hospitable to women. In the 1970s and 1980s, the end of the rapid rise in the American standard of living put a different pressure on the traditional patterns of married women's withdrawal from the workforce. Rising divorce rates (which, as analysts have pointed out, had been rising since the turn of the century, but only in the 1970s overtook the combined rates of death and divorce) have also tightened women's connection to the world of paid employment.

Employment patterns among middle-class women now resemble those of their male peers to a far greater degree than would have been imaginable to women one hundred years ago. Yet as in education, there are still vast differences between male and female experiences of work, whether in the marketplace or at home. Most people are familiar with the persistence of the wage gap between women and men and recognize that women are still ghettoized in certain occupations or occupational specialties. More recently, sexual harassment has risen to public prominence not just as an experiential reality for many women at work but also as one mechanism of discrimination. It is also significant that women still bear the brunt of the responsibility for what sociologist Arlie Hochschild (1989) calls "the second shift" of housework and child care—which leaves them with less leisure (and proportionally more exhaustion-related stress) than men experience. And the timing of careers, which often demand maximum commitment during a person's twenties and thirties (what economists call a "tournament model" of competition for rewards in later life), creates a structural tension in women's lives between childbearing and child rearing and the imperatives of paid employment. Work conditions in the United States are also inflexible compared with those of Northern Europe, particularly in the areas of family leave, part- and flex-time scheduling, and retraining for those who have been out of the workforce.

In effect, the world of work has remained doubly gendered, with troublesome consequences for women. On the one hand, housework or nurturing work—the work that economist Nancy Folbre calls "caring labor"—is not recognized as real work, either in terms of financial remuneration or in terms of what economic indices such as the GNP count as "productive." Despite praise from mass circulation magazines, segments of the clergy, and other fractions of the intelligentsia, women at work in the home have good reason to experience their way of life as being culturally devalued. Moreover, as fewer women stay at home for shorter and shorter periods of their lives, working at home can be isolating. It is precisely this isolation from other adults—as well as from the mainstream of the culture in general—that motivates some women at home with young children to join reading groups.

On the other hand, the structure of paid work in the marketplace, especially full-time employment and professional careers, assumes an employee with no family responsibilities except to earn money. This means, in effect, that paid employment as we know it is built around the assumption that the employee is either totally autonomous or is constrained only by the responsibility to others that has traditionally belonged to the male within the family. So professional careers and most other occupations can be characterized as structurally gendered male.[3] And indeed, women often feel a distressing lack of fit between their aspirations or imperatives as women and the demands of the marketplace.

In sum, the extension of "universal" categories to cover women without taking into account their differences from men—differences relating to biology, especially to reproduction, as well as those relating to the traditional middle-class family form and division of labor by gender—has left women's realities and concerns still fairly marginal to the core institutions of the American mainstream. My argument here is that women's inclusion in education, the economy, and the polity has been different from that of men because of a gendered division of labor within the family, which has never been adequately addressed. Because the public realm has a masculine cast, women have found themselves somewhat at odds with its proscriptions, somewhat out of phase with its expectations.

This difference was easier to understand during the nineteenth century, when formal exclusion from public life was coupled with a strong ideology of domesticity and natural difference. The twentieth century has been more confusing because informal barriers often feel like individual choices rather than social constraints. Indeed, the very successes of organized womanhood in the past have won significantly more options for the women of today. Similarly, during the twentieth and now the twenty-first century, it has become unclear whether (or under what circumstances) women are better served by claiming similarity to men, and when, on the other hand, it is strategic to highlight their important differences. Under such institutional and ideological circumstances, reading groups have continued to be important for women, in particular, because of women's need to negotiate life choices and identities that are, as argued earlier, both significantly more open and uncharted than in the past and yet are still not really well served by the major institutions of our social order.

How Are Contemporary Groups Different, and Why?

The broad changes in middle-class white women's lives explain not only why contemporary reading groups have continued to be important forums for women but also why they differ from nineteenth-century groups.[4] I have already mentioned the change in members' educational level and the ways reading groups have shifted in function from supplementing nineteenth-century women's meager formal education to continuing some of the pleasures of twentieth-century women's college experience in a more informal venue.

Women's reading groups have also ceased to give detailed reports on the books they select each month. In the nineteenth century, women spent long hours preparing such reports, which they often wrote up for presentation and even for distribution to other clubs. Today, if there is a member who is responsible for presenting a book, she usually introduces it briefly, drawing on biographical information about the author and on reviews in periodicals such as the *New York Times Book Review* or *Publishers' Weekly*. Sometimes she is only responsible for generating discussion questions. Groups may even dispense with preparation altogether, hold no one responsible for presenting a book, and just jump into groupwide discussion.

This difference may be related to the busyness of contemporary women's lives, but it also has a performative dimension (Butler 1990). By their earnest application to scholarly research, nineteenth-century women were communicating their seriousness of purpose to themselves, to each other, and to the world at large. They were enacting an equivalence (even if only approximate) between their endeavors and those of a college class-room. Contemporary women do not have to acquire—or prove—their competence in this way, because they are already college educated. The in-formality of their book discussions expresses a level of ease with literary analysis that comes with prior experience. Often they cite the fact that they enjoyed talking about books in college as a reason for their participation in reading groups. The format of contemporary groups communicates a self that is already so well acquainted with books and book discussion that book talk is easy and "natural," pleasurable rather than laborious. These modern selves are the heirs to decades of struggle to establish and broaden women's higher education. The very "naturalness" of informal reading groups is a his-torical construction, the sediment of efforts contributed in part by earlier reading groups, who would probably be both surprised and gratified to see the casual competence displayed by their descendents.

Contemporary groups have also shed much of the procedural formal-ity that marked earlier groups. Gone are the slates of officers, the meticulous attention to parliamentary procedure, the elaborate minutes, slogans, mot-toes, and yearbooks. Again, time pressures may contribute to their disap-pearance, but again, the expressive dimension of present-day informality is important. Where once such groups provided women tutelage in the skills of running a formal organization and an education for citizenship and lead-ership in the public sphere, now other groups and organizations provide that tutelage. Contemporary women come to their reading groups with a sense of how to set up an agenda and delegate tasks, a sense so deeply inter-nalized from participating in other kinds of organizational meetings that their reading groups can afford them the relief of informality. Similarly, they have already established that they are citizens, organizers, and leaders, so they do not need another occasion to practice these skills or demonstrate them to each other or to the broader world.

Most strikingly, women's reading groups today are different from those of their predecessors in that they have no larger or more social mission than to gather women together for the companionable discussion of books, ideas, and experiences. Indeed, the procedural informality of their meetings may also be expressive of this more purely cultural intent. Many women who participate in reading groups are involved in other socially relevant ac-tivities. Yet only a small number of book discussion groups see themselves, as groups, expressing a social mandate in any way resembling those of nine-teenth-century literary groups and the women's club network those literary groups spawned.

The earlier organizations claimed to represent all women. This was never the case, for the movement was limited by both class and race, but the illusion was served by two factors. First, literary clubs and the broader wom-en's club movement avoided both religion and politics. Second, middle-class women were more confined to domesticity and did not have the possibilities for imagining or living through the many divergent lives that middle-class women have today. But after a century of broadening options for middle-class women, those older organizations have been overtaken by a host of more specialized and ideologically divided associations that serve the immense variety of women's contemporary concerns and speak with the many different voices women now claim. For example, academic groups such as the Sociologists for Women in Society or the International Association of Feminist Economists address the work/home question at the level of both theory and practice. Almost every professional group has a women's association concerned with equity, advancement, and issues relating work to family, sexual orientation, and other aspects of domestic or private life. Broader-based and more issue-oriented groups address general problems from sexual harassment and domestic violence to questions surrounding reproduction. Other more explicitly ideologically based groups also proffer analyses and solutions for the gender dilemma as they define it, whereas umbrella groups such as the National Organization for Women attempt to reach broad constituencies for political interventions.

It is not surprising that reading groups now have no integral connection to social reform. Other organizations have taken up that mission, or more properly missions, because the unity of nineteenth-century middle-class women (always somewhat illusory) has fractured into a bewildering array of possible orientations toward the opportunities and constraints structuring middle-class women's lives at the end of the twentieth century.

It is also true that during this same period, a constellation of factors has reshaped the literary field, making more tenuous the ideological connection between reading good books and reforming the social world. The late nineteenth and early twentieth century witnessed the decline of the cultivated amateur "man of letters" who wrote for a general audience of people much like himself and who saw literature as part of a broad civilizing process. Literary studies became professionalized when they were institutionalized as departments in the university around the turn of the twentieth century. By now, creative writing itself has become another academic discipline, offering advanced degrees. Along with departmentalization, literary studies developed specialized professional journals. This rewarded academics who wrote for each other rather than to a broad audience. Reinforcing this tendency is the decades-long rise in special interest publications and concomitant decline in the "general interest" periodical in which men of letters spoke as citizens or cultural critics.

Some scholars claim that professionalization has democratized recruitment into literary studies by making it possible for any talented student to master textual analysis. Certainly, the content of curricula in literature reflects a broader definition of literature than was true in the middle years of the twentieth century, and the umbrella of cultural studies has extended literary studies not only into popular culture but also close to the borders of history and anthropology. But there is a cross-cutting tendency within the field for scholars to speak in specialized technical terms that rival the arcane terminology of the social sciences. Linked to professionalization, this development has isolated academic literary discourse from a broader middle-class audience, despite literary critics' often genuine desire to link literature to its social and political concerns.[5]

Despite these developments, increasing numbers of middle-class women have continued to join reading groups since the 1980s. Reading groups appear to provide a particularly valued kind of social and intellectual support for middle-class women, even if participants have also turned to more activist groups to deal with other concerns. In the latter part of this book I describe in more detail how contemporary women's reading groups function and characterize some of the needs and desires they fulfill, but I briefly address these questions here in relation to the social-structural changes I have already described.

The radical transformation in women's lives over the past century, and the widening options it has brought in its train, may have made the kind of interaction provided by reading groups especially valuable, although differently so than in the past. For one thing, as discussed earlier, all of today's much vaunted choices are to a certain degree problematic. Traditional women find their lives more culturally devalued than ever before because fewer and fewer women participate in this way of life, and because the ideology of separate and morally superior womanhood—with its implicit critique of the marketplace—has lost its hegemonic place in the middle-class worldview. Career-oriented women find the world of remunerative jobs and professions gendered in ways that make it hard for women to compete as equals to men, whereas women who withdraw from paid employment during their child-rearing years face demanding transitions. Moreover, men's lives have not changed in ways that are symmetrical with the changes in twentieth-century women's lives.

Even if one were to disregard such issues as problems to be debated, they entail a need for adjudication, negotiation, and self-reflection. Moreover, because of the range of possibilities and the rapidity of change, the lives contemporary women are forging for themselves lack clearly defined role models, and there is even less that speaks to what might ideally be possible. Finally, many women no longer have automatic access to what Carroll Smith-Rosenberg (1985) calls the "world of love and ritual" that nineteenth-century women—who were more separated from the worlds of adult men—created together in close relationships with other women, whether kinswomen or friends. Instead, women at home often face isolation from other adults, and even if they are not precisely cut off from adult companionship, they often feel a distance between their lives and the intellectual mainstream of our culture. Women at work, perhaps especially in male-dominated occupations, can often feel set apart from other women, and most occupations are so specialized that they do not validate a persona characterized by broad interests or holistic humane and aesthetic concerns. This is, of course, a problem for men as well as for women, but women's historical self-definition has been that of "guardians of culture" and cultural generalists (even dilettantes), so there may be more resistance among women than men to being forced into narrow occupational slots.

Reading groups have become a cultural form that can help women with many of the lacunae, complexities, and contradictions in their lives. In their present form, reading groups can provide a forum for self-reflection that is not narcissistically self-referential but involves learning through literature—both fiction and nonfiction—about the most important objective and subjective developments of the contemporary world. For women whose lives entail the uncertainties of unmapped territory, they can offer the comforts of discussion with like-minded peers. This discussion often blends lives in books with lives lived by others, whether those gathered together or those known to a member of the group. This kind of contemplation can offer the security of similarity, the challenge of divergence, and the possibilities of the hitherto unimagined. And because groups tend to continue over decades if they are satisfying to the members, they offer women a chance to deal with major life transitions in the company of well-loved books and companions.

Reading groups can offer women both support and the wherewithal to explore their identity and negotiate its complexities over time. In this, reading groups resemble therapy groups and consciousness-raising groups, and many who do not know about reading groups draw that comparison upon hearing of them for the first time. Yet reading groups are different. For example, reading groups do not generally deal with the inmost reaches of subjectivity, and indeed, groups often perceive members who become too preoccupied with their own personal problems as difficult or disruptive to the real purpose of the meetings. Reading groups also do not pathologize members' personal issues, so they are not contributing to the spread of a "patient" or "victim" mentality. On the other hand, reading groups do not generally have a political or even a public mission. Yet they allow members to think about themselves and the social world in ways that, if not collective, can often provide critical purchase on the dilemmas facing contemporary women. This kind of discourse appeared in the feminist movement of the 1960s and 1970s, but even during the height of the second wave of feminism, most middle-class women were not mobilized, and many did not agree with feminist ideology.

Herein lies the most salient difference between reading groups and the plethora of other support groups or political groups women may participate in. Reading groups are centrally focused on books and ideas. They may engage issues of identity and provide validation for many different inflections of womanhood, but their primary mission, today as in the early years of the nineteenth-century literary club movement, centers on reading, the pleasures of the text, and normative conversations that consider both books and life experience. Reading groups still serve middle-class women as time spent for self-improvement, for personal fulfillment, and for exploration of personal identity, but most particularly as time for the development of a self that is engaged with the literary imagination and dedicated to the discussion of ideas, meaning, and values in the company of equally dedicated companions.

FOUR

Exploring the Social World of Houston's Reading Groups

Houston and its environs are the venue for my research on late-twentieth-century white women's reading groups. I chose this site largely for reasons of convenience: it is where I have a job as a university professor and where I could most easily locate and spend time with groups. However, it is also a very large metropolitan area, with substantial claims to represent the American populace.[1]

In this chapter I describe the setting and social world of Houston reading groups and then discuss how and why people join reading groups, arguing that this process always involves some kind of thought about the social order and their own lives. I also explore issues of group structure and interaction, including the processes of selection and discussion as they relate to groups' social nature (as well as what people "get" from reading groups). Here I argue that at their best, such groups provide their members with a compelling synthesis of the pleasures of reading and sociability, revealing the book through the lens of other people's perception and illuminating other people's experience through the lens of the book.

In the following chapter, which is organized around the ways groups form and enact their particular identity, I deal with questions of conflict, departure, and group demise. These also have a social dimension but engage the emergent normative solidarity that gives each group a special tone and a special position in regard to literature and the social world.

Houston and Its Literary Infrastructure

Houston's reading groups are conditioned by the urban geography and literary history of their location. The city itself, founded in 1837, is by now the largest city in Texas and by many measures the third largest city in the nation, although this sounds strange to anyone who has seen the huge conurbations of the Northeast corridor or California. Houston is also the nation's second largest port, and that, as well as its proximity to Mexico and Latin

74

America, has contributed in large part to its ethnic diversity. In the early twentieth century, Houston, like most of East Texas—an extension of the cotton and timber economy of the Deep South—was largely a city in black and white. Beginning after World War II, and with gathering speed in the 1970s, the booming oil and aerospace economy drew immigrants not only from across the country but from beyond its borders as well. Now Houston's largest minority population is made up of Mexican Americans, followed closely by African Americans, but there are significant groups from Southeast Asia, China, India, the Caribbean, and Latin America, as well as from Greece, France, and Eastern Europe—not to mention the newcomers from every region of the United States.

Among the experiences and traditions brought to Houston by the people who have made their lives here is their previous acquaintance with reading groups as a cultural form. Like their nineteenth-century predecessors, contemporary Houstonians often form or join reading groups because they have brought that idea with them from other locations. So, in terms of literary traditions, as well as in more obvious ways, Houston is a latter-day regional and global melting pot, ensconced within a fiercely individualistic, free-enterprise, and almost nationalistic Texas culture: the city has no zoning, for example, and a strong open-shop history.

Physically, Houston has all the characteristics of a relatively new Sunbelt city. It is a car city—in part because of the stunning heat and humidity, which also make it green and lush for much of the year—a city of suburbs and strip malls. Its downtown sports a group of elegant skyscrapers that grace the skyline and advertise in stone and steel the corporate or financial institutions they house. Here too one finds the equally elegant structures expressing elite Houstonians' concern for high culture: the Wortham Center, home of the Houston Grand Opera, Jones Hall, which houses the Houston Ballet and Symphony Orchestra, and the Alley, home of a respected regional theater. As in many new American cities, until recently the downtown was dark and inhospitable after working hours. Now a loft district to the north, renovated urban condominiums, and ranks of chic new apartments have begun to draw after-hours life to the clubs and restaurants springing up in the center city. A little farther south lie the museums, Hermann Park, Rice University, and the medical center. Almost a city in itself, the medical center has recently become the largest employer in Houston, although the oil industry and aerospace technology still largely condition the economy, which has boomed, stalled, and reconsolidated with those industries. With the exception of some gentrified areas in the east and north, Houston's upper middle classes tend to live near these institutions, in the southwest quadrant of the "inner" city.

In a process of expansion and suburban incorporation, Houston has grown outward from its center in all directions. Nodes of development such as the Galleria area serve as mini-downtowns, and concentric bands of highways record successive eras of urban growth. At present, the 610 Loop marks the inner city from the outer suburbs (people live "inside" or "outside" the Loop), but Beltway 8 marks another stage of suburban development, and to the north, the FM 1960 semicircle delimits a yet farther band of housing, malls, and strip centers. Generally, the wealthier suburbs lie to the north or west of Houston, with the Clear Lake/NASA area to the southeast representing another burgeoning concentration of largely aerospace-related prosperity that lies approximately forty-five minutes away from Houston itself.

The literary scene in Houston has become quite vibrant over the course of the past few decades, both drawing on and contributing to the strong regional literary culture that Texas has nurtured since frontier days. Some of Houston's literary infrastructure, however, has been closely related to reading group activity. For example, the city's first public library—by now the center of an extensive city and county library system—was founded (as detailed in chap. 2) in large part by the Ladies Reading Club, which celebrated its centennial year in 1985. The creative writing program at the University of Houston was founded in 1979 and has achieved a national reputation in the decades since then. Other local colleges and universities also offer creative writing courses. By now, Houston claims as its own a surprising number of authors, whether native-born or residents by choice, and even attempts to lay claim to those who have long left the city and the state behind them. These authors, as well as some of the faculty members at local universities, are sometimes invited to book groups. Occasionally they serve as consultants or lecturers for continuing education courses, book-and-author luncheons—most notably the B'nai B'rith's annual book festival and the *Houston Chronicle*'s book-and-author luncheon—or the Women's Institute and Houston Club classes, which are organized by educated and civic-minded women who are also often members of book clubs. All of these literary institutions stimulate readership.

When I arrived in Houston in the late seventies, the bookstore situation was unpromising for readers. Near the city's center, there were a few high-quality independent bookstores with close connections to both national and local literary-intellectual culture. A few of the early chain bookstores, such as Cokesbury and Waldenbooks, could also be found, mainly in the suburbs. At about the same time that coffeehouses, bagel shops, and bakeries began to proliferate, another generation of chain bookstores sprang up in Houston. Now Bookstop (a Texas-based division of Barnes and Noble), Borders, and Barnes and Noble have entered Houston in force, incorporating cafés as part of their marketing strategy to make bookstores a welcoming social setting for reading and buying books. The cultural effects of these chains are a matter for intense debate in the publishing industry, and their competition poses a real threat for the independent booksellers, but they have clearly made books more easily available to readers. In turn this helps make the local environment more hospitable for the formation and sustenance of reading groups.

The Social Landscape of Reading Groups in Houston

Exploring the social world of Houston's reading groups provided an introduction to the variety of upper-middle-class lifeways in a Sunbelt metropolis. In the course of research, I drove several hundred miles through neighborhoods of the sprawling city and its far-flung suburban subdivisions to visit and observe meetings of women's reading groups. My notes from these observations—which ranged from one or two meetings with some groups to many months of attendance with others—as well as results from a survey that I administered to six women's groups contribute to my comments in this section.

Before I definitively settled on women's reading groups as the topic for this research, I attended several coed groups and one all-male group. The coed groups included Great Books groups meeting in the Heights Library and a social center in the Woodlands—a prosperous planned community to the northwest of Houston. There was also a Not-So-Great Books Group of university professors and other professionals that selected a wider range of books but maintained some of the formality of Great Books discussions. Genre groups tend to be mixed-gender groups, although the science fiction groups included more men than women, and the two romance groups I met later in the project were all-women groups. The mystery group that met at Murder by the Book (a specialty bookstore) was organized as a class but also held a holiday party. Members, many of whom attended several such "classes" over the course of two to three years, included librarians, accountants, retirees, engineers, and homemakers. Their generic tastes ranged from literary British mysteries to hard-boiled detective novels, and many participated to broaden their mystery reading. Of the two science fiction groups, one was held in the LaPorte Library, led by an elderly and very near-sighted female librarian who had read the genre for several decades. Members, whose ages varied widely, included people from Baytown south to the NASA–Clear Lake area, home to many aerospace-related engineers and scientists. The other science fiction group met inside Loop 610, which vaguely delineates the city from its suburbs. Members ranged in age from their late twenties to their early forties, and most had occupational links to engineering and information technology as well as friendships formed within the subculture of science fiction conventions or "cons." On the day I attended, the group gathered in a modest 1960s era single-story house whose yard had been so ignored that a large bush obscured the house number, made it difficult to enter the front door, and darkened the living room, which was casually furnished in "graduate student" style.

Couples groups of general fiction and nonfiction readers included a small group of six people meeting in the Meadows subdivision of southwest Houston—who selected mainly very serious fiction and planned menus to coordinate thematically with the books—and a larger group centered north of Rice University. The larger group was composed of engineers, scientists, and a couple who ran a home-decorating store featuring furniture, textiles, and design elements from Latin America and Asia. The singles group I attended for the longest time drew members from the Leisure Learning course catalogue. It met in a classical music café in the Rice University/Museum District and had a small core of long-standing members, whose numbers swelled to twenty-plus every time another six-week Leisure Learning session began. Participants included geophysicists and journalists, medical writers, engineers, lawyers, and a secretary from one of the science departments at Rice University.

The one all-male group I attended was inspired by the annual Men's Night discussion in a women's group. The majority of members were lawyers, many of them partners in prestigious Houston firms. For their meetings, conducted over dinner in reserved rooms at a variety of upscale restaurants, they selected mostly nonfiction titles about public affairs, although one member pushed for more fiction and spirituality related nonfiction. The meeting I sat in on, feeling more than usually conspicuous, centered on Nicholas Lemann's book *The Promised Land,* which is about the great migration of African Americans from the rural South to Chicago. It inspired a lively debate of issues ranging from inner city poverty and the failure of urban renewal to the merits of affirmative action. I also heard of four other all-male groups, one that began in the philosophy department of North Harris Community College, one among ministers, one that drew a generally professional and scientific membership, and one composed of Shell engineers that had disbanded as members were transferred out of Houston.

I attended my first Houston women's book club before I began this project. One of my friends invited me to discuss a paper I had written on several "feminist" novels. Members had attended the University of Texas, were married to doctors, lawyers, and businessmen, and were all considering careers or further education after an interval of stay-at-home motherhood. I remember driving into a very private circle of large older homes north of the university and entering a gray-green living room with an unusual kimono-esque piece of textile art above the fireplace. Groups of neutral-colored modern furniture made oases of comfort in the serene room, and a few large abstract paintings on the walls drew the eye into volumes of space below the high ceiling. During the discussion I was equally struck by the very existence of nonacademic women's reading groups and by the way this group had used women's literature to reflect on their own lives and desires for the future.

Next, I was invited by a colleague's wife to join a book group she was forming. This group, which I refer to as My Book Group, drew together women who mostly had some connection to Rice University or to a small, liberal Protestant congregation. At the beginning, I was one of the youngest members of the group and the only one who was single. The group met for over ten years, losing and gaining some members, and seeing all of us through life changes of varying degrees of intensity. My own feelings of being slightly distanced from discussions of marriage and children were one source of the realization that book clubs could be an object of study.

Early on in the project, after a brief newspaper article about book clubs and my research, I was contacted by several groups that made me aware of some real differences even within this largely college-educated constituency. For instance, a woman named EC invited me to two groups she belonged to. The first met in Houston's northwest suburbs. I sat in on a meeting in a member's home and then went on an outing with the group to another member's cottage on the shores of Lake Conroe, where the group of fifteen let me interview them for about an hour. Although at that point everyone in the group was staying at home with children and all but one had been to college, they were very conscious of their differences. They had married and had children at very different ages. Some had grown up in Houston, but many had come from other regions of the country, and some had spent a considerable time abroad. Their religious affiliations and levels of religiosity varied, as did their political orientations. Some were divorced and remarried, whereas others had remained in first marriages, which varied a great deal in emotional tone. Some had always been readers, others began reading seriously in college, and one member had taken to reading as a way of dealing with life in an American compound of oil industry families in Saudi Arabia. They saw their own social characteristics as evidence of the wide variety of life choices available to women in the late twentieth century. EC, whom I contacted later at a job she had taken in a bookstore, told me that over the next three years, most of the women had taken full- or part-time jobs and that the group had amicably dissolved during this transition.

When we first met, EC also told me about an older and more "serious" book group she had joined when she made friends with some members of the League of Women Voters. I came to a meeting in a two-story house with a small circular drive and what real estate ads call "mature plantings" in a 1950s in-town subdivision. The group was discussing E. O. Wilson's *On Human Nature,* and they referred back to mainly nonfiction selections such as Nietzsche's *Beyond Good and Evil* or Teilhard de Chardin's

The Future of Man. Members were mostly in their late forties to early sixties. Many were career volunteers, thus well off financially and seriously involved with civic and political issues. Perhaps because they were secure in their married identity, they did not discuss their families much; their own public organizational concerns took up most of the "chat" time. They wore little makeup, no nail polish, and low-maintenance hairstyles and were more plainly dressed than most prosperous Houston women. Refreshments were equally plain: coffee and store-bought cookies. The hostess's house was furnished with comfortably worn antiques, modern Scandinavian furniture, and somewhat faded color photographs that chronicled the family's trips to Europe and Latin America during the 1960s and 1970s.

About that same time, I was contacted by the founder of a small group that met in the far northern suburbs of Houston. LS's group had six members and had only been in existence for six months. As she drove me from her house to the meeting, LS confessed to me that she was worried about whether people would stay in the group because almost everyone was busy with young children, and some weren't really confident about reading and discussing books. She had initiated a policy of individual book selection, she said, to make everyone feel their choices were valuable, which she hoped would motivate them to keep coming. On that same drive, after asking me whether I found the directions hard to follow, she spoke at some length about the differences between living in the suburbs and the city, which she noticed whenever she visited an old friend who lived in central Houston. I found it ironic that she felt such a gap in lifestyles in a city that itself seemed to me an agglomeration of suburban developments and malls. Even my cynicism, coupled with the familiarity of the subject (the safety and blandness of the suburbs, the exciting diversity and dangers of the city), could not keep me from noting the seriousness with which she highlighted what she perceived as a deep fissure in Houston's middle classes.

I met with LS's group several times. The members were in their late twenties to mid thirties, and those who had worked had, with one exception, been elementary school teachers. Husbands were salesmen and middle managers. The houses where the group met were new, two-story, multibedroom houses in equally new subdivisions. This was not as cosmopolitan a group as, for example, the in-town University of Texas group. More people decorated in a "country" style, with pine-framed mirrors, bric-a-brac, and samplers with cheery mottoes on kitchen walls. One pre-Christmas meeting was suffused with the sweet scent of maple-vanilla candles, and the hostess served an elaborate and delicious chocolate dessert with layers of pudding, brownie mix, and Cool Whip. This was not a "take-out from the French bakery" crowd.

During the course of the research, I developed long-standing relationships with several groups, but I sat in on most just one to three times because they wanted to maintain their groups' privacy. I met them in three different ways. First, some heard about my project and invited me to visit, usually because they wanted to hear about the research or be included in it. Second, I contacted some because they were recommended by members of other groups or by people to whom I had mentioned my work. Third, as I undertook more systematic outreach, I asked groups rather randomly whether I could meet with them. Again, I was struck by individual group differences within a broad commonality of backgrounds and education. I attended three meetings of a feminist group with strong connections to the lesbian community, which was listed in the newsletter of a center-city Unitarian Universalist church. A sense of deep concern about feminist theory and practice informed all the group's book choices, from Margaret Atwood's *Cat's Eye* to Gerda Lerner's *The Creation of Patriarchy*. Their book discussions were among the most focused and "academic" of the Houston groups. Even the informal talk about films, concerts, and other cultural events that took place after book discussions was suffused with a sophisticated awareness of the politics of culture, and the group's cultural judgments were rarely cast in a purely aesthetic mode.

At the other end of the spectrum in terms of gender relations, I sat in on a very traditional women's group that met just south of the Rice campus. When I met with them, most members were in their late forties and fifties. The three original members had begun meeting every two weeks when they had young children. They, too, read many books by women. We met in a slightly unkempt but roomy two-story house whose owner was developing a part-time career as a writer after her children had left home. Husbands were professors, doctors, and other professionals, and most of the women were highly educated in the liberal arts. They had discovered a shared commitment to domesticity within traditional marriages. Several years later, I was unsettled to hear that the meeting's hostess—one of the most vociferous defenders of the group's social beliefs—had divorced.

Groups differed economically and socially as well. At one end of that spectrum, I attended two meetings of a socially and culturally elite group that annually ordered a full season's worth of hardcover books selected in conversation with the owner of Houston's best-known literary bookstore. The first meeting was held in the Cleveland Sewall house, a 1926 Spanish revival mansion that was one of the earliest homes in River Oaks (a very wealthy enclave) and that had been lovingly restored by its present owner. As we served ourselves from an elegant buffet prepared by a family employee, people laughingly informed me that not all of their houses were this splendid and that this visit was a treat for everyone. The group was very welcoming, although they asked me to remain on the sidelines rather than participate in the discussion. Under the circumstances, this made me feel rather like a latter-day Jane Eyre sitting in the corner. Procedurally as well as in ambiance, the group maintained some nineteenth-century traditions, with a relatively formal agenda and a program committee that selected the next year's reading.

In sharp contrast, I also met with Networking, a suburban group that grew out of a literature class taught by a feminist faculty member at North Harris Community College. In the words of one member, the founder had envisioned "a group of women who were interested in reading and in helping each other find a sense of self and place." We met in a member's modest apartment, decorated with self-assembled bookshelves and other slightly transient-looking pieces of furniture. The group began among women completing college as adults, and when I visited them they mostly had undergraduate degrees, and except for one retiree, all were working full time. Husbands' occupations included control-systems engineer, production manager, and supervisory investigator. Five out of seven members who completed the survey answered a question about income. In 2000 dollars, the average family income fell in the category of between $61,001 and $83,000, whereas two of the seven reported incomes in 2000 dollars of between $21,001 and $42,000, which was the lowest category or range of reported incomes for all groups surveyed (only two other women reported household incomes in this range).[2] The group Networking had provided an important support and source of ideas during a time of great transition for most participants: marriages had dissolved or changed drastically; women had acquired new skills and forged new identities. Even years after its formation, the group had a palpable feeling of deep camaraderie.

I developed more long-standing relationships with four reading groups. This did not happen randomly but because one or more members (with the implicit consent of the whole group) felt drawn to my research strongly enough to open their meetings to me for several months. Doubtless my own feelings of warmth toward the groups also contributed to the process.

One of these groups was a predominantly Jewish group of doctors' and businessmen's wives that had close connections to the psychoanalytic community. The women were familiar with urban high culture and generally liberal in religion and politics. The average household income of members who answered that question fell in the range of $139,001–$174,000, in 2000 dollars. I particularly remember meeting in a high-rise condominium with so many broad views over the treetops that it made me feel slightly dizzy. The rooms were decorated with modern art and contemporary furniture in shades of aubergine, and the women—mostly in their fifties to late sixties—had a similarly urbane and assured personal style of their own. I heard of the group from a member of a Rice literature department who had been meeting with the group as their discussion leader. They said her knowledge made discussions more substantive. This connection provided an easy entrée and made the group not only hospitable but also, I think, curious about what another Rice professor could bring to the table. I sat in on several meetings of the group but felt, in the end, that I was intruding on my friend's relationship with them. Most women in the group were active volunteers, and they were considering forming a group to discuss menopause and aging ("without whining," as one woman said).

I met another group, which I call the Interns' and Residents' Wives Group, in the early stages of my research. The group had begun about fifteen years before among the wives of the house staff at a Houston hospital. Several of the original members were still married to doctors, but some were divorced and either single or remarried to other professionals. They had recruited other members from neighborhoods or friends they met at work or at children's schools. They, too, were married to professionals (lawyers, geologists, managers, or the above-mentioned doctors). All had completed some college, and more than half the group had completed some postgraduate education. Ten of these eleven women were working outside the home (six full time), in occupations from attorney, nurse, and teacher to bookstore clerk. I became friends with two members. One was becoming a serious artist, and this personal transformation had unraveled her marriage. She was drawn to me in part because I was also single and my life was more similar to hers than were those of many other members. Another member, married and mother of five teen-aged children, felt very sympathetic to my situation as a single, adoptive mother. She was considering taking a part-time job and was curious about prospects at Rice University. Eventually she got a job at Rice, where she still works. I think she also saw me as a scholarly role model for her eldest daughter, who baby-sat for my son and with whom I became quite close during her final years in high school. I attended many meetings of this group, becoming in the words of one participant, an "honorary member."

I learned about the group I call here Readers Inc. because I became friends with one of its participants, who was a professor at another college in the Houston area. She had become intrigued by the project, invited me to attend her eight-member group, and was the linchpin of a friendly research relationship that lasted several years. Although "Katherine" was single and two other members had been divorced, most of the women were in their first marriages and had (at the beginning) teen-aged children. Husbands were professionals: doctors, scientists, a minister, and a lawyer. All of the women had college degrees except one, and three held advanced degrees. Four of the members had worked all their adult lives, and the other four were returning to work after staying at home with children.

The last group I met with for a long time actually became research partners with me for a summer. As detailed in the Preface, JG gathered other book club members, friends, and kin to help with a large outreach effort. I also attended ordinary meetings of the book club for over a year. All of the members were college educated, many in Texas. Married to lawyers, doctors, independent entrepreneurs, and corporate executives, almost all were dedicated volunteers. For example, several had served on the board of the Natural Science Museum. The group had grown from such connections, other friendship circles, and the neighborhood—most participants lived in the pinewoods of Memorial, one of the city's wealthiest residential areas. JG's own house, where we performed much of the work of the outreach campaign, had been designed by one of Houston's leading architects. It had a contemporary but very warm feeling and showed loving attention to even the smallest details. JG was a knowledgeable cook, and even after a decade I still enviously remember her kitchen, with its professional stove, ranks of copper pots, and large windows looking out into the trees. Most of the group was politically liberal, and they had been thinking of starting an activist group to address women's concerns, although to my knowledge they never went beyond several preliminary discussions.

These groups were very much like other Houston groups on several dimensions. All read a mix of classic and contemporary fiction and nonfiction, for example, and their recruiting practices resembled those of many other groups, as did the ways they structured their meetings. They were very much like other groups in educational, marital, and employment patterns as well. All four, however, were probably more liberal than most Houston groups, and they certainly were "successful" groups in that they had all been together very companionably for some years. To me, all four groups seemed both happy and outgoing. The fact that two had considered forming other activist groups around women's concerns probably makes them atypical as well, but I wasn't well-enough acquainted with other groups to have known whether any of them had also harbored unrealized ambitions of this nature.

Sociologically speaking, whether or not these four groups represent other Houston reading groups is only an important question if the research builds explicitly or implicitly on that claim. I have not explicitly stated that information gleaned from these groups is typical for others, but many of my tapes come from their meetings, so I have often used them as examples. However, I do not think of these groups as representative. Precisely because of this problem I have drawn on transcripts from these four groups mainly for illustrations of behavior or processes that are common to other groups as well.

More subtly, relationships with these groups may have affected the findings by compromising my own objectivity. Objectivity has been a vexed issue in sociology since its emergence as a discipline, and this is not the place to rehearse the complexities of the debate. In terms of practice, most sociologists rely on a notion, loosely adopted from Max Weber, that one's values may guide the choice of research questions but should be left behind once one begins the process of discovering the answers. This simplifies even Weber's position, for one of his inheritances from the debate about methods (*Methodenstreit*) that permeated German historical and social sciences in the late nineteenth century was a conviction that sociology had to understand—*verstehen*—human action in terms of its meanings for those human beings, rather than just explaining—*erklaren*—social causation in the fashion of natural science. This implies that (subjective) interpretation of people's subjectivity is one integral aspect of social science knowledge. Typically complex and ambivalent, Weber's formulation inspired a protracted twentieth-century debate about objectivity among sociologists. During the latter part of the twentieth century, postmodernists, feminists, followers of Michel Foucault and other poststructuralists, and scholars in the social study of science joined the fray. They critiqued the claims to disinterestedness on the part of seemingly objective research methods or disciplines. In some cases they also argued for the benefits of understanding all knowledge as conditioned by the social situation of the individual researcher or the social composition of the research community. This discussion has highly politicized and "metatheorized" the issue of objectivity, which is not always useful for scholars who are trying to generate fair and accurate knowledge of the social world.

These issues are particularly troublesome for those who practice participant observation or ethnography, which is the methodological keystone of this book. Participant observation depends much more than do "distant" methods such as survey research on developing relationships between the researcher and those being studied. Such relationships are crucial for understanding cultural nuances or subjective meanings, yet they necessarily raise the specter of bias. Bias doesn't haunt mathematical modeling or statistical analysis so doggedly, in part because of the logical and mathematical precision of these methods, which can obscure biased assumptions in the formulation of questionnaires or in decisions about how to choose data to model. Like most participant observers, I have tried very hard to remain fair during the research process and to keep research as the overriding goal in my developing relationships with book group members.

One piece of feedback indicates some success in this endeavor. When my name came up at an antiwar artists' meeting, the artist in the Interns' and Residents' Wives Group said she knew me. People asked for details. She then realized that in fact she knew almost nothing about me, because I was there to observe them. She recounted that she said to her friends, "It's like she's Jane Goodall and we're the chimps." I said, "I hope I don't make you feel like chimps." She replied, "No, but you know a lot more about us than we know about you." Seeing a somewhat stricken look on my face, she then said, "I think Jane Goodall must be a perfectly nice person. After all, the chimps tolerated her observing them for years at a time." The ironies of this exchange are numerous. It certainly pointed out how I had manipulated social similarity and "niceness" to gain access to groups, while keeping a certain distance so I could control the nature of the interactions and the use of the information gleaned from them. It also showed that book group members were interpreting me just as I was interpreting them and that they were using their resources (including my desire to be perceived as "nice") to try to control my behavior and interpretations of them.

The sophistication that reading group members displayed about social research gave them the ability, in fact, to control my interactions with them quite substantially. They decided whether or not I would tape meetings and whether or not I would participate in their conversation. This one quote from a member of the Traditional Women's Group gives a flavor of the kind of negotiation I often entered into, which ethnographers often refer to in discussions of "studying up," or working with populations who are the social equals or superiors of the researcher. As MT said to me during a discussion about a visit to her group,

> As we all know, an event being observed is changed, and we just don't want the event to be changed. The idea here is that this is the opportunity that people have to talk a certain way and that's precious enough in all our busy live and schedules that people just don't want any interference. The way you would be most welcome is if you tried to be as nearly invisible as possible. Please don't misunderstand. The people who will be getting together today do want to be cooperative. It's just that it's such a valuable event that we don't want to be essentially sacrificed by your being there. (Interview, 19 July 1990)

Fieldwork also involves the researcher's own demographic characteristics and social situation more than other methods. This is both beneficial and problematic. The ease of my access to white women's reading groups, for example, would have been hard for a man to duplicate. But the very social similarity of these research subjects raises problems. As the anthropologist Renato Rosaldo (1988, 78–81) says, studying familiar groups confronts us with a "zone of cultural invisibility," a social landscape so much like our own mundane reality that its inhabitants seem to be "people without culture." If studying people with strange customs and unfamiliar mores can create problems of stereotyping, exoticizing, or romanticizing a group, then studying "people like us" may not challenge the researcher's own blind spots or taken-for-granted assumptions about the social world. Natural scientists rely on peer review and replication to handle this kind of dilemma. Of those correctives, only peer review is usually helpful for the fieldworker, given that field studies are rarely replicated. Aside from such collective oversight, field-workers rely on reflective self-criticism.

Two aspects of this project, especially, called for this. First, because reading groups are generally middle to upper-middle class, the social group I belong to, it was hard for me to focus on their exclusivity. Like many informal associations and even some that are more institutionalized, such as religious congregations, reading groups draw from informal social networks. Because such informal networks are usually socially homogeneous, reading groups are as well. This seemed so "natural" to me as a participant observer from the same social stratum that I only gradually became aware that the easy fellowship of reading groups arose, in part, from keeping people not "like us" outside the circle. An important moment in this reflective process came when I lectured about early Texas reading groups to my sister-in-law's mainly working-class sorority. A talk that had been very interesting to more elite local audiences, some of whom even knew the names of nineteenth-century Texas reading clubs or members, generated no comments and not one question. As I looked out over ranks of obviously disinterested listeners, I realized that I was speaking to women who would never have been invited to the Ladies Reading Club of Houston. In conversation after the lecture, when one woman said she knew of someone who had once tried to start a book club, it became clear that even today this is a cultural form that almost entirely passes by women who have not graduated from college—approximately three-fourths of adult American women.

Second, it was also hard to recognize that some book clubs are competitive, conflictual, even interpersonally nasty groups, and that members of even "nice" book clubs can feel alienated, marginalized, or looked down on. It is likely that conflicted book clubs did not volunteer as research subjects. It is also probable that book clubs presented themselves in a good light when I came to visit, and that those clubs that allowed me to sit in for several months were especially companionable and self-confident. Members are apt to leave if they are discontented with a group, so in a sense the project itself was biased against finding them, because it was based on observing ongoing groups. Here entered some bias of my own, given that I began the research feeling that women meeting to discuss books were doing a good thing. In defense, after recognizing this "zone of invisibility," I made efforts to locate people who had left or felt alienated, and I searched out accounts of groups that had foundered on irreconcilable differences. At another level, I remain convinced that many groups are pleasurable for participants and that they make efforts to ensure that all members are satisfied. Otherwise, being voluntary associations, they would dissolve.

The Survey

To check some of the insights I arrived at through participant observation, I handed out a survey questionnaire to six groups, a total of 48 women.[3] The survey supported the ethnographic findings while providing some additional information. For instance, the survey confirmed that this was a very highly educated group of women. Of the 47 women who answered a question about their education, 10 (21 percent) had either master's or advanced postgraduate degrees (Ph.D., M.D., J.D., or equivalent), 11 (23 percent) had completed some postgraduate work, and 12 (25 percent) had graduated from a four-year college. Just 3 (6 percent) held only high school diplomas.

If the women's reading group members were highly educated, their husbands were even more so. Of the 40 women who answered this question and the one about their husbands' work situations (for 6 it did not apply), 22 (55 percent) said their husbands had attained an advanced postgraduate degree, whereas only 1 husband had not completed high school, and all but 4 held a four-year college degree or higher. Of the husbands, 36 (90 percent) were working full time, and four were retired or disabled. Not surprisingly, these men were for the most part involved in upper-level professional, managerial, and entrepreneurial positions. The most common occupations listed for husbands were physician (9), attorney and professor (4 each), and various kinds of engineer (3). Among the other occupations listed were investment banker or investor, business owner, production manager, computer consultant, real estate developer, export salesman, geology vice president, geophysicist, manager of financial systems, furniture store owner, international managing director, and supervisory investigator.

Given these educational and occupational levels, it is also not surprising that the average household income reported—in 2000 dollars—was in the range of $104,001–$139,000. Eight women reported a family income of $208,001 and over, whereas at the other end of the spectrum only 5 women (14 percent), including 3 who were retired, indicated family incomes in the $21,001–$42,000 range. This was, in other words, an affluent as well as an educated group.

Although husbands were employed as professionals, managers, and entrepreneurs, it is interesting that 27, or 63 percent, of the 43 women who answered a question about their own work situation were working either full or part time, with 5 more full-time than part-time workers. Just under a quarter of the respondents (10 women) described themselves as homemakers, whereas 3 women were either retired or disabled. Another 3 were either students or had been laid off. Given that most respondents were in their forties, I speculate that this group of women participates in the currently common pattern of returning to work as children return to school, although some respondents may have worked throughout their adult lives. Women listed occupations ranging from attorney, accountant, psychologist, and professor to bookkeeper, artist, nurse, or teacher. In fact, in response to a question about teaching, almost half of the women (22 out of 45 answering) said they were or had been teachers. This surprised me, but I think it reflects the perception of this generation of women that teaching was one of the few occupations open to women that provided both social prestige and a flexible schedule that could accommodate raising children. One thing that draws women to book groups is a love of learning and reading, so the numbers of women who had been involved with teaching may reflect such a connection as well.

All of the respondents answered questions about their marital status and religious affiliation. In relation to marriage, this was a quite stable, even traditional group. A total of 38 women (79 percent) were in their first marriage, and another 4 (8 percent) were in their second. The same number were divorced, 1 was widowed, and 1 had never been married. In terms of religion, 26 women (54 percent) indicated they were Protestant, 1 (23 percent) Jewish, and 5 (13 percent) Catholic. One person marked "Pagan," and 4 claimed "no religion." The high proportion of Jewish reading group members can partially be explained by one group, all of whose members but one were Jewish.

A total of 42 women answered a question about their age. The average age was 51, but ages ranged from 25 to 78, with the largest concentration, 25 women (60 percent), in their forties. Of the 38 women who answered, 20 (53 percent) said that politically they were moderate/middle of the road, whereas 11 (29 percent) said they were liberal/left, and 7 (18 percent) said they were conservative/right. This marks a slightly larger percentage of liberals than I would have expected in Texas at the beginning of the 1990s, but otherwise it is not surprising.

When the six reading groups were examined as groups, some were quite homogeneous on one of several dimensions. For example, despite the fact that three of the groups had members who differed in age by twenty-five years or more, two of these groups were highly concentrated around one decade, with a couple of "outliers" who were much younger or older. In one group with an age spread of from 25 to 51, four out of the six members who responded were in their forties; in another group whose oldest member was 64 and youngest was 39, eight of the ten women who answered the question were also in their forties. The remaining group with a large span between members' ages showed a more even pattern of distribution, with three women in their forties, two in their fifties, and two in their seventies. The three other reading groups spanned at the most a thirteen-year difference among members' ages.

This kind of generational concentration has interesting consequences for the life span of reading groups. The earliest that most women either found or join reading groups is in their mid to late twenties, during a transition from college into the occupational world or life at home with young children.[4] If these women find themselves in small and relatively informal groups, a common pattern is for the membership to remain close in age and for the group to continue through their lives—or at least until retirement, ill health, or failing eyesight intervenes. If the group is cohesive and fulfilling for its members, they will change their reading and their schedules to accommodate changes in participants' lives. They may meet at night rather than during the day if participants return to school or work, for example, or reduce the number of meetings per month (or the length of books selected) to compensate for increasingly busy schedules. So if the group is small, it tends not to reproduce itself but rather to survive only as long as its founder or central core of members does.

Larger and more socially elite groups, on the other hand, seem to have at least a chance of a very long life. For instance, a club in San Antonio, Our Book Group, has been meeting since the last decade of the nineteenth century. The Ladies Reading Club of Houston celebrated its centennial year in 1985 (although it has ceased to be primarily a book group). These groups tend to recruit from among middle-aged or elderly women of their city's social elite. Belonging to such a group becomes a badge of social distinction, an award, as it were, of having attained a certain social position. As one relatively young San Antonio woman was told at her first meeting with Our Book Club by an older woman who had disapproved of her candidacy, "Young lady, women have died waiting to join this club."

As is the case with age, patterns of concentration applied to certain groups along dimensions of education or work, but these were not necessarily the same groups. So, for example, one group of ten women that was fairly homogeneous in relation to education, with eight members who had completed two to four years of college (the outliers being one high school graduate and one member with a master's), showed a much more mixed pattern of involvement with work. Half of the members (5 women) were keeping house, three worked full time, one part time, and one was retired/disabled. Another group with ten of the eleven members working either full or part time (six worked full time) showed less similarity in education, with two members having completed between one and three years of college, two members with B.A.'s, five with some postgraduate work, and two with M.A.'s.

In terms of marriage, because almost 80 percent of all the women were in their first marriage, there was not much variation, but two groups were more diverse along this dimension than others were. One, with seven members, had two women in their second marriage, one divorced, and one who had never been married. Another group of eight had one widowed and two divorced members. Perhaps women who are in less traditional marital situations feel more comfortable in groups such as these, where everyone is not in a first marriage.

As for religion, the group with nine out of ten Jewish members was the least diverse. Most groups were overwhelmingly Christian and largely Protestant but also had two to five members of non-Protestant faiths (Catholic, Jewish, Pagan) or women who claimed no religion.

The way groups ranged along a scale of incomes was interesting, showing variation from one group to another but also variation among members of most groups. The wealthiest group was the least diverse in terms of income. The range here was (in 2000 dollars) between $139,001– $174,000 and $208,001 or more. But of the seven members who responded, six were at the income level of $208,001 and up. The group lowest on the dimension of incomes ranged between $21,001–$42,000 and $104,001–$139,000 for the five out of seven members who responded. This group showed no concentration, with members evenly distributed along the scale. The results, then, show important differences between groups, which range along a rough continuum of incomes, yet show significant ranges of incomes within each group except for the most wealthy. Overall, despite variations of income and education both between and within groups, reading groups are by and large a middle- to upper-middle-class phenomenon.

Founding or Joining a Reading Group

Groups grow out of existing social or institutional networks. Of the seventy-seven women's groups I located in Houston, for example, nineteen had some institutional connection, at least at their inception. Sixteen of these groups grew from networks formed in "women's" institutions, such as college sororities, the League of Women Voters, the PTO, or the AAUW. Three began as an activity in the auxiliary organizations for women associated with predominantly male workplaces. Examples include the group that began as the Interns' and Residents' Wives Group or the book discussion group associated with the Rice University Faculty Wives (now the Rice Faculty Women). Reading groups have begun as classes in, for example, women's literature or as discussion groups at churches or synagogues. Bookstores themselves have provided the springboard for several groups, as in the case of Nia Bookstore and Gallery, which is the point of purchase and has been an important organizational focus for about a dozen African American women's reading groups currently meeting in Houston. Brazos Books, Houston's preeminent literary bookstore, has served this function for several decades. Bookstore chains such as Barnes and Noble make a conscious policy of initiating book groups and providing a setting for existing book clubs. Libraries can also serve this function. In Houston, for example, libraries have served as meeting places for at least five women's groups and host at least four coed Great Books discussion groups as well as the LaPorte science fiction group mentioned earlier.

Like women's groups, coed and men's groups display a pattern of institutional and social linkages related to participant's nonliterary lives. For instance, as mentioned earlier, men's groups in Houston have sprung from occupational links such as the clergy, a philosophy department, and an engineering department at Shell. Coed groups have garnered membership from associations of University of Texas alumni or from singles groups at churches, the Jewish Community Center, and Mensa as well as from Leisure Learning Unlimited.

Despite the clear importance of formal institutions for facilitating the foundation of many book groups, fifty-six of the seventy-seven women's reading groups grew from neighborhoods or informal circles of acquaintances. Previous social connections with other women are not necessary, though. One of the groups described in *The Book Group Book* (Slezak 1995) began when a woman took out an ad in a local paper and put up a notice at a local bookstore. Even if participants are already known to each other in some fashion, they make it clear that their reading groups are not simply friendship groups or organizational spin-offs. In fact, many people stress that their reading groups are not made up of people they routinely socialize with. Participants may be friends with one or two other members. Indeed, this is usually how recruitment takes place. On the open-ended survey questionnaire (which garnered only a small number of responses), respondents were almost equally divided between those who had known no one or just one other person when they joined their group and those whose groups began among acquaintances or friends. If a group lasts several years, women may count several members among their friends. For example, of the 47 women who answered a question about the number of people in their groups they counted as close personal friends, only 3 (6 percent) said none, and only 7 (15 percent) said one. Fully 20 (43 percent) said they had two to four close friends, and another 17 (36 percent) said they had more than four close friends in their group. But even though the groups may include connections drawn from everyday social networks, their members view them as transcending these connections, just as the discussions include but go beyond ordinary conversations.

What people value about these book discussion groups can provide some clues about what is missing from their "real" lives. To put it more positively, it is clear that the act of founding or joining a reading group and deciding what its program will be provides an occasion for people to define who they are culturally and socially and to seek solidarity with like-minded peers. For many, joining a reading group represents in itself a form of critical reflection on society or one's place within it, because it demands taking a stance toward a felt lacuna in everyday life and moving toward addressing that gap. This action, in turn, reveals both to participants and to the analyst some of the ways in which contemporary society fails to meet its members' needs—needs that correspond in patterned ways to their social situations.

Housewives with young children and technically oriented professionals provide obvious examples of this process. Many women join reading groups during the time they find themselves isolated in the suburbs with young children. Members of the FM 1960 group were very articulate about this. "This group was a lifeline for me," claimed one member, while another said, "Days would go by when I hardly talked to another adult. What I missed was adult conversation." These women agreed that they didn't just miss talking to other adults but felt particularly deprived of substantive intellectual conversation. Another member of this same group, who had become a serious reader while in Saudi Arabia as the wife of an oil company manager, said she had tried to form a book discussion group there but that other women "didn't know how to talk like we do—they only wanted to chat." Yet another participant said she had been standing in line in a bank with her boisterous toddler and felt so worn down that she said to the woman ahead of her: "I'm at the end of my rope. I haven't read a book for months, I feel like I never talk to anyone over three, and my mind feels like it's just going to dry up and blow away." The other woman recruited her for the book group (comment at a book group meeting, 24 March 1992).

Many other women echo these group members' comments. One woman said, "I founded the group with several other young friends who were mothers and wives. We wanted to have some intelligent interaction among a group similar to ourselves: educated women who spent a great deal of our days washing diapers and planting caladium balls." Another who also answered the questionnaire in June 1991 said, "At the time I began going, I was at home with two young children. Book Club filled a void in. I lacked anything truly stimulating in my life except for my conversations with my husband. . . . I felt [Book Club] saved me from an otherwise drab existence. I loved my children and home life, but it was nice to have something outside of that existence to look forward to and be stimulated by" (both responses from the open-ended portion of the questionnaire).

Amplifying this line of thought, another said,

B If women are at home with children, they become children: their dialogue, their association is with younger people. . . . But the problem is that that adult woman doesn't mature as well. She doesn't prosper. There is no nurturing of her. And so, you want to go out and find out about the world? Ok, well, you know, Johnny is in a booster seat and Sara isn't even out of diapers. But when a woman [joins a book] group, there is a communal spirit, which I think women do better than men anyway because we were all sitting around the fire while they were out hunting.

D S So why now are we looking for community?

B Because we're still in the same place. I mean if you choose to be a mother, a woman at home with your children, you still are an adult woman alone with children. None of that has changed. (Interview by DeNel Sedo, February 2000)[5]

The comments of men and working women in single-gender book groups form an implicit critique of the narrowness and isolation of the occupational world. The Shell engineer who had led an all-male reading group for three years said, "You may not believe that engineers read a lot, but we do," and he told me about his co-workers' thirst for general and intellectually challenging reading. Other men mentioned a desire to read something less specialized than business or technical reading, and one lawyer in a men's book group commented, "I really feel isolated as a reader at work. You'd be surprised how few educated people read" (interview with TB, June 1997).

Professional women echo such sentiments and mention, in addition, their isolation from other women in male-dominated work settings. The founder of My Book Group told me, "I wasn't seeing any of my women friends any more, hardly any women at all, and I was spending my days talking technical 'oil-talk'" (conversation, 10 October 1986). She and others like her seek fellowship with other women readers to overcome the peculiar kind of gender isolation felt by women who have honed themselves to the narrow range of activities and behaviors congruent with a professional career.

One of the disjunctions that fuel people's desire to be part of a book group is the one that occurs between the broad, engaging intellectual discussions that often characterized their experiences in college and the life they find themselves living afterward, at home or at work. Postcollege shock may be a strong motivating force among groups founded when members are in their twenties, but even much older men and women mentioned wanting to join a book group because they missed the forum that college provided for humanistic discourse.

Joining a group also demonstrates members' recognition of their own, sometimes critical, position toward either literary or social values. Sometimes this positioning is explicit from the group's inception, as was the case with the feminist group that began by advertising meetings through Houston's First Unitarian Universalist Church (a local center of progressive social activity) and the *Women's Community Newspaper,* a publication that targets the feminist and lesbian communities. One romance group, although less public, is similarly self-aware that they are flying in the face of traditional literary judgment. Sometimes, however, the process of self-definition is more complex, as I discuss in the next chapter.

Group Structure

Part of what gives each reading group its distinctive character is how its members structure their time together. In one sense, there is very little *to* structure. The major organizational tasks involve deciding when and where to meet, how to handle membership (recruitment, conflicts, and departures), how to select what the group will read, and how to organize the discussion.

As I discussed in chapter 2, nineteenth-century groups tended to deal with all of these issues formally. Some of the larger, longer-lived, and more socially elite book clubs of the late twentieth century still adhere to a set format. Our Book Club in San Antonio, for example, still features written reports and a formal agenda. Literatae, a Houston group, continues to appoint a committee to select an entire year's reading. But on the whole, contemporary reading groups are much more informal in nature and would find the notion of a group constitutionalist, for instance, quite amusing. In fact, one of the few ways these modern-day groups resemble their progenitors organizationally is in their tendency to schedule the "book discussion year" along the lines of the academic year. Groups usually assemble for their first meeting of the season in late August or September and hold their last in May or June, with a hiatus for the summer months. Despite this general looseness, contemporary groups do have structure along a variety of dimensions. Later in the chapter, I discuss some of the "rules" groups have developed to shape their individual group structure and procedures.

Leadership

One of the qualities that make most contemporary groups very different from their predecessors is their lack of formal leadership. Where nineteenth-century groups tended formally to elect not only presidents but whole slates of officers, it is rare for modern groups to choose even a yearly president. Especially in larger groups or those that have complex schedules and rotation of functions such as hostess and discussion leader, one person will often be elected or "volunteered" by other participants as the group coordinator. But many times this function as well as others—such as keeping records of books the group has chosen—simply falls to whoever is willing to be responsible for it. As CS said about her group: "We have no president. Whoever's there at the meeting who asks, 'Well, what should we do now?' and has a piece of paper and a pen gets to be the secretary" (interview, 12 July 1991). Modern-day book clubs find themselves hard-pressed even to carve out the time to meet at all, so participants feel happy to give up responsibility to anyone who has the personal desire or ability to assume it.

Some members carry more authority within the group than do others. The founder(s) or original core members have the authority that flows from their initiative in forming the group. Consequently, they often display a feeling that the group "belongs" more to them than to latecomers. In many groups, one or two people have special literary authority, either because they have graduate degrees in literature or because they are integrally involved with the world of books, whether as teachers, librarians, or book-sellers. If a book group has emerged from a class, as did Networking in north Houston, these two functions may be united. But in most cases, group members regard the desire to take charge as a personal idiosyncrasy and welcome it as a relief. There are few rewards for assuming leadership, aside from the intrinsic pleasure of seeing the group flourish. Whatever modicum of control leaders can exact because of their authority is undercut by the voluntary nature of these groups. If people are not happy, they can leave. So despite the fact that some members are more involved than others and some exert more authority than others do over either organizational or literary decisions, book clubs generally display an egalitarian ethos. As one member of the Interns' and Residents' Wives Group said, "You see, but we're all lead-ers" (comment at a meeting, 10 July 1990).

Meeting Format

Whether its members are notified by printed schedule, telephone calls, postcards, or e-mail, groups usually meet once a month at the same day and time. This is often reflected in group names: the Tuesday Club or Second Friday Night Book Club. Depending on whether or not members work outside the home, these monthly meetings take place during the day or in the early evening, although, as I mentioned before, groups often change their meeting times to accommodate members if, for instance, women re-turn to the paid workforce.

Most commonly, groups meet in members' homes, although libraries, bookstores, and cafés or restaurants are also popular venues. Meeting in members' homes structurally limits most but not all groups to somewhere under twenty or twenty-five members. This also seems to be a "natural" ceiling for fostering informal discussion, although some groups are larger. Conversely, groups find it hard to meet if they are under seven or eight in number, for a group smaller than this will become uncomfortably small if only one or two members are absent.

Many groups make some effort to split the demands of hosting and leading a book discussion, either by scheduling these functions separately or by making sure that other members supply refreshments if the hostess is also the main discussion leader. Usually there are refreshments of some kind. This, too, marks an arena of similarity between nineteenth-century and contemporary groups, some of which celebrate their "discussions over the teacups" in much the same way as did their foremothers' groups; witness one African American Houston group called Sisters Sippin' Tea. How ex-tensive the refreshments are, however, varies widely.

Some groups elaborate the metaphoric link between reading and eat-ing as a central part of the group experience. The Meadows Book Club, a group of married couples, connects the subject matter of the book to the cuisine for that month's meeting: when reading Kafka, they ate sauerbraten. Others, like the League of Women Voters Group with their store-bought cookies, downplay refreshments, celebrating instead the difference between their book-centered sociability and other kinds of socializing. Another group of suburban women located in the wealthy Memorial area meets at approximately the same time of day as the League of Women Voters Group, but this group provides a magnificent buffet that made the phrase "the groaning board" come immediately to mind when I was first ushered into the dining room. This group appears more traditional than does the League of Women Voters Group: the house was a conventional Georgian mansion decorated in a bright, English-influenced style, and the women embraced a Southern mode of dress and makeup and congratulated the hostess on her refreshments with the comments of experienced cooks. In these groups as in the world beyond, food serves an expressive as well as a utilitarian function.

Book club meetings have a particular rhythm. Generally, they last about two hours, with the first twenty to thirty minutes passing in greetings and sharing of news. This chat ranges from personal issues related to work or home to events in the world of politics and culture. The last thirty to forty-five minutes move outward from the book discussion to more personal talk as members take their leave. Whatever administrative or ancillary issues there are (book selection, establishment of place for the next meeting, mention of absent members' health or family issues) tend to occur during those times.

Group Practices

Book selection and discussion are the central and defining activities of all reading groups, and many groups are concerned if they do not spend at least close to an hour discussing the book they have chosen. In these two defining activities, groups display a range of practices.

Book Selection Procedures

Formal Programs. Groups use several different procedures to select books. Each procedure tends to structure intragroup relations somewhat differently as well as to bring groups into different kinds of dialogue with literary authority. The most formal method, in which either a committee or one person develops a program for several months' reading, harks back to the large, strictly organized book clubs of the nineteenth century. When this model occurs in contemporary groups, they too are likely to be large and formally structured in other respects. There is also an association between this method of literary selection and participants' relative leisure and social distinction. The two Houston groups I know that delegate a committee to select a year-long program of reading, for instance, have rosters of more than twenty members, many of whom do not work outside the home, and can count on participants being able easily to afford to buy all the books for the year in hardcover at one time. Less stringently organized and socially elite groups are apt to take up organized reading programs of several months duration if they find a certain topic compelling. I have encountered such multimonth topics as Contemporary Southern Writers, African American Women Writers, and Commonwealth Literature.

Deciding on a program, even informally, makes book selection rather serious business. If the group delegates the responsibility for organizing the program to a committee or an individual, then one's reputation as a literary provider for the group can be at stake. So this method appears to engender the most dependence on cultural authorities, whether bookstore owners (who sometimes help plan an entire year's program), college professors, or respected journals and lists of notable or award-winning books. Working with such authorities appears to alleviate the responsibility for picking several months' reading and to add luster to the choices the selectors finally present to the entire group for approval.

Yet the program planners must not simply represent the dictates of cultural authority to their group but represent the group's interest and desires as well. I watched this process at work when I attended the large lunch-hour meeting in the venerable Cleveland Sewall mansion described earlier. In this case, the head of the program committee, while giving an interim report, said that because they were reading contemporary literature this year (that month, the group was discussing work by Donald Barthelme), her committee had thought to engage with social or cultural issues for next year's program. They had discussed tackling a country, but the committee was wary after their experiences with a recent year's program on China. As the group might remember, although the help of a professor of Chinese history at Rice University had been invaluable (here people murmured about how wonderful he had been), they had all grown a little tired of the topic by the end of the year. This statement elicited general support. People agreed that although they still had a lot to learn about China, they had felt a certain lack of variety after several months of reading about one country. Then a member suggested that one way to get more diversity in choice would be to select a topic that could offer more cultural breadth or cross-cultural comparisons.

The most popular proposal of such a topic came from a woman who suggested they read about "trouble spots of the world," which would include the Middle East, Eastern Europe, Latin America, and parts of Asia. People took up this suggestion with enthusiasm, but then one woman said that frankly, although she hated to sound socially irresponsible, she wasn't sure she wanted to read about world conflicts for an entire year—it sounded too depressing. Furthermore, she felt that discussing literature was the central purpose of the group, and this program looked as if it would all be "issue" books. After more discussion, the group decided that their next year's topic would be Literature from Trouble Spots of the World. The head of the committee noted all the titles that group members generated in response to the general idea and promised to consult with the owner of Brazos Books and get back to the group with next year's final reading program very soon. With this method of choice, there is group input, but the program committee has the final word.

Consensus. The second mode is consensual choice, which is sometimes coupled with rotation of individual responsibility for suggesting books. In some ways, this is the least formal group process and often feels the most comfortable because of its informality. But this very informality also makes it relatively easy for some members to be deprived of influence over the selection process. Because equalizing measures such as voting are not explicitly structured into the process, this mode of selection rests on the structural assumptions that all members have equal voice and that there is enough common purpose within the group so that achieving consensus will not suppress either individual opinions or possible conflicts within the group. Oftentimes this is true, but consensual selection also offers opportunities for the indirect expression of power within the group. A group's informal leaders may support a book enthusiastically or may remain noticeably silent at someone's suggestion. For example, a woman who was the newest and least conservative member in My Book Group, as well as the only person in the group who had not finished college, proposed an autobiographical book by Shirley MacLaine and expressed enthusiasm for it because of the author's mysticism and defiance of social conventions. She was met with a blank and sustained interval of silence. The suggestion disappeared like a stone dropped into a well, and the group's founder proceeded with the discussion of what to read as if MacLaine's book had never been mentioned. Here, an informal mode of choice was coupled with informal group sanctions (the "silent treatment") that not only effectively silenced one member but alienated her from the group as well. In fact, significant differences of opinion about selection are an important factor leading to discomfort, feelings of marginalization, and even departures from reading groups. On this, more is discussed later.

In achieving consensus, groups often move toward relatively more "serious" reading, because it offers a culturally legitimated way of transcending conflict within the group: all can agree on an "objectively" excellent book. Here is another example from my tape recording of Readers

Inc., which was at that point vaguely pursuing an interest in literature about Africa (although one of the members was trying to interest the group in a biography). This excerpt from the discussion of the next month's reading shows the group's founder (Sarah Grace) and two other members appealing to various levels of cultural authority in order to persuade the group to come to a consensus about *Waiting for the Barbarians* by J. M. Coetzee.

The selection discussion arose abruptly after someone in the group compared *West with the Night* (that month's book) to Isak Dinesen's work.

SARAH GRACE (the group's founder): And the same area produced them both.

KATHERINE And Doris Lessing's *African Stories,* which are also wonderful and are also very focused on the place and the people of the place.

LACEY So, let's do a biography and then do Lessing. [*Laughs.*]

Katherine then discussed Doris Lessing, mentioning *African Stories* and *In Pursuit of the English.*

SARAH GRACE Well, I'm embarrassed to admit it, but *The Golden Notebook* bored me. I'm not a real Doris Lessing fan.

KATHERINE The first thing I read of hers was these stories. I've stopped reading her too.

SANDRA Then we could move maybe from there to South Africa. Lately I've been hearing a lot about it.

JOANNE Oh yes. There's a really good—the Nobel Prize went to this South African writer, for the first time.

SANDRA Yes. Does it have "barbarians" in the title? The other day someone said start with that one, and "barbarians" was in the title and the author's name started with a C.

Group members' conversation clustered excitedly about this remark, struggling with the author's name, and finally spelling it: "Oh yeah, he's the one—He's the one who won the Nobel Prize."

SANDRA If you want to be au courant at cocktail parties—say you're standing and talking to Donald Barthelme in Austin—you talk about "commonwealth literature."

PEGGY [*In an ironic inflection, that seems to poke fun at literary trendiness*] We have now moved on from South America and are dealing with "commonwealth literature"?

SANDRA It's commonwealth, and by that you mean South Africa and Australia, and, you know, the British Commonwealth—and it's the "in" thing.

[*General murmurs of assent, including "Neat stuff" and "Neat books."*]

JOANNE Well, what about this South African guy? The one who won the Nobel Prize, just a month or two ago.

A few members then said that Lessing also might be interesting, but Katherine, her initial sponsor, deferred to the group's emerging consensus, saying: "I don't want to retract it necessarily, but it's been so long since I've read them [*African Stories*] that I'm not sure it would offer you anything that would be different from this one."

Someone else then asked about availability. Susan had just bought *Waiting for the Barbarians* in paperback, and Lacey left the circle to call bookstores, discovering that it was available in a Penguin paperback for $5.95.

SARAH GRACE So, are we going to do that then? Or the Doris Lessing?

KATHERINE I think I'd rather do this.

SANDRA Mary Seton is doing her dissertation on this "commonwealth literature." I said, "Tell me some things to read," and she said, "Start with that one," and she was quite clear.

LACEY So we're going to do *Waiting for the Barbarians?*

The group murmured assent and then moved into a discussion of the date for the next meeting (Readers Inc. meeting, 10 November 1985).

This passage has several points of interest. First, the sponsors of *Waiting for the Barbarians* deployed cultural authority of three distinct kinds to persuade the group. The weightiest was the Nobel Prize. Second, the reference to cocktail parties raised the authority of literary culture in general and the desire to shine in the imagined company of a famous author in particular. Third, late in the discussion Sandra mentioned a doctoral dissertation by a student who had, as members of the group knew, returned to graduate school after running a literary bookstore, thus uniting the authority of literary culture in general with that of the academy.

In all three of these instances, people rhetorically demonstrated proximity to cultural authority and, if possible, personified it. Joanne brought the Nobel Prize closer in time ("The one who won the Nobel Prize, just a month or two ago"). Sandra brought literary culture to Texas in the person of Donald Barthelme, while also communicating that she was enough of a literary insider to know that Barthelme was in residence in Austin at that moment. Similarly, after some early general comments about commonwealth literature being the "in" thing, Sandra clinched the discussion with a detailed reference to Mary Seton, the topic of her dissertation, and her "clear" advice to read Coetzee's book.

The almost magical power of proximity to cultural stars is something scholars usually discuss in relation to mass-culture fans. It seems not coincidental that in this passage a similar construction of high cultural authority appears both in Sandra's reference to the trendiness of commonwealth literature and in Sarah Grace's remark about Doris Lessing ("I'm not a real Doris Lessing fan"). Although no one contested Sarah Grace's feelings about Doris Lessing or the way she phrased them—this being a matter of individual taste—Peggy called into question trendiness as an appropriate criterion of literary judgment when she said sarcastically, "We [are] now . . . dealing with 'commonwealth literature?'"

The passage also illuminates the group dynamics of consensus building. The members with the most dominant voices, who led the movement toward selecting Coetzee, were the group's founder (Sarah Grace) and Sandra, a woman who was close to her on several dimensions. Both were married to geophysicists, both had children, both came from Texas, and both were active in the same church. The two people who were the most invested in other choices, Lacey and Katherine, were also the most socially different from the other members. Katherine, a non-Texan, was the only single person in the group; Lacey, who had no connections to geology, and knew only one other member well, was also the only divorced woman in the group at that time. After being very active in the decision-making process, they eventually deferred to Sarah Grace and Sandra, perhaps because of their more peripheral status within the group. After initial comments that set them, already more "marginal" members, apart from the emerging majority, they became very accommodating, almost as if they had to demonstrate extra loyalty to the group to work their way back in. Lacey, for instance, tried early on to represent her interest in biography and at the same time to forge an alliance with Katherine, Lessing's sponsor—although laughingly undercutting her own case. Then she investigated the availability of Coetzee's book and was the one who articulated the group's final consensus. Katherine, who first spoke positively about Lessing at some length, later expressed distance from Lessing ("I've stopped reading her too"), then retracted her proposal, and finally stated she would rather read Coetzee. Apparently, because she was initially the most vocal and concrete counterspeaker, a clear signal of her assent was necessary for the consensus to hold.

Voting. The third mode of choice, direct voting on suggestions, appears to express and encourage a certain populism in book choice as well as a democratic ethos in meeting structure. Among women's groups in Houston, I have encountered this mode of selection in two groups. One, called

The Bookies, operates almost like a small lending library, although members do briefly evaluate the different books they read each month. One member of The Bookies discussed voting as one way in which they were able to undercut an early tendency to choose what they "ought to read" instead of what they really wanted to read (comment from a meeting, 17 September 1986). Because the group buys up to ten different books each month, this tendency was quite literally a costly problem.

The Leisure Learning Group also chooses by voting on suggestions. Because it recruits members through the nonacademic continuing-education organization, it has a high turnover around a stable core of membership. It is populist in its reading choices (they are known as "the group that reads trash" in one Great Books group), and it is very egalitarian in tone. In part, this is the result of structural constraints. Many new "members" sign up for each several-weeks-long session, but retention is always a problem, and the group's solution is to give everyone a say in selection, hoping that their democratic outlook and the choice of reading material with wide appeal will keep people coming back.

Individual Choice. The fourth method, strict individual choice, allows or challenges groups to encounter books that do not necessarily appeal to everyone. It offers one way of dealing with the tension between a narrow and a more expansive reading mission, which is, after all, one reason why people gather in groups to choose books to read in the first place.

The policy of individual choice offers each member the possibility of expressing her particular interests to the group. This can be exciting for other members because it opens up new literary territory for exploration, and it can be empowering for the individual if the group validates her choice. For instance, Sandra of Readers Inc. chose A Year in Provence by Peter Mayle, introducing her choice by saying how much she admired Mayle's "travel" writing and wished she could develop a similar career. Delighted by the book, members of the group also expressed warm support for the idea of writing about travel. Mayle's sponsor took up her ambition and has now published travel essays in local, regional, and national magazines.

Groups often welcome individual choice because it also brings openness to social or cultural concerns. For instance, members of the FM 1960 group mentioned mysticism and the black experience as subjects they would never have confronted without their policy of individual choice (meeting, 24 March 1982). LS's small suburban group devoted what all agreed was a very interesting session to a science fiction fantasy by Piers Anthony, the choice of one dedicated fan, even though several members had worried that there would be "nothing to discuss" about the book (meeting, 22 January 1986).

Individual selection, like voting, works to enfranchise participants.

This may be of particular importance to members whose interests are devalued, whether for purely cultural reasons (the science fiction reader in LS's group) or for reasons that engage social issues. For instance, two essayists describing their groups for Slezak's The Book Group Book (1995, 118, 12–30), said that their mixed-gender groups only began discussing women writers when the groups began selecting books by individual choice.

One of the overriding social concerns at play in the selection process is keeping everyone satisfied with what they are reading and with the amount of "voice" they have in the choice. Sometimes this means that a group establishes a method of book selection early on that suits everyone for the life of the group. Other groups such as Readers Inc. shift back and forth between these methods. Still others combine features of several. Some, for instance, delegate a member or two to investigate a several-month topic, then choose by consensus or vote among the titles brought forward. One group I observed was using two methods at once for a period: every other month they concentrated on African American women novelists, and on the alternate months they chose by consensus from suggestions of classic and contemporary fiction and nonfiction brought up by members. Another group I attended was using Great Books selections every other meeting and voting on titles for their alternate months. My Book Group, which began by reading Southern novelists for several months, turned to selecting books by informal consensus. After a year, they again took up a several-months-long reading program, this time concentrating on European novelists suggested by a knowledgeable member and voted on by the group. Next, the group spent several months selecting by individual choice.

Differences in selection practices may seem relatively insignificant, especially given groups' ability to move from one to another with relative ease. Yet each practice sets group members in slightly different relationships with each other. Each method also encourages different relationships between groups and literary or cultural authority. Formal programs of selection appear most commonly in formally organized groups, which are apt to be larger and more socially elite than are less-organized ones. As they deliberate over yearlong programs, selection committees tend to draw on advice from cultural authorities, from booksellers to professors, whose very accessibility to group members and willingness to serve them is another mark of these book clubs' cultural distinction. Selection by consensus gives the appearance—and sometimes the reality—of intimacy and shared values, but if there are differences within a group, this method can work to enforce informal power relations, silence minority opinions, and create feelings of marginalization among some members. Yet this practice can enable groups to respond quickly and flexibly to changes in their own interests and/or in the universe of available books. Selection by vote, individual choice, or some

combination of the two often sacrifices some of this flexibility in the interests of preserving equality in the decision-making process. These practices
appear to enfranchise all members, perhaps especially those whose literary
interests are not shared by everyone. Voting or individual selection opens
groups up to reading that is not as legitimated by traditional cultural authorities as are books that might be chosen by consensus. In turn, this means
that these selection practices are often more populist in nature and can generate expansive reading choices.

As I discuss further in the next chapter, each reading group achieves its
own special identity in large part by negotiating how it selects books. The
enthusiastic and iconoclastic tone of one group's pre-vote wrangling over
next month's choices ("Serious? I'd say that one was deadly serious!"); the
careful and scholarly report of another group's committee chair about its
upcoming annual reading program; a suburban club member's hesitant but
determined recommendation of a mystery novel for her choice of reading—all of these interactions are what feed into the variability that makes
each group, as members often say, so unique.

Book Discussion Practices

If rules about book selection tend to engage the complexities of literature
as commerce and hierarchy of cultural values, rules about discussion or
group process tend to be more exclusively focused on the creation of a normative order that will allow everyone in the group to feel she has an equal
voice and equal attention from other members. (Selection processes, too, as
mentioned earlier, tend to be formulated with this notion of an equal voice
in mind.) In turn, this formulation allows the group to benefit as much as
possible from the full participation of the diverse range of opinions and
perspectives represented in the group as well as ensures that individuals experience the sense of ownership and power of voice that comes from active
participation. Indeed, when asked on the survey how much they felt they
participated in discussions, the majority said they felt they participated
equally, whereas only four (9 percent) of those responding said they participated less than others and fifteen (32 percent) said they talked more than
most.

Variability characterizes book discussions as well as procedures for selection. Here I will confine myself to how discussions are organized; chapter 6 takes up their content. As with the selection of books, there is a whole
gamut of ways that groups manage discussion. Some groups use discussion
leaders, although in Houston this approach appears to be less common than
it is in, for example, the Midwest, where Rachel Jacobsohn (1994) mentions
it as an ordinary practice. Historically, the role of the book reviewer was

common in the South, but although I have heard mention of a few well-known older women who have served this function, I have not attended a book club that uses them. On the other hand, several book groups have invited me to special meetings to discuss my own research or to serve with other academics as part of a panel of experts. Authors, professors, journalists, and other cultural authorities occasionally figure as special guests in many book clubs. In one of the groups described above, a guest from Rice University became a discussion leader for several months after a visit that impressed the group.

Generally, however, the groups I have attended structure their own discussions. Some simply begin or, in the words of one member, "We all just jump right in." Others follow a format I am most familiar with from the early days of the women's movement with its consciousness-raising groups: in order around the room, each member is afforded a time period in which to express her own opinions and questions without interruption, and then the meeting is opened for discussion.

The majority of groups, however, welcome at least some delegation of responsibility for leading the discussion. For some, this means that there is a designated discussion leader who provides some biographical and critical information about the author and the book. Usually, this task falls to the woman who has been responsible for suggesting the book, but almost equally often the duty is simply rotated without regard for "whose" book is under discussion. Just how much scholarly preparation is expected varies widely from group to group.

Other groups highlight the importance of raising good questions for discussion rather than setting the text in its historical, biographical, or literary critical context. This seems to reflect the Great Books discussion mode. The Great Books program considered each text to be a timeless expression of truth and value and, like the New Criticism of the 1940s and 1950s, considered the reader's task to be that of making sense of each text internally. The Great Books model also encouraged taking whatever insights from the text that could be brought to bear on contemporary issues or enduring philosophical problems. Although some Houston groups appear to have invented this approach spontaneously, others refer back to various members' time in Great Books groups to describe how they came to their question-driven discussion format. For example, the Interns' and Residents' and Wives Group consciously modeled their discussions on the experience several members had had in Great Books groups, taking seriously the responsibility of raising questions that would tap into the most significant aspects of the book under discussion. Eventually, they decided that this task was important enough to be shared, so now two members meet in advance to formulate the questions for that month's discussion. They have found this practice helpful both for ensuring the quality of the discussions and for enabling members to get to know each other better.

Rules for Groups to Live By

Some codifications have clear social ramifications, and these I discuss here. Other rules or practices that bear more centrally on the literary aspects of group life I discuss more fully in the next two chapters.

Most rules demonstrate consideration for the exigencies of members' lives outside the group. This is particularly true of guidelines for book selection. For example, many groups choose only paperbacks, because hardcovers are expensive. My Book Group instantiated a strict paperback policy after having bought a newly issued hardcover that nobody liked well enough even to give away as a gift. Another Houston group has what they call the ruler rule: they do not consider books unless they are under two inches thick.

Similarly, groups take into account the social demands of women's yearly schedules. It is common for groups to pick lighter reading for the summer. One group in Houston chooses a particularly demanding book for the first meeting after their summer break, to give members a long interval to get through it. Winter is apt to be a time for more difficult or longer selections, although many groups choose short books during the holiday season or schedule purely social meetings for a time of year when reading takes a back seat in members' lives. Such rules show that groups take members needs into account and recognize that reading is only one of many commitments in each person's life.

A more subtle way that group rules demonstrate a need to provide a pleasurable experience for members is by placing controls on the selection process. First, many groups require that someone in the group have actually read a book if it is to be considered for selection. For example, one of the groups I observed put this rule in place after a member recommended *The Cinderella Complex* on the strength of a magazine excerpt and everyone else decided that the book had no more depth than the recommender's synopsis. This is both a defense against commercial "hype" and a mechanism to ensure that the group's own particular literary interests will mesh with the broader universe of available reading material. A related rule—that groups ought not select books only because members feel they *should* read them— recognizes that there may be a gap between abstractly defined "worthy" books and books that will be most pleasurable for groups to read. I discuss both of these rules in more detail in the next chapter.

Most such rules show a concern for the satisfaction of all members in the group, and therefore they promote a democratic ethos. This orientation, which works to ensure everyone's participation, is not uncommon in voluntary associations, where everyone has the choice to leave. Such rules also recognize something that goes beyond the requirements of formal democracy, for they speak to the positive benefit to the group of the inclusion of diversity or difference. As one woman said on the open-ended questionnaire: "What happens because of the continuity of relationships is as important to me as the content of the discussions. The members have various experiences, backgrounds, which I love to hear about. Perhaps it is how we are alike and not alike and the universal themes of human nature that we see in this microcosm that appeals to me."

Some of the "rules" for good discussions resemble the requirements of the "ideal speech situation" described by social theorist of democracy Jürgen Habermas (1989). In his model, such situations allow a free and open exchange of ideas, accompanied by a strong egalitarian ethos that encourages expression of and respect for other people's opinions. This means that the best arguments can win adherents by virtue of their superior rationality, without regard to the speaker's rank or social status. Book clubs ideally follow his model in that they discourage bullying, domination, or personal attacks and attempt to work through both substantive issues and interactional problems with tolerance and broadmindedness. In point of fact, reading group rules in some cases make explicit what Habermas himself leaves relatively unexplored in his account, which is somewhat naive about the insidious nature of power differentials and how they might distort the process.

There are also important differences between Habermas's ideal and that intimated by reading group discussion rules. Because he is interested in outlining the conditions for a vital public sphere that can provide support for participatory democracy at the political level, he foregrounds rational persuasion that can usher in innovative political ideas or policies. Contemporary reading groups have no such political mission, so people are not necessarily expected to shift their opinions because of rational arguments; rather, they are expected to entertain the possible validity of other "takes" on either literature or life. In fact, excursions into the personal, unless they range too far afield, are a valued aspect of reading group discussions. These conversations recognize the validity of experiential truths and the perspectival nature of knowledge in a way not fully explored or even entertained by Habermas, with his interest in more objective rationality. Also, such discussions do not usually end in instrumental action or public policy, although they did spark a social movement among women in the late nineteenth century, and even now they are important for women negotiating personal or social change. Rather, reading group discussions encourage a repeated dialectic of social, moral, and aesthetic reflection. It is this process that lies at the heart of what keeps groups together and that can make them, when successful, a source of validation, support, and even personal transformation for their members.

The Cradle of Familiarity, the Challenge of Difference

When I began to explore the social world of reading groups, I was repeatedly struck by the way participants insisted on the differences among the women who belonged to their groups. They mentioned differences in age, marital status, college major, occupation (or husband's occupation), and sometimes religion, regional background, or even place of residence in Houston. For instance, participants in one suburban group enthusiastically justified their method of strict individual book choice by outlining the major areas of social diversity this method tapped into. They mentioned ethnic heritage, work experience, marriage, singlehood, divorce, and the age at which they had had their first child. Just the other day, a friend who is in a book group remarked how diverse it was, mainly referring to family status: four of the members have children, three are married, two divorced, and three single.

To a sociologist used to dealing with large-scale registers of social difference along dimensions of class, race, and gender—not to mention nation, region, religion, or political ideology—such differences seem rather small. The groups I observed drew on only one racial group and were composed of women who were both college educated and middle to upper-middle class. Many groups, in fact, recruit members from among those who share not only their race and social class but also their marital status, age, neighborhood, and sometimes occupation, religion, or political orientation as well.

I formulated various ways of understanding this striking divergence in perception. For instance, early on in the research I thought I saw less difference because I had seen many groups, whereas most participants experience only one or two. Later, I developed an explanation based on the perceptual difference between a sociologist and a layperson in a highly segmented social order: "I am professionally used to dealing with very large differences. Given our age-graded, class-stratified, racially divided, and even occupationally segmented society, most people's direct experience brings them into close contact with persons much like themselves. Therefore, relatively small social differences *feel* large when experienced in the context of a small group." I also hypothesized that race and social class might be ideologically "invisible" to people living within a white, upper-middle-class environment, thus leading them to ignore their all-too-taken-for-granted commonalties. And indeed, in one session about a book on poverty among a group in Houston's wealthy Memorial district, a participant said, to generalized murmurs of assent, how easy it was to forget that most Americans make under $100,000 a year. Another of my explanations highlighted the intimacy of reading group settings, which, in combination with the fact that many members are not personally close to everyone in the group, might be enough to cast their differences into stark relief.

All of these factors partially account for the stress that group members place on the differences spanned by their groups; however, this stress also seems to me more closely connected to the nature of the experience that people hope to gain from their discussions. This experience is predicated on members revealing their different perspectives on the book under consideration, but it is also predicated on discussants revealing things about themselves when they explain how they responded to the book or how they relate it to their own lives. It is only through the sharing of differences that a book discussion becomes something more than reading a book alone. On the other hand, people must have enough in common to be able to talk to rather than past each other and, as well, to be comfortable enough with each other to sustain a deep and sometimes personal discussion. In a sense, this is the background or precondition for discussions; in the foreground are the novel insights and perceptions each member can contribute. Thus, what people in book groups notice most, even celebrate, is the kind of alchemy that brings a group of people together to a new level of understanding—of books, self, others, or the world—that is achieved through the expression and appreciation of their divergent perspectives.

Differences lead to learning, both about the book and about self and others. The lens of other readings gives members a broader and deeper access to the book under discussion; conversely, the lens of the book reveals the inner lives of coparticipants in a particularly meaningful way. The survey and open-ended questionnaire show that respondents could definitely point to changes in their reading or knowledge because of participating in book groups. Of the thirty-nine women who answered, thirty-two said they "know more about certain subjects, authors, and types of literature than before"; nineteen said that now when they read on their own, they "read some types of literature or authors" they did not before; eighteen said they "read more critically now"; and seventeen said they "read about some topics or subjects" that they did not before.[6] In open-ended comments, people said such things as "I am much more willing to try new authors," "I love books and reading and like to discuss other perspectives about them," "More discriminatory in selecting books to read on my own," "More eclectic in my reading," "Certainly broadens cultural horizons," and "Broadening of perspectives, awareness of written criticism, author's bias, stimulus to reference materials." One member responded rather crisply, "It has enriched my life and probably expanded my taste. But it has also sharpened it."

At its best, this process accomplishes several things, among them a broadening and deepening of a participant's engagement with literature and the ideas that the books themselves, approached in this way, contribute to the discussion. This leads to an expansive and critical literacy. In this context the books are important not only in and of themselves but as signifiers of critical thinking, reflective conversation, and a discourse at once abstract and morally and emotionally informed. Such practices are not always encouraged—but perhaps differentially inhibited—in the differing social worlds these book discussants inhabit. Over and over, participants speak of a process that couples reflection about literature with self-reflection in the company of others who bring similar reflectiveness, but different selves, into the process. And over and over, they speak as well of the surprising closeness that emerges from this kind of talk.

The intimacy engendered by such discussions may be enabled by the externality as well as the substance that books provide. They give distance yet promote a discourse that gives access to parts of the self not usually mobilized either by the hurly-burly of everyday life or by the disembodied rationality required by technical, bureaucratic, even academic thinking. Yet books can only further such discourse in a discussion that encourages the airing of personal interpretations, even excursions into personal life that the book may inspire but that leave the book far behind. As one woman said of her group: "We share news and feelings about relationships, births, miscarriages, loss, joy, and sadness. We discuss gender, a woman's power (and lack of it), and moral choices. . . . By the end of the discussion, we have experienced some shift in perception. Our combined perspectives have enriched our understanding of the book. We do not change who we are, but we become more than we were" (Slezak 1995, 94–95).

Contrary to this woman's feelings about her book group, women in Houston reading groups indicated that participation has brought change to many of them. Above, I spoke about their changes in reading habits. Women were just as definite in their survey responses about the changes in their social and personal lives as stimulated by their book clubs. Of the thirty-three who answered this question, thirty-one said they had made new friends, twenty-two said they had become "more reflective" about their lives, seventeen said they had become "more tolerant of others," and seventeen said they were more confident about their ability to deal with people in groups. In a couple of instances they said other members had become among their closest friends, and one said her marriage functions better for "having a separate cultural and social outlet." In open-ended responses, women said things such as "The group affirms me as a woman who thinks,""I am a more confident person—self-image enhanced," "I have decided to give myself the freedom I need to be a whole person," and finally, "It has broadened my scope of reading and given me a greater sense of self-confidence and feeling of being an important part of something worthwhile."

Only half of the women who answered a similar question about whether their book group had affected other cultural activities affirmed that it had. Of those twenty-two women, seventeen said they participate more in other cultural activities, and fifteen said they enjoy different kinds of cultural activities than they did before. Nine said they watched less television than before, which also indicates a cultural shift. The reasons for these changes appear to be of two kinds. First, several women commented that they attended cultural events with either the group as a whole or friends within the group. Second, women mentioned that belonging to a book group had "broadened their awareness of art, music, ideas, and lifestyles" and of "cultural events in the city," or as one woman put it, "I've become more curious and more critical of other cultural activities."

Far fewer women registered religious or political changes because of book group participation: only seven out of the forty-five women answered this question. But the direction and content of those changes were indicative of the leavening process of reading "with" others. Five of the seven indicated that they had become more politically aware, and five also indicated becoming more politically active. Three said they had become more religious, and an equal number said their religious or spiritual perspectives had changed. Two said they had become more politically liberal, whereas none said they had become more conservative. Their comments indicate a "broadening of perspectives," or as one woman said, "Perhaps, in general, I have become more broad minded." Clearly, the fellowship of books and valued co-readers provides a gentle catalyst for women to expand socially and as readers, whereas some find that the fellowship of their reading groups encourages change even in realms of life we now classify as far afield from literature.[7]

It is this fellowship that often spills over into the elaboration of group traditions, where the intimacy itself becomes the substance of the time the group spends together. Group traditions represent one of the most substantive ways that contemporary reading groups resemble those of their nineteenth-century foremothers. The traditions are not always the same. Instead of the nineteenth-century New England Women's Club "Dickens Night," which featured members dressed in the costume of their favorite Dickens character, contemporary groups tend to substitute attendance at a play or a movie or a getaway to a beach house or retreat. One Houston reading club became known, for example, as "the group that goes to Mexico." Other traditions include special sessions on topics such as members' autobiographies, spirituality, or one group's erotica night, when each member brings a favorite erotic book and something chocolate to share as each reads a passage aloud. (Surely, the connection between women's sexuality and chocolate was not so clearly elaborated a hundred years ago!)

The annual "meeting with the men" is another common and important ceremonial occasion for many women's groups, and it encourages book selection by what one might call "masculine projection." The "meeting with the men," which often happens near the holidays or during February (Valentine's Day month), is a ritual of inclusion that celebrates a connection—between women and their men—that is in fact abrogated every other month of the year by the all-female reading group meetings. So, in a sense, it is an occasion that reaffirms both the heterosexual bond that structures so many women's lives outside their groups and the importance of the all-female space represented by the groups themselves. Some of these meetings are purely social, but many others bring the husbands in to participate in a book discussion. And although such meetings are atypical on one level, they represent to the men in at least some of its essential substance (and seriousness) what the women do most of the year without them. For these meetings, women usually choose books they think their men will like— World War II, international relations, or biography are common generic choices—and sometimes ask men to lead the discussion.

Some traditions are almost uncannily similar to those that women in reading groups enacted a century ago. The Ladies Reading Club of Houston finished each year with their annual "pic-nic," and picnics have seemingly lost none of their savor for twentieth-century reading clubs. Others hold annual dinners to celebrate the group itself. These traditions make it clear that despite the huge sea change in women's lives that has marked the last century, and the lesser changes that would make a nineteenth-century clubwoman amazed by a twentieth-century book club meeting, these groups still offer a mix of literature and life, intellectual discussion, and personal support that makes them—at their best—an extraordinarily creative social phenomenon for their members, a potentially transformative way of being in the world.

FIVE

Book Selection: Negotiating Group Identity through Literature

During my initial contact with a reading group, the first thing participants wanted to tell me were what books they had read. In fact, members' impatience to talk about books led me to revise the brief telephone interview form I used to "inventory" each book club I encountered. I had planned to question members about the composition and history of the group and then to move on to what they did with books. But everyone I interviewed—after politely answering a question about how their group began—launched determinedly into a discussion of what they had read, forcing me to shuffle my papers just to keep up with enthusiastic descriptions of titles, categories, and special favorites. This was one indication that what groups choose to read is at the heart of their identity as reading groups and of each individual group's particular identity. If we are what we eat, book clubs are what they read.

Sometimes this identity is reflected in the names groups give themselves—the Feminist Book Club, the Not-So-Great Books Club—or are given by others—the group that reads trash. The same holds true for genre reading groups: the Romance Group, the Mystery Book Club, the Biography Club, and the Poetry Group. But usually, if a group is more mainstream in orientation, it takes a longer discussion to reveal its special interests as well as the "reading boundaries" by which the group defines itself.

Book selection is also the process that members of reading groups are most curious about when they ask about other groups. This curiosity is a signal of both its centrality and complexity. Selection inspires curiosity in part because book group members are always on the lookout for promising titles: they want to know what books have circulated among other book clubs, and in particular which have generated good discussions, because good discussions are their lifeblood. They are also curious about how other groups select books. Their curiosity entails an implicit recognition of the problems inherent in matching critical evaluations of books to members' varied "reading expectations."

From the scholar's point of view, book selection is important because it reveals the negotiations at the boundaries of the institution of literature. It also reveals the social and personal worlds—full of nonliterary preoccupations, interests, and yearnings—that bring people to books in search of fulfilling reading experiences (and, in book groups, in search of fulfilling discussions).

This juncture has not been much researched. Scholars have studied the publishing industry, authorial careers, the rise and decline of literary forms, literary reviews, the ways people learn to read, the development of "literature" as an academic specialty, the canon and its vicissitudes, the psychology of textual interpretation, library use, and even (although much more rarely) individual reading patterns, popular literary fandom, and the manner in which readers experience genre books such as the romance. There are also numerous interpretive studies of what canonical books mean, at least to the one reader who writes the study.

How actual readers choose from the vast universe of possible books to read—how they sort through it, make it manageable, and finally settle on a title that they have some reason to believe will provide them with whatever reading experience they are seeking—has remained mysterious. In this chapter I discuss only a specialized part of this large issue. Reading groups are not the same as individuals: they make collective rather than individual decisions, and those decisions are not wordless, private, or impulsive (as many of our individual book choices are) but are themselves a matter for open and sometimes sustained debate. Moreover, reading groups are looking for "discussible" books, which, as I elaborate later, directs them toward evaluative criteria that are irrelevant to many individual reading choices.

Examining the process by which reading groups choose what to read reveals much about the way all readers find and choose books. The selection process reveals what the institution of literature looks like from the audience's perspective, that is, how readers engage with various aspects of that institution, from authors and booksellers to "professional valuers" (Bourdieu 1984, 4) such as literary reviewers, college professors, or even the compilers of CliffsNotes. It also shows these groups in dialogue with literary and cultural authority—and often more deferential to that authority than they are during book discussions. Groups feel constrained to decide what will be both worth reading and good reading, which moves them into a complex process of negotiation with the arbiters of legitimate culture. This process reveals an "evaluative hierarchy" that most reading groups accept as a taken-for-granted ground of the literary universe, even if in particular instances they contest it. It also brings into focus fissures in the cultural universe—such as the one between the university and even very well educated "civilian" readers—that have heretofore not drawn much attention.

Book selection also shows how the exigencies of people's social and personal lives shape their reading choices. On a very concrete level, as I discussed in the last chapter, this means that reading has to be sandwiched in with women's other responsibilities and activities. At another level, it shows reading groups responding to changes in their personal worlds and our broader collective life by searching among books for pleasure, enlightenment, solace, or expansion of their perspective. And at the level of social and personal identity, book selection shows groups to be involved in a process of exploration and self-definition that is mediated by literature. One of the major reasons that members of women's reading groups choose specifically to meet with other women is that they want to read a significant number of books by and about women and to explore issues that have particular resonance for them as women. The same principle holds true for members of reading groups composed of African American women, feminists, or lesbians. Book selection, then, provides the mechanism that gears groups outward into the world of literature or social issues. It also permits them selectively to incorporate that world into their more internal group processes of reflection, self-development, and the evolution of their group's particular identity.

In this chapter I move from a discussion of the varying ways that book selection engages the world of literature to an analysis of some of the issues that come into play as groups develop their own identity through their choice of what to read.

Book Selection and the Institution of Literature

The Marketplace and Book Selection

The marketplace and the institutional processes of book distribution limit book selection among reading groups, for they must choose among available books, and, given their time constraints, they usually choose books that are easy to find. Yet the complex commercial and cultural process whereby publishers decide to accept a book and then decide on the basis of predicted sales how to price, print, and "push" a title—which then has implications for the related decisions of book wholesalers, bookstore owners, and librarians—lies largely outside the awareness of reading group members. They confront the book industry only when they are deciding what to read, and because availability is a precondition for choice, it is the lens through which they survey the literary marketplace. Only two aspects of availability are of conscious importance to their deliberations: whether a book has been issued in paperback and whether it is available through local bookstores.

The hardcover/paperback distinction relates to price. Because most groups have a "paperback requirement," publishers' commercially based decisions about whether or not to issue a paperback edition are reinforced by these groups in their processes of book selection. The effect for reading groups is nonexposure to those very books that publishers have decided lie outside the cultural mainstream. In this case, the marketplace narrows choice further than groups might desire.

Bookstores and booksellers occasionally figure as topics for fascinated discussion. These discussions also reveal the complexities of institutions or relationships that operate on the borders of culture and commerce. Bookstores become a topic of discussion first, when participants account for why they have not read a certain book. It is a valid excuse if one has tried but not been able to find the book at nearby bookstores or libraries. Reading groups do not expect members to have to work hard at getting a book, because they construe the groups themselves as a leisure-time activity. This confirms the findings of surveys of reading and book purchasing (see, for example, Yankelovich, Skelly, and White, Inc. 1978, 220–22)—that the ease of obtaining books is one factor in supporting the activity of reading in general. Chain bookstores in suburban shopping malls have profited from this fact, taking advantage of shifting residence patterns.

Chain bookstores have often been cast as industry villains that reduce books to pure commercial commodity and threaten the livelihood of the independent literary bookseller. Indeed, some reading group members complain that the chains stock mostly self-improvement books and "trashy" novels. Were this the whole truth, book superstores would represent censorship by commercial viability and an intensification of marketplace pressures toward mass cultural homogeneity, perhaps even an example of Habermas's colonization of the lifeworld (1987).

The picture is more complex. To begin with, even the most literary bookstores are also business ventures, so booksellers occupy ambiguous positions: part friendly cultural authority, part profit-seeker. For example, several reading groups use a Houston bookstore that can rightly claim to have expanded their range of literature for discussion. Yet in at least one instance, the owner pushed a recent title by a well-known Latin American writer rather than the author's more famous earlier book simply because he had the new book on his shelves. This irritated some group members in the wake of what they considered an unsatisfying reading experience. Chain bookstores are also appealing to readers for more substantive reasons (as I discuss in chap. 7), including their wide range of titles and inclusive, nonjudgmental atmosphere.

Cultural Authorities and the Hierarchy of Taste

The institutional work of cultural authorities, from booksellers to what one analyst calls "literary post-processors" such as critics and professors, remains largely invisible to group members, in the same way that the commercial apparatus of the book industry is not noticeable to them. This very invisibility may well be crucial to the extraordinary power that cultural authorities have in framing groups' understanding of literary worth, which in turn significantly influences their processes of book selection.

An important criterion for selection is the "discussibility" of books, which is centrally related to the discourse and function of the groups as reading groups. On a sheet of members' names, FM 1960, for example, states that the books chosen may be current or classic but "should contain literary merit and be very discussible" (meeting, 24 March 1982). When asked about what makes a book discussible, a member of Belles Lettres said, "It's a book people can take different opinions on and find evidence in the text to support" (conversation, 4 October 1983). This raises a number of issues.

First, it implies a hierarchy of taste. Groups negotiate interestingly varied positions in relation to this literary hierarchy, but everyone seems to know of its existence, and it has the stability of an almost natural feature of the cultural landscape. No mainstream group considers romances, for example, to be discussible. Women sometimes read romances privately, and occasionally groups meet to consider them as a cultural phenomenon ("We wanted to see why they are so popular"). By this analytic move they set themselves both above and at some distance from this genre. Similarly, FM 1960 members agreed that any reading was better than none, but they deplored the "trashy" nature of much currently available fiction (meeting, 24 March 1982).

Distinctions such as these, which rank genres as well as individual novels, show that reading groups generally accept without question the categories of classification and evaluation generated by cultural arbiters such as reviewers or professors. Their acceptance of this evaluative framework as the criterion for demarcating what is worth discussing from trash is the clearest evidence of their dependence on cultural authority. Conversely, what gives cultural authority to literary professionals such as teachers or critics is their ability to frame the "reading boundaries" within which these groups operate. The cultural work of these authorities is to articulate the bases for aesthetic judgment and canonical inclusion or exclusion—whether of one novel, one author, or a whole school or genre—and to win adherents for their representations of the literary universe.

Their role is especially powerful because their work remains largely invisible to reading group members. Hidden in the taken-for-granted cultural background, the social process whereby these "professional valuers" create and defend cultural legitimacy becomes opaque. The evaluative hierarchy they produce acquires an aura of inevitability and objective, even transcendent, truth. This hierarchy, which reading groups all recognize no matter what attitude they choose to take toward it, is encoded in the bedrock of assumptions about literary merit that inform each group's over-

all definition of worthwhile reading. These assumptions constrain book selection, notwithstanding most group members' vision of themselves as ad-
venturesome and broad-minded readers.

When questioned about their reading, most members say initially,
"We'll read anything." But groups usually do not deal with either end of the
literary spectrum: most do not read poetry, plays, or difficult postmodernist
novels, and if they do, they will mention it proudly. At the other end, groups
rarely even consider genre books to be part of the relevant literary universe.
When queried, "How about genre books like mysteries or thrillers or romances?" typical responses were: "We did read one spy novel and nobody
wanted to do *that* again. It's nice to have something to stimulate conversation" or "No, not that we might not read them on our own" (interviews
with MW and SG, June 1991). Such responses show that women's reading
groups generally accept traditional categories of classification and evaluation. And the fact that these categories and distinctions structure discourse
rather than become themselves a matter for discussion further conceals
their complex but nonetheless hegemonic origins.

This is especially clear in the case of classics, which stand at the pinna-
cle of this hierarchy.[1] Classics offer the legitimization of tradition and the
worth of self-improvement. Groups rank the relative worth of reading different kinds of books under the rubric of a rarely articulated humanism that
defines reading truly great books as a morally and intellectually enhancing
experience. So, groups sometimes retreat to reading classics when there is
conflict over selection, and they often use these volumes to establish cultural
legitimacy. The leader of the Leisure Learning Group, for instance, feels they
should undertake reading a classic at least once in every two-month "program," and aside from this dictum she does not attempt to control selection.
Here the classic serves as ballast that keeps the group from flying off into
cultural limbo. Other groups read a classic at least once or twice a year,
which is one way of identifying with the humanistic traditions that underwrite reading groups themselves. Interestingly, groups often choose classics
near the holiday season, as if there were some elective affinity between a tra-
dition-imbued time of year and books reflecting tradition's aura.

Classics also call forth unstinting interpretive effort because they offer
a secure investment in self-cultivation. Groups approach them with respect—
"You'd be proud of the way we discussed it," said one group leader of The
Bookworms about a classic (conversation with SG, January 1986)—often
preface discussions with historical and critical introductions, and put forth
considerable energy to understand and appreciate books that are not always
as accessible as contemporary fiction. I have observed several groups labo-
riously answering CliffsNotes discussion questions about classics, subjecting themselves to what they thought was a "hokey" process in order to "get
the most" out of such a book—like miners working a particularly rich lode.

119

Classics, then, are low-risk reading because they provide guaranteed cultural worth.

By and large, however, the historical sedimentation of authority that gives classics their aura remains invisible and unquestioned. The social sources of literary judgment have been so lost in time, so buried in reaffirmation across generations, that they are altogether obscured, and the classic becomes an icon for our general cultural heritage. Deference to this heritage, in fact, is what gives reading groups their cultural mission and distinction. I have never heard anyone question the stature of a classic, even if they found it disappointing in the reading, which happens surprisingly often.

Contemporary "serious" fiction and nonfiction (such as biographies, history, science, and philosophy) and the classics form the main fare of many reading groups, which, in turn, achieve the reputation of being "serious" if they exclude everything else. The most socially elite groups aspire to the status of serious readers, but so do others that are distinguished by literary credentials. This implies that Bourdieu's analysis (1984)—that high culture confers social distinction, which is, in turn, marked by adherence to high culture—has some validity.

Slightly lower on the evaluative hierarchy are "good" best-selling authors such as James Michener or Herman Wouk, whom some groups reject and others enjoy. Below this category are mysteries, mass-market blockbusters such as *Princess Daisy* that do not aspire to literary status, and most thrillers. Choosing where to draw the reading boundary along this continuum can be a delicate business, as shown by the following example (which also shows links between social and literary distinction). When asked what sorts of things her group reads, CW responded,

> Well, mostly women authors. We try not to read just junk. That is anything that is just a step above Danielle Steele. But we did read *The Shell Seekers* at one point, and one of the people in the group said that she really liked it because it was junk but you didn't feel like you ought to put a cover over your paperback. It was acceptable junk that you weren't embarrassed to be seen reading at the airport. (Interview, June 1991)

Science fiction falls toward the bottom of the hierarchy, followed by westerns and romances. Westerns give rise to the same kind of cultural contempt as do romances, and they provoke even less interest, especially among women's reading groups. Referring to westerns, one respondent from a couples group said, "The closest we've gotten to that in the group is Larry McMurtry's *Lonesome Dove*" (interview with JP, June 1991).

This hierarchy of taste is more fluid than it first appears. From the inception of my research, there have been genre reading groups dedicated to both mysteries and science fiction, although more mainstream groups still do not discuss them. These genre groups are mixed-gender groups, so I only refer to them tangentially in the course of this discussion. During the late 1990s, two women's reading groups dedicated to romances emerged in the Houston area. These are women's groups mainly because romances appeal overwhelmingly to women. Like the loose group of romance readers discussed in *Reading the Romance* (Radway 1984), these two groups sprang up through the efforts of two women involved in bookselling: one was an employee at a SuperCrown store and the other the owner of an in-town secondhand bookstore. Both groups understand that romances are culturally denigrated books, and their aim, in part, is to revalue both the books and romances in general. I discuss this in more detail in the next chapter. Here I want to point out both that every book group I observed is aware of the hierarchy of taste and that some groups contribute to its historical development by contesting it.

The groups I observed judged nonfiction not on literary merit (although people did criticize such books for being too long or boring) but on social relevance. Several of the groups were aware of the ways in which their nonfiction reading had linked them to wider social currents. FM 1960 read about black Americans in the mid-1970s; the League of Women Voters Group had felt the need to "take on" mysticism. All the groups had used books to understand the women's movement. Whether they agreed with feminist ideas or not, all groups felt they had to come to terms in some way with such a historical movement by and for women. Books provide a signal that people must come to terms with change, and they mediate between people directly involved in activism or analysis and those who feel the impact of social change more subtly or more indirectly in the routines of daily life.

Using Cultural Authority: Expertise and Information

Aside from relying on a relatively stable hierarchy of taste, women's book groups, like individual readers, use cultural institutions of opinion formation to sift through individual titles. My research has already indicated that two institutions not usually accorded great weight in models of cultural dissemination are crucial in this regard. One is the independent bookstore. Like the "opinion leaders" described in early communication research, such booksellers are influential in part because they mediate between other authorities and the general public through a face-to-face relationship that both includes and transcends commerce.

For instance, book selection in several Houston groups demonstrates that a fine independent bookstore can expand the scope of books considered for discussion. Women in these groups often mention titles they found by browsing at Brazos Books or by working with its owner and his staff to plan suggestions for one meeting or an entire year's program. This bookstore has close ties to Houston's intellectual and literary communities as well as to the national literary scene, and its owner advises more than ten reading groups. Other stores in Houston also follow this model. Because their owners usually consider books as more than a commodity, they serve not only as marketers of books but also as cultural resources or authorities for the community of readers.[2]

Universities also are important in providing access to authoritative literary opinion, especially for members not in the habit of reading the *New York Times Book Review* or the *New York Review of Books*. I have observed several selections—including titles from *Germinal* and *The Gnostic Gospels* to *The Color Purple*—made on the basis of books brought into the home by college-aged children. Moreover, the Belles Lettres group was eager to have syllabi from Rice University English courses to give them a broader idea of what serious modern literature they should be tackling.

If booksellers and professors are authoritative because of their expertise, friends are influential because of intimate and reciprocal knowledge of taste in books. Women often cited friends' recommendations, adding remarks like "We always agree about books." It is possible that many of these personal chains of recommendations will lead, as one analyst of best-sellers found, back to literary publications such as the *New York Times Book Review* (Ohmann 1987, 72). They may also explain how one or two novels become overwhelmingly popular among book groups every year.

Certainly, book reviews do matter, whether they appear in the media or on book jackets. Here there is also a hierarchy of authority. Group members weigh the placement, length, and authorship of reviews in literary magazines and rank magazines' and newspapers' prestige. One woman mentioned that the *Kansas City Star* had called a novel "a jewel"; when her group burst into laughter, she said, "Oh well, I just thought I'd lay that one on you," implying the quote was not worth much (Readers Inc. meeting, 10 May 1984). Literary awards and annual lists of notable books also help members choose books. Best-seller lists, however, have lost some authority as genre books have become increasingly popular. All this indicates how closely reading groups follow the dictates of traditional cultural authorities and their estimation of literary worth.

Reading groups make use of cultural authority during the process of book selection for two major reasons: to legitimate choices and to predict the outcome of their reading experience. The first needs little explanation; it refers to readers' desire (for whatever motives) to read good books and, correlatively, to the critics' function as gatekeepers. But these cultural authorities, as well as other people who have no claim to expertise, are also valuable because of their informational function. Literary reviews, especially at the time of publication, often devote a surprisingly large amount of attention to description, as if intuitively understanding the needs of their audience. But for this purpose the informed judgment of a trusted adviser can suffice, which is why literary booksellers, friends, and other reading group members are so important. They help mediate between the wider world of literary judgment and a particular group of readers, and they can also be questioned.

This brings to the fore the dialogic nature of the relationship between women's reading groups and the institution of literature. Although groups may defer to cultural authorities in the process of book selection, they selectively choose from the range of available books and topics for discussion on the basis of their own reading interests. To be "discussible" a book must be interesting as well as good; otherwise, reading and talking about it will fall into the category of the onerous and unpleasurable "shoulds" that reading groups such as the Bookies are anxious to avoid because they bury members' own desires under the pressure of an obligation to legitimate culture.

This is ironic, because participants in reading groups are convinced that there is something inherently fulfilling about engaging with literature, usually meaning meritorious or critically valorized literature. So on one level, reading group members accept the legitimacy of the system of cultural hierarchization that also legitimizes their own practices. Yet they also keep a kind of critical distance from it. This indicates an awareness of the potential divergence between their own judgments and those of professional cultural critics. It also shows some consciousness of the potential distortion of their own group process—a distortion that may result from choosing a book only because of its cultural cachet. To put it another way, book groups approach the institution of literature with some deference, but also with all the issues, desires, interests, and what Raymond Williams (1977, 128–35) called "structures of feeling" born of their social identities and individual life experiences. So to understand book selection, we must understand what limits the sway of cultural authorities.

Self-Definition as a Source for Change: Rhetorical Variations on the Serious

However stable the evaluative hierarchy may appear at any one point in time, it is always under construction. The earliest American women's reading groups, for instance, did not discuss novels because in the late eighteenth and early nineteenth centuries, the novel was a highly suspect literary genre. Over time, the constituencies (authors, critics, educators, and audiences) that make up the world of literature have changed both internally and in relation to each other. Sometimes these changes are publicly recognized as transformative, as when technological changes (the printing press, the Internet), literary movements (romanticism, surrealism, the rise of the novel), or institutional changes (the development of English as an academic discipline) are at issue. Audiences—in this case, reading groups—also help to rework the literary world, in part by the ways they characterize who they are in relation to literature and what they want out of it. This dynamic process of self-definition or cultural framing expresses their ideas about what literature ought to be and how it should be read and evaluated. Reading groups do not simply fit themselves into the field of literary value but rhetorically reshape and sometimes dispute it. Such cultural reinterpretation and contestation has been analyzed most extensively in relation to popular cultural forms, but it also takes place among audiences for more legitimate culture. One hallmark of this process among reading group members, however, is that the contenders for more expansive reading boundaries often deploy the language of cultural legitimacy in the service of quite different hierarchies of taste.

To show the complexity of this cultural practice, I discuss the different ways groups use the word *serious* in describing themselves. I have chosen this adjective because it is a particularly powerful boundary marker both within academic circles and in the cultural world beyond the university. It is loaded in two senses: it carries heavy cultural freight, and it can be deployed as a discursive weapon to stake out or defend a cultural territory. Because of its power, I became sensitized to this word early in the research. Both academic colleagues ("But do they read serious books?") and group members themselves used the word so often that it was clearly important.

One meaning of the word was deployed by EC when she described one of her book groups as "very serious." The core members of the group (as noted in chap. 4) had met in the League of Women Voters, and all were involved with politics and social action. This group mainly discussed intellectual nonfiction. *Serious* in this context meant nonfiction, abstract knowledge, and a concern with the public sphere. These members were suspicious of most fiction and especially of popular or genre books. They teased one member twice during a meeting in April 1982 for having chosen James Clavell's *Shogun* some months before. Their amusement was particularly pointed because she had not even attended the meeting at which the book was discussed. At that same meeting, they likened another member's penchant for mysteries to a "nervous tic" and "wasting time by doing crossword puzzles" (League of Women Voters Group meeting, April 1982). They asserted their own seriousness vis-à-vis cultural authority as well: they had formulated a policy of not inviting experts to lecture them about even the most difficult books; they refused to let me tape the meeting "because it might interfere with discussion"; and they do not appoint a discussion leader. In their words, at the first meeting they all "just jumped right in," and they have been doing so ever since.

The founder of another all-women group, the Harpies, advanced another definition of *serious*. When asked, in an interview in March 1991, "Are there any kinds of books you definitely don't read?" she answered, "We don't like to read anything too simple . . . because most of us have a serious background and are serious readers—or were at the time we were in school." She characterized the group as "very well educated. Everyone has at least a master's. A lot are involved with writing." The group wanted to replicate graduate school discussions. They usually read fiction, and their choices reflected a feeling of being entirely at home in the universe of canonized writing. As the founder said, "We read across countries and historical movements; for instance, we might read something by Jane Austen, then something current, something by Henry James, and something current. We've read *Anna Karenina* and some French novels in translation, but one women who reads French really doesn't like to read in translation."

Here *serious* is closely linked to academic definitions of great literature. The humanities, rather than politics or philosophy, provide the grounds for judgment. Moreover, members see themselves as self-confident cultural evaluators and masters of their cultural heritage in that their book selections are unfettered by temporal or cultural constraints. As this founder said, "Discussion is loud and can be very mean. Someone will walk in and say 'I liked this,' or someone may start out by saying, 'I hated this, it's really shit.' Comments can be very personal. It's a scary group. A real high-powered group of people with strong opinions who are not at all reticent about voicing those opinions."

Both of these groups use the word *serious* to mark their affiliation with the realm of high culture, although each has appropriated a different sphere within that world—one more closely allied to the public world of politics, science, and other abstract knowledge, and the other to the traditionally more feminine world of literary culture. They affirm a distinction not only between trivial or nonliterary talk (which they characterize as "chat") and their own literary discussions but also between serious and nonserious books.

For other participants in reading groups, seriousness does not accord so easily with traditional cultural hierarchies. Such people often manifest a critical distance from the academy and its strictures or show an unabashed appreciation of the vitality of more popular cultural forms. These attitudes are often expressed by women who are very well educated and who possess a great deal of what Bourdieu calls cultural capital, which may legitimate what from a traditional viewpoint look like transgressive cultural choices.

This kind of perspective on the world of literature can lead members to draw somewhat innovative literary distinctions, even in the name of the serious. Certainly, at least a few Houston reading groups are working with "maps" of the literary world very different from the two mentioned above: maps that flatten the generic hierarchy or raise the claims of lowly genres to serious consideration. The two groups I discuss below are coincidentally mixed-gender groups, although the evidence from the Houston romance groups is a clear indication that women's reading groups can also manifest distance from high cultural dictates about literary worth.

An advertisement for the mystery group that meets at the Houston bookstore Murder by the Book shows how seriousness can be mobilized to underwrite a challenge to traditional cultural authority. The headline for their fall 1987 announcement of what they called their "continuing series of 6-week seminars" read "For the Serious (?) Mystery Reader." "Seminar," of course, harks back to the academy. Yet the parenthetical question mark seems to indicate an ambivalence toward the category of "the serious," asking, in effect: Can reading mysteries be serious? And do we want to ally ourselves with this notion of the serious? It may further posit that compulsive reading—sheer volume—indicates seriousness, as in the "serious" fan. These questions run through the group's discussions in different ways.

There is a tendency among members of the group to redefine mysteries as serious books. Members accomplish this, first, by claiming that they are important sociohistorical documents; as one member said, "I read somewhere that mysteries are the best books to read if you want to really understand another culture or period in history." And second, members accomplish this by subjecting the books to the same processes of categorization and evaluation that literary critics apply to the entire universe of literature. In particular, the mystery experts—those who spend time at the store and lead the group discussions—are heavily involved in elaborating subgeneric categories such as the "British cozy" or the psychological thriller, which they call genres, and in discussing what makes a mystery great. These discussions quickly become quite arcane, although each person in the group is also asked to rate the week's book on a scale of one to ten and to justify his or her evaluation. The group discusses mysteries as books that are morally serious because of their insight into character and motive. In fact, after the initial rating process, group discussion then focuses on the characters, usually initiated by the question, "Which character did you like the most and why?" Such discussion makes an implicit claim that the books are serious in and of themselves because they can sustain serious discourse about moral values. One member seemed uncomfortable with this, saying to me at the break, "Sometimes I think we take these books too seriously" (Mystery Group meetings, October–December 1986).

His discomfort points to an assumption that has pervaded literary studies: that there is a correspondence between the level of difficulty or quality of the text and the level or quality of its discussion. The educational system inculcates this assumption early, by legitimizing only certain "great" books as worth class discussion time. Yet linking literary worth to worthwhile discussion also provides an opening for potential contestation of the traditional literary hierarchy if a lowly genre such as the mystery can elicit morally serious talk.

The last usage of *serious* points to a dichotomy between readers and nonreaders that may be more important to American culture in general than that between readers and "serious" readers. It is found in an advertisement for the Bookpeople, a group I have called the Leisure Learning Group because it is listed in Leisure Learning Unlimited's free catalogue of various recreational and self-improvement activities. The January–February 1987 schedule included this reading group under the catalogue's general category "Serious Stuff," along with groups on speed-reading, writing, mathematics, and current events, as well as test-preparation study groups.

Under the general rubric of seriousness, the advertisement itself emphasizes enjoyment. It reads: "Do you like to read good books (fiction and nonfiction) and enjoy discussing them with others? If so, participate in these fun, informal gatherings. Read *Black Elk Speaks* by John Neihardt for the first week and bring suggestions for the remaining sessions. This isn't a group for literary snobs, just an ongoing group (now in its fourth year) that's always looking for new energy." Reading itself may be serious, this implies, but with this group you will find fun and excitement. The description of the group's leader also distances her from an overly serious stance toward literature. It reads: "DS has been an avid reader all her life. She has managed several bookstores and has led this group since 1983." This both establishes her reading credentials and sharply distinguishes her reading from the academic mode, with the word "bookstores" implying her connection with popular demands and usages for books, and "avidity" implying a voracious and catholic reading habit rather than purity of taste.

This is "the group that reads trash." Their leader presents the group to new members by saying, "We'll read anything. We're not snobs. If you can get enough people to vote for your book, we'll read it." They have read science fiction, mysteries, and a Louis L'Amour western as well as classics. Several members of this group have advanced degrees, but not in literature, and although two members teach at universities, others have scientific, professional, or business careers. Less connected to the literary establishment than, for example, the Harpies, they show a similar cultural confidence in their discussions.

Readers such as these may be not just rebelling against cultural snobbery but reframing the traditional evaluative hierarchy in literary studies. Saying you will read anything is a way of implying that the dichotomy between books and other kinds of culture is a more crucial distinction than that between different kinds of books (only important to "snobs"). It is also a way of privileging the discussion over the text itself. This stance tends to flatten the generic and categorical hierarchy into a continuum of different but equally valuable kinds of reading. Indeed, members often subject classics to merciless criticism. Some of their meetings are suffused with an almost illicit sense of taboo breaking, which heightens the group's pleasure. This tone may indicate that they are implicitly defining themselves as advocates for a new "map" of literary culture and possibly as claimants for a new kind of cultural authority based on open-mindedness, literary populism, and reading competence across generic boundaries.

There are at least two crucial conceptual underpinnings to this cultural renegotiation. One is a redefinition of *serious* that privileges the moral seriousness of discussion rather than the formal qualities of a given genre or individual book. In turn, this relies on uncoupling the quality of discussion from the abstract notion of literary worth as something inherent in a given text that is, if "worthy," automatically morally or aesthetically elevating. Second, this position privileges the distinction between reading and not reading rather than that between worthwhile reading and "trash." Both cultural moves challenge the autonomy of high or academic literary culture while maintaining allegiance to literary culture and moral seriousness in general.

One reason reading groups express distance from the concerns and dictates of more academic or "professional" cultural authorities is that their lives are not so wholly bound up with literature as a vocation. An earlier generation of cultural analysts encapsulated this difference with the term *middlebrow.* To classify these groups as middlebrow assumes that they are failing to achieve an academic formalism in their reading and may miss the point of their activity altogether, along with the related possibility that reading itself may not be a uniform activity. This kind of static cultural ranking obscures the delicate renegotiations that change the boundaries of legitimate culture. Conceptualizing reading as a variable social practice, however, reveals the give-and-take between literature and life experience by which audiences constantly dismantle and reinscribe the seemingly stable hegemony of the evaluative hierarchy.[3]

Different Meanings of Literary

Some of the experiential distance between reading groups and academics or other literary professionals is revealed by their discourse and assumptions about "the literary." For reading group members, literary quality, to begin with, necessitates a minimum level of craftsmanship; *literary* presupposes literate. Most academics do not have to cope with questions of literacy, except when grading student papers, so discussions of merit rarely touch on this issue. Reading group members must negotiate a world teeming with noncanonical books, in which judgments based on grammatical correctness, for example, are often not only relevant but also necessary to defend the stature of good books. As a case in point, most reading group members despise romances not only because they are formulaic but also because they are not written well. "The sentences weren't complete; the grammar was wrong. It was a terrible book," said one member about a romance given her by a friend. Ungrammatical books offend, in part, because by definition they cannot be improving.

Literariness is also evidenced by references to other "things literary," such as things academic and things British. One reason that detective fiction outranks science fiction, for example, is that many mysteries (often written by academics) are peppered with literary epigraphs and word play. Within the Mystery Group, members most often rank what they call the "British cozy" highest among the subgenres they differentiate. Some members, in fact, will only read British mysteries, because they are so much more "literary." Contiguity with other sources of high culture, then, is another source of literary value for reading groups.

Significantly, Dorothy Sayers, who is both British and literary, most often occupies the crossover slot among mystery writers. Reading groups classify this kind of author as a transcendent representative of a literary category or genre. Authors such as John Le Carré or Sayers serve in the same way that tokens of a minority group do in the social world. They are the high-quality exceptions within their humble genre, and groups can read them without questioning the evaluative boundaries that they draw around their reading in general. As one reading group member said: "We've never read a murder mystery or a science fiction book—I don't think there's any prejudice. There's no reason we couldn't read something by Ursula LeGuin, for example. We never did sit down and consider what we were going to read" (interview with EM, July 1986). Crossover authors have a more literary reputation than do other representatives of their genre, yet exactly what quality makes LeGuin more generally acceptable than science fiction writers such as Mary Gentle, Orson Scott Card, Sherry Tepper, or William Gibson is much less clear. As in the social world, the literary meritocracy may owe something to pedigree and connections. The Bantam edition author's note in LeGuin's books mentions that she is the daughter of the famous anthropologists and writers Alfred L. and Theodora Kroeber, that she was educated at Radcliffe College and Columbia University, and that she had a Fulbright year in Paris (LeGuin 1975, 278).

For reading groups more than for academics, literary merit stands, first, for adherence to certain standards of linguistic competence, standards that themselves are an integral part of high culture, if we follow Basil Bernstein's discussion (1971) of class and language. Second, it is established by association with other loci of "literariness." And third, it refers to a reading experience that is personally significant and enduring. As one reading group member said about Gustave Flaubert's *Sentimental Education:*

> Woody Allen said, "What is there to life?" and he named some jazz singer . . . and then *Sentimental Education.* I don't have that much leisure time to read. But I just think—it's a *classic.* I want to read something that I can remember a year later. I'm tired of reading stuff that doesn't stick with me. I really like something that's substantial. I'm certain this is substantial. There's no doubt about it. (My Book Group meeting, 20 October 1986)

There are echoes here of the literary doctrine that great books are those that have endured through the centuries, but the standard is subjective—instead of the judgment of the ages, there is judgment of the individual's memory. Trash lasts only a week or so; classics for a year at least. Like a hearty meal, they stick.

This reader also defines a classic in experiential terms. A classic is great because it *does* something for someone: it provides a reading experience that can transcend the ephemerality and flux of daily living, and it enriches or moves the reader in such a way that it finds a permanent niche in her memory. This stands in direct opposition to the intellectualist tendency to produce formal aesthetic analyses. Even if intellectuals and reading group members categorize the same book as a classic, they may expect something different from the book and subject it to somewhat different standards of judgment, because the "ordinary reader" is working with an existential or psychological definition of greatness that subsumes it to the criterion of personal enhancement. Even those readers who automatically defer to cultural authority may stand at some distance from it because they are amateurs who look to books for the pleasures of deep emotional involvement, meaningfulness, or illumination of their experience rather than for the more rationalist pleasures that come with analytic distance.

Book Selection and Social Identity

Naturalistically exploring the world of reading group members points up one of the aspects of their engagement with literature that is difficult to perceive when one begins from within the world of texts and "vocational" reading. Reading group members read, it is true, and read enthusiastically, but their reading is dependent not only on various aspects of literature (e.g., availability of books, the evaluative hierarchy) but also on their sense of literature's relationship to their everyday lives beyond literature. In regard to literature, the daily life of reading group members has the weight to structure book selection in various ways.

Literature as Equipment for Living

Reading group members tend to select books that can bring them pleasure and illuminate (in the sense of enlighten or inform) their experience. In this sense, they are using literature, in Kenneth Burke's memorable phrase (1957, 253–62), as "equipment for living." This is a rich and evocative notion, urging consideration of literature less as a platonic ideal than as something that is pressed into service for a task beyond itself, a tool employed in the construction of human lives. As such, it opens our vision of literature to encompass the people who read it and the various contexts that influence the variable nature of people's engagement with books. In regard to book selection by members of women's reading groups, this way of conceptualizing literature points toward at least two aspects of the relationship between books and the group members' lives beyond them: the interest that reading group members have in books relevant to their "social selves," and the reason that groups' self-definitions can marginalize some members, making them feel so alienated that they leave.

As to the first issue, we see that participants' desire to elucidate their world and lives through book discussions means that who they are outside of these literary groups conditions what they wish to read in them. This is just a special case of a more general phenomenon among audiences for books. In relation to gender, for example, even the broad national surveys of individual reading habits show that men read more nonfiction than women do. Women not only read more fiction than men do but they also form the primary audience for certain genres, such as the romance. Men have historically outnumbered women as audiences for thrillers and mysteries, especially hard-boiled detective novels. Region, political values (broadly defined), and race also influence book selection both within reading groups and among individual readers.

For us to understand the process by which social identity figures into book selection, it is not enough to simply relate reading choices to large-scale structural variables such as gender or race, as many cultural analysts have done. For example, women's groups tend to choose more fiction and nonfiction related to psychological or spiritual issues, and men's groups tend toward book choices involving the public spheres of politics, business, warfare, and science. Yet structural variables alone are not enough to account for the book choices of the different women's groups. Taking their self-definition into account is crucial. Perceiving that participants are using literature (and each other) as a tool for normative discussions of their lives and their world is necessary for understanding why they choose the books they do and how they read them.

The Case of Gender

Gender figures into reading groups' selection of books in complex ways. Men and women sometimes find different books engaging, given their different life experiences and socialization. Gender is an issue with variable salience among both men and women, however, so there is no automatic association between men and Men's Books or women and Women's Books as some kind of essentialized, internally homogeneous, and dichotomized categories. Nonetheless, women's experiences in coed groups with the kinds of literary selections they would like to make show that women at times choose different books than men do, and that these books—especially if they are by women authors or about women's concerns—often encounter either disinterest or denigration.

During my research in Houston, I came across one instance in which this gender divide in book selection—which can leave women feeling marginalized in mixed-gender groups—spurred a coed group to accomplish some creative cultural work regarding the conceptualization of gender during meetings from fall 1986 to spring 1988. The example is interesting in part because it reveals the way in which women's concerns appear to be culturally coded as special and provincial, because at least until this group worked through the issue, men and their concerns tended to be equated with the general and universal. The setting for this extended discussion was the Leisure Learning Group, which was quite catholic in its reading choices and voted on suggestions by members to accomplish book selection. One of the more persuasive women in the group generally pushed for books about modern women's issues.

Resentment among the men about books they perceived as hostile to their gender finally came to a head when the woman "sponsored" a discussion of Lisa Alther's *Other Women,* a book about a woman who is very depressed, gets little pleasure out of men, and finds happiness through therapy and a lesbian relationship. Deeply offended by this representation of gender relations, the men began teasing her every time she suggested another book: "Is this another book about women in pain?" This tactic silenced her for a while. But gradually she began to renegotiate her participation in the group by accepting "women in pain" as her literary genre of choice, saying, for example, "I know I'm always suggesting women-in-pain books, but this is much more interesting than most of them." By reformulating their derision as a literary category, she worked herself back into the group's conversation.

The men then decided that women had no monopoly on pain and began a search for men-in-pain books that could serve as a moral equivalent to women-in-pain work so they would not be marginalized or silenced in turn. Both categories became a routine part of the group's generic mapping of modern literature. "Women in pain" is a recognizable, although trivializing, label for women's literature from the nineteenth century on, but to work themselves back into the group's conversation the men had to articulate publicly something new about modern literature, gender, and their own emotional makeup. By negotiating through their deeply felt differences about how each sex views the other to a common ground, the men and women in the group invented new cultural categories that articulated a new framework for literary and social experience. This framework involved conceptualizing both male and female experience as inflected by gender. In combination with the "in pain" formulation, which they used for both sexes, the group not only articulated feelings that modern existence is difficult for both men and women but also removed the mantle of "the universal" from men's experience and thereby the stigma of provincialism from women's concerns.

This example indicates two things. First, women, like men, want to engage in a dialogue with others that links literature to their lives. Therefore, they may be interested in exploring different authors and different books—even different aspects of the same books—insofar as their lives are different along the axis of gender. Second, although books by women have gained more critical acceptance in the past decades, many men still tend to see them as either unimportant or uninteresting. This view is still so generally accepted that men (and perhaps women) in mixed-gender groups feel authorized in dismissing women's choices of books by women or about women's experiences.

What this means is that literature divides along gender lines in a way that cannot be conceptualized simply as different but equal; difference here, as in much of the social and cultural world, is weighted in an asymmetrical or hierarchical fashion. These intersecting structures of lived experience and cultural value are consequential for women's patterns of book selection. This is also one reason why they form women's book groups. For instance, one group founder, JS, when asked during an interview (June 1997) why she conceived and began her group as all women, answered, "Book selection—I guess I wanted to read a lot of books by women." DLS, another woman who also belongs to a women's book group, indicated that she is very sensitive to the gender component of narratives. She understands her reading choices both inside and outside of her book group as almost a form of resistance to or compensation for a literary culture that devalues women's concerns.

> Books by women are more likely to address concerns that are important to me as a woman. Books by men often give visibility to particularly masculine hang-ups and a preoccupation with competitiveness and manliness. Some authors who are very much admired present women in an offensive light and only include women as less

well-developed characters. Women authors don't often present women as hunks of meat, as does John Updike, or as Lady Macbeth–type dragon women. In school and college I read mainly books by men. But I'm tired of being implicitly insulted as a gender through books that don't give a fair perspective on women's concerns or that treat women in a shallow way, so I mostly read books by women. (Interview, 28 September 1998)

However, it is clear that men's attitudes about women's writing or about discussion of issues that are culturally coded feminine rather than masculine are not uniform. For example, TB, a Houston man who founded an all-male group, told me during an interview in 1997 that he is frustrated by the group's desire to read almost entirely books about politics or public affairs. He is also frustrated by the group's responses to the books he chooses, which are apt to be concerned with psychology or spirituality, and by what he sees as an inability among other group members to hold discussions that are introspective and open and that allow a certain level of personal vulnerability.

Enlightened men notwithstanding, many women either find themselves in all-women groups because they want to read more than a token few books by women or narratives that do not marginalize women or because, having joined a group of women for more social reasons, they find themselves among co-discussants for whom such choices simply make sense experientially. Of course, gender composition is not an automatic guarantee that all women's groups will read a lot of books by or about women: witness the League of Women Voters Group that reads books mainly by men about public affairs and science. Understanding how groups define themselves and why is crucial here. But in general, it appears that all-women reading groups are engaged in the kind of dialogue between literature and life that makes women's experiences or concerns particularly compelling for them.

Sometimes, the reasons for wanting to read books by women are not easily articulated by group members. In 1990, I informally interviewed a friend who had belonged to an all-women reading group in California. I asked her what they had read. "Biography," she said, "and almost all biographies about women." When I asked her why only women's lives were chosen, she twice puzzled over the question. She then discussed the biography of Margaret Sanger the group had read and how poignantly it brought up for her the question of having a great cause and doing tremendously important work in the world, and yet abandoning one's children. We discussed various ramifications of that question for about ten minutes, and it was not until I reflected back on the interview that I realized that she had both evaded an explicit formulation of her answer and demonstrated exactly why women's biographies mattered to her.

Group Tone and Subtler Levels of Group Identity

Book selection is crucial for group formation and group cohesion: both what a group considers worth reading and what it considers interesting to read powerfully shape that group's identity along the axis of legitimacy or "seriousness" as well as along substantive dimensions of content and genre. In combination with how a group organizes itself, a group's reading boundaries and the evolving nature of their discussions make each group different from the others.[4] As mentioned earlier, these boundaries can be an explicit part of the group "compact" at its formation, with the group defining itself in relation either to literature (the Not-So-Great Books Group) or to the social world (the Interns' and Residents' Wives Group). Sometimes what brings women together and gives them a sense of group identity and common purpose is more subtle and idiosyncratic and cannot be easily subsumed to "macrocultural" structures. As Rachel Jacobsohn (1994, 5) says, groups evolve in different directions: "Purpose, syllabi, and method of leadership separate one group from another and play an important part in establishing a group's tone and behavioral norm."

Sometimes this is a gradual process, as was the case for a group of by now avowedly traditional women. Three members started a reading group without an explicit social or literary program. As the group grew in size, the members gradually recognized both that they were using the group to explore literature about women, in the main, and that discussing such books revealed how much they shared certain deeply held convictions about womanhood. As EM, one of the group's founders, said in an interview in 1988:

> We have a joke that you have to be married to your first husband to belong—it's an expression of commitment. Everyone cared for her own children when they were young, and there's an open commitment to that. And an open wonderment at people who live differently—at people who have children and then leave them in other people's care, or who think they should leave their husband to find someone "better." It's such a pervasive joke I'm not sure it's a joke. It does function —though there are conflicts—I don't want to call it a consciousness-raising group because these are *traditional* women—but there's a support aspect to this group. We're fighting to hold the tide back.

In some cases, groups can identify a "defining moment" in their history, as noted by Stephanie Patterson (Slezak 1995, 63):

The discussion of *Cat's Eye* was the defining moment for us. The story of Elaine's torment at the hands of her friend, Cordelia, struck a chord with all the members of our group. We discussed not only the book, but also our own struggles with classmates we had admired and feared. We were clearly a group of Elaines. Even now when friends inquire about our group, we suggest they read *Cat's Eye* and tell us with which character they identify. But we're not really sure Cordelias join book groups.

Such moments are often linked to the books under discussion because it is precisely in the discourse about a book the group has chosen that the group creates itself as this particular and unique group saying these things and no others about this book's meanings. At times like this, *literary interpretation* seems an impoverished term for the embellishment or creation of a common reality that shimmers into existence as the group brings its own register of personal relationships with the book into play in their talk about it. This is a very rich vein that I explore in more detail in the following chapter about book discussion. Here, suffice it to say that a noteworthy aspect of book clubs, especially successful ones, is their ability to acquire what members recognize as "a life of their own," which is a distillate of a collective identity often referred to by members. In fact, the issue of how people describe their groups—which I call the group tone for short—came up so often in informal discussion that eventually I included a question about this on the revised version of the short group "inventory." A few examples of responses to this question give some of the variety it elicited:

> Depends on who you ask. One friend comments on tension. I never notice. It's an amiable group. We've had some good fights over books, but we tend to refer back to those fondly, like "Remember the big fight we had over Barbara Pym and whether she was worth reading?" (MT, Book Club)

> Friendly and loose-knit. Positive, fun loving, happy. Everybody has a pretty positive attitude toward their lives. And there's never been a great tragedy, just normal family problems and break-ups, and generally we don't talk about family problems a lot. (SW, Revista)

> Honest! It's amazing we've gotten along so well. We accept criticism from each other better than from anyone else. We have a heck of a lot of fun, really roll with things. (JB, Networking)

> It's a scary group. One woman said this week that she thought people knew boundaries. I'm not so sure. (LP, Harpies)

It's not particularly an intellectual group. Which I think everyone thought it might be. It really evolved. I mean you don't start at the college class level and work upward. . . . We have certain standards, but they're not that high. [*Laughter.*] (JG and CS, Book Group)

It's energetic, enthusiastic; it's an escape and a special treat. The people in it are not connected except through the book group. There's an intensity and an intellectually stimulating, maybe competitive, environment. But it's acceptable to disagree. (EW and GC, Book Group)

Our group is the group that usually talks about how we think we would have liked the book if anybody had gotten around to reading it. (CW, Book Group)

Leaving the Circle

Most reading groups develop a balance between homogeneity and diversity. At least some diversity is necessary for an enriching book discussion. Homogeneity enables groups to draw on a substrate of shared values and experiences to create the atmosphere of fundamental understanding and trust that sustains an enjoyable and mutually revelatory conversation. Without such shared assumptions, which implicate both literature and life, some members will find book choices too simple, too difficult, or simply irrelevant to their concerns. Or they will feel bored or alienated by the discussions.

Departures from reading groups reveal this most strikingly. When members decide to leave a reading group because it is no longer meeting their needs, that choice forces both them and other group members to reflect on what binds the group together. This relates to book selection and discussion because people's reasons for leaving often refer to the literary quality of selections and the intellectual quality of the discussion. For example, one couple left a small suburban group because the level of book choice and discussion intimidated them. As DN, one member of the group, said,

We weren't trying to intimidate them, but when we'd pick books we liked they would spend hours studying for our discussions, using CliffsNotes. It was like a class for them, when we were just enjoying ourselves. Then one time they picked *The Thorn Birds,* and we all said, "Oh, won't that be fun. We've never read a book like that together," and they felt really insulted, because for them, it was a good book. (Interview, October 1983)

In this instance, competing understandings of literary quality were at play. From a member's perspective, this lack of intellectual fit can be painful. In an interview that was remarkable because the memories had such freshness even after several years, CD described her departure from a reading group:

> I was booted out. I have a degree in computer science, and I think the girls in that group just couldn't handle logic or clear thinking. I really didn't like reading trash and low-level books, so I guess I just didn't fit really well. This must have been around the time I was starting to go back to school, so I hadn't always been able to attend the meetings. The president got together with me and said, "Since you haven't been attending meetings regularly, you really can't belong to the group." I mentioned another member who also hadn't been attending really regularly. That made her mad. But Lynn was acceptable, and my ideas weren't. They were too challenging of the general level of the group, which was quite childlike. When I suggested that *Watership Down* was built on anthropomorphism, they found that difficult to accept. They really thought those rabbits thought like that and talked like that and lived like that, and they couldn't accept that that might not be the case. They were in many ways real shallow. They would accept girls who were having affairs with each other's husbands easier than someone who didn't think like them. That's when I thought, "I can't handle this group." They're very suburban and very wealthy, and in one sense educated and in one sense not. I wasn't obnoxious about it. I had meetings at my house, and helped organize, and enjoyed the socializing. But they couldn't handle my mind. They sort of forced me out of the group. (Interview, 14 June 1990)

Such differences are among the most common reasons for members' departures from reading groups. In June 1991, during an interview, three members of one Houston group discussed members who had left because they wanted, in JG's words, to read "a lighter level of fiction. I think they want to read the best-sellers so they can discuss them with whoever they're playing tennis with or at a cocktail party with or something like that. Because that is a subject of conversation. And any time we have read a best-seller it has basically not been the kind of book to discuss." But during the same interview, CS mentioned a member who seemed to feel alienated from the group because the tone wasn't analytic enough: "I think that she's not going to be in the group any longer. Somehow it's just—It's not for her. Maybe because it's not intellectual enough."

Groups often find a definite niche in the literary hierarchy. Consequently, it can be difficult for an individual to find a group whose level of discussion fits her own orientation toward literature. M, a woman interviewed by DeNel Sedo, explains her departure from two groups, one too intellectual and one not intellectual enough:

> Frankly, there were quite a lot of lightweights. That was the problem. It was a bit superficial. I'm not saying that I am any great intellect. Well, actually the first group I belonged to was definitely superficial. In the second group there were quite a few really intellectual people and I was nowhere near at that level. They were Ph.D. English grads kind of thing, and they were way more into it than I was. And I just lost interest. Also when you have a kid, life can change. (Interview, February 2000)

Sometimes more personal qualities are at issue. This becomes particularly problematic because most reading groups are informally structured and are predicated on an assumption that everyone gets along. It becomes very difficult for members to speak plainly when someone dominates the conversation, takes too much group time to discuss personal problems, or otherwise behaves in ways that violate the group's often unspoken assumptions about appropriate conduct, because there are no real rules to refer to. I have heard rumors of groups that were so reluctant to confront a difficult member that they pretended to disband the group and then started up again without her. Examples from my data are similar but less dramatic. For instance, CW described a situation fraught with indirect communication:

> CC was driving us all nuts. She was dominating the conversation, and she was too argumentative, and we tried everything we could do. Finally, we decided that we were going to do facilitator-course-type stuff so that when CC started talking too much we would all turn our backs or no one would respond. We would try to get the message across, and it didn't seem to be working at all. But I think somebody told CC what we were trying to do, because she never came back one time. (Interview, 16 May 1991)

In other cases, socioeconomic status or differences in social identity make people feel marginal to the group. For example,

> I found the book club a little cliquey because of the nature of a few of the people who were in the same profession who were less respectful of those that weren't. That bothered me a little bit. Also the choice of the books was great, but I was on a limited budget at the time. If I tried and couldn't get the book in the library, I wasn't in a position to purchase the book to keep up. [Without the book] I kind

of felt like an imposter. I didn't want to go to a group when I hadn't read the book and sit there and not say anything. (Interview with B, November 1999, by DeNel Sedo)

When telling My Book Group's founder why she had decided to drop out, one woman analyzed the hitherto unremarked-on social bases for the group's solidarity and her own sense of marginality. She pointed out that with two exceptions, everyone was married to her first husband, had adolescent or adult children, and had stayed at home while the children were small. Most maintained some connection to Rice University, and most belonged to a liberal Protestant church. She failed to meet several of these "criteria," because she was younger than most of us, had no connection to Rice, and had decided to start graduate school while coping with a new baby. She also pointed out that I also did not fit very well, because I was single, childless, and unaffiliated with a church. I recognized the truth of her analysis, and in fact, over time I tried to recruit two women who were more like me. Both were more iconoclastic than the rest of the group, and each differed from the dominant majority in other ways as well. One was Jewish, had no children, and was interested in politics and social movements. The other had been divorced, was interested in spirituality but was not conventionally religious, had not yet finished college, and was working as a secretary at Rice. Neither lasted more than a few months in the group. I stayed with the group much longer, in part because they became for me the object for academic study—a sociological solution to marginality.

If not related to social, personal, or literary factors, alienation and departure can implicate the roles and hierarchy that develop within the group. These are slippery and painful issues because often groups sustain an illusion of egalitarianism, which can make informal leaders the more influential because they are less accountable. One colleague of mine (CB), who came to a university in another Southern state from a Commonwealth country, told of an especially difficult experience she had in this regard during an interview in July 2001. Searching for a women's group (her minor had been women's studies), she was told of an on-campus reading group. As she said: "What I had anticipated in my naiveté was that it would be an egalitarian, sharing get-together, sort of informal and cozy. That I would be welcomed. That had been my experience where I came from." Although the group had been described as leaderless, it was in fact under the totalitarian rule of one professor, as she discovered when she made the "huge mistake in actually speaking up at the first meeting about the content of the book. It was very clearly a hierarchical arrangement, which I really didn't understand. I went in boots and all. I should have just kept my mouth shut." "Until?" I asked her. She replied: "Until invited to speak. There were about three people who were permitted to speak, and the rest of us had to sit there and say nothing."

CB's only notice that she had broken a group "rule" was the hostility and irritation displayed by the woman who ran the group. A couple of meetings later, CB made another mistake: "The only books we read were about women in other cultures who were always oppressed, abused, or suffering. Finally I said, 'You know, women are sort of subjugated everywhere. Why don't we look at one of the texts that deal with women in America or [this state]?' That was the very worst thing I could have said."

"The final straw," as CB said, came after three or four meetings, when she suggested reading a book on menopause during the group's solicitation of titles for the next meeting. "A couple of the women jumped up and said, 'Oh, we'd like that!' And her [the leader's] face turned purple. But she sort of agreed to it, and next time we went along and we discussed it. It was the liveliest discussion we'd had. But she refused to come." At the end of the meeting, CB asked a woman she'd become quite friendly with whether there was a problem. The woman responded that the leader didn't want to attend " 'if this is the sort of book that's going to be discussed.' I said, 'Oh, then she has a problem not only with the book but with my being there.' And she said, 'Yes,' so I left the group."

The informality that can give book group leaders so much power, however, also makes their power fragile, as the two following accounts show. The first recounts a leader's voluntary departure, and the second, a mass rebellion.

The funny thing about the group is that everybody was a friend of this one woman. Everybody knew her. And finally she ended up quitting because she asked this one person to join who had kept asking her: "Can I join your book club?" and she finally said yes. She realized that she couldn't stand this woman. Couldn't stand her opinions and the way she sort of harrumphed around about some things. She just couldn't stand her, so she quit. [*Starts to laugh.*] Quit her own book club! (Interview with M, February 2000, by DeNel Sedo)

MB decided she wanted a group that would support each other in reading classics. So at the beginning they would read Shakespeare one year and southern women writers the next year, and go back to Shakespeare the next year. But eventually the other members rebelled and MB dropped out. It was a coup d'état! (Interview with CW, July 1991)

In reflecting on homogeneity and diversity among reading groups, I think diversity is the greater challenge because of two factors, both of which relate to a group's informality. First, most groups grow out of participants' informal social networks, which are apt to be composed of other women very much like themselves. Reinforcing this basis for homogeneity is the organizational informality that characterizes most groups. This can foster a group dynamic based on unspoken assumptions about literary quality, right conduct, voice, and the proper scope of leadership—assumptions that are difficult to discuss because they are uncodified and consequently difficult to articulate. Diversity offers a challenge to preconstituted value judgments, whether literary or not, so it is a particularly important challenge for keeping reading groups open-minded and self-critical.

Group Demise

Conflict can tear groups apart, but my Houston observations do not include examples of this problem. Rather, two interviews show reading groups gradually dissolving because their members' lives changed to the point that they no longer needed the literary and social support the groups had provided. In the first case, the group had formed among women at home with young children, and it disbanded as women returned to work. The interviewee (EC), for instance, held a full-time job at a suburban bookstore. As she explained the situation:

> Well, the group is not functioning on a regular basis any more. [There have been] a lot of changes over the years. Many of our members have returned to the world of full-time work, one member moved away, and another is seriously ill. Most of us are still in touch with each other, although not as regularly as when we were in the group. [The group lasted] about twelve years, which is a long time for a group that was as totally informal as we were. We all watched our children grow up and change and move on. It was a very good experience. (Interview, May 1990)

The second case provides a clear example of how empowering a book group can be for the women involved. It shows women literally reshaping their identities through the group's discussions and support. Early on in our conversation, the woman I was interviewing—JB of Networking—said that the group might be falling apart:

> The reason for this appears to be that the group has been very successful. Most of us have conquered the big problems we've had and that the group helped support us with. We've had two divorces and two or three marriages and five of us have graduated college, and we've had the support of each other through all of this. It's been a really positive experience. People's lives have changed so much, be-

cause of the group. The basic thing that's been very important is the encouragement to go on. The encouragement to keep looking for yourself. You're so used to being for others: someone's wife, and someone's mother. The group has made us ourselves more than anything else. (Interview, June 1990)

In contrast to these groups, which provided an experience that helped members negotiate challenging periods in their lives and then faded in importance for their members, other reading groups evolve over time, changing meeting times and reading choices to accommodate the stages in their members' lives. Of such a group, one member said in October 1985, "We're so close, I guess we'll just grow old together."

SIX

Conversing with Books, Fashioning Subjectivity, Dealing with Difference

Originally, I had thought of book groups as places where I might have access to members' individual interpretations of books.[1] Informed by questions about the variability of people's interpretations and evaluations of literature, I understood reading groups mainly as sites at which the results of solitary reading experiences would be voiced and could be captured on the wing, as it were, by the assiduous ethnographer. Book club members do bring their individual interpretations and ideas about books into their meetings. But any formulation of their central cultural practice as simply reporting what each thought about a book almost entirely misses the point of why the participants are there at all.

What goes on in the meetings is primarily a conversation. As such, it is an intersubjective creation that takes on the weight of reality, however ephemeral it may be. This reality comes into being because of the strands that comprise it, but it cannot be reduced to them, for it is out there, between, or hovering above, in much the same way that the music played by an orchestra or jazz ensemble hovers in the well of air above the individual players. Alfred Schutz (1964, 159–78), the phenomenological sociologist, referred to this process in an essay titled "Making Music Together," an essay that only came to life for me when I participated in an early music group. In that group I noticed that occasionally we indifferently gifted musicians were able to create something between us that was so moving, so musical, that we could hardly bear to hear the last notes disappear into silence.

In the same fashion, participants in book groups create a conversation that begins with the book each woman has read but moves beyond the book to include the personal connections and meanings each has found in the book, and the new connections with the book, with inner experience, and with the perspectives of the other participants that emerge within the discussion. At its best, this kind of discussion is profoundly transformative. Linsey Howie's work (1998, 229) on Australian book groups claims that they are, in fact, spaces in which participants can "speak, imagine, or live alternative subjective positions," and I have observed that process in some Houston groups.

Such conversations are in some ways much less than a classroom discussion about a book, for they move back and forth between using people's remarks as windows into the text (the primary imperative of literary analysis) and using the text as a window into people's lives or various aspects of the cultural and social lives we live together. In this sense, they are perhaps not very indicative of how people in other solitary or interactional settings "use" literature. Yet again, they can become much more than a class or a solitary reading. It is as if the discussion is a lens that reveals the books under discussion and the inner lives of coparticipants and, through this process, allows participants to reflect back on their own interior lives as well. In these conversations, people can use books and each other's responses to books to promote insight and empathy in an integrative process of collective self-reflection. In that sense, reading group discussions perform creative cultural work, for they enable participants to articulate or even discover who they are: their values, their aspirations, and their stance toward the dilemmas of their worlds. The centrality of this intersubjective accomplishment helps explain several aspects of book discussions in reading groups.

Conversing with Books

Freedom and Lack of Boundaries

If reading groups appear very sensitive to the dictates of cultural authority and the hierarchy of taste in selecting books to read, they are much freer from that authority in their discussions. Participants talk about books with deep engagement, but very differently than literary professionals do, and they sometimes interpret characters and evaluate novels with marked disregard for the critics' opinion. This activity can be construed as one form of culture constitution or cultural resistance, although usually group members do not understand it in this light. The women are aware that their book discussions are, in their term, "playful." Several women noted the freedom to leap from topic to topic and the stream-of-consciousness structure of their discussions. The League of Women Voters Group, at a meeting in April 1982, had consciously decided not to invite experts to their rather analytic meetings because, in their words, they did not "want to be informed"; they wanted "to spin the ideas out" by themselves.

One reason these groups can be playful is that they are not held accountable for their interpretations in the way that "professional readers" and their students are. Group members do not have to assert their interpretations in a serious way or defend them with tightly reasoned arguments from the text. Indeed, women often expand on an opinion by discussing their personal reasons for making a certain interpretation, using the book for self-understanding and revelation of the self to other participants rather than for discovery of meaning within the book.

For instance, a member of the Harpies said: "One woman was going through a divorce and we were reading *Absalom, Absalom,* and another woman started talking about the mean father in the book, and we had a big fight about the character of the father, but it was really just a fight about the husband" (interview, June 1991). Here, she was not describing an inappropriate eruption of the personal into a literary discussion. Rather, she was observing the interweaving of literature and personal experience through which group members routinely crystallize their values. This reflection occurs in solitary reading as well. Yet, at their best, these groups provide a "special" interactional setting that enables self-discovery and collective affirmation.

Crucial for these discussions is the sharing of different perspectives. It is for this reason that the "best" books do not always lead to the best discussions. As one member of the Traditional Women's Group said, "It isn't always the best books that give rise to the best discussions. Sometimes we just sit nodding at each other and saying, 'Isn't it great?' It's like you don't want to muddy the water by sticking your finger in" (interview, 22 May 1990). In fact, general approval may work against precisely that airing of differences that seems to make for the best discussions, whereas passionate disagreement often elicits the most interesting ideas.

Another striking quality of these conversations is that although they may change people's opinions about the book and each other, they usually do not lead to anything resembling closure or even, necessarily, agreement. Sometimes members of women's book groups claimed that men were less able than women to enjoy the open-endedness that marked their book group discussions. This constitutes an implicit (and probably inaccurate) gendered critique of men as more closely linked to an instrumental or pragmatic attitude toward ideas, an attitude that would prevent them from appreciating the richness of a conversation that appreciates differences without needing to resolve them. FM 1960 members, for example, said that the men they knew could not understand how one could "just throw ideas around" without coming to a conclusion or at least a point of resolution (meeting, 24 March 1982). Members of Les Belles Lettres maintained, during a group interview, that this was one reason they enjoyed book groups more than their husbands would. One woman claimed that men like to "get somewhere" with an argument and can't understand just wanting "a forum for opinions." Another said that the arguments were enjoyable in and of themselves:"It's a kind of therapy: a chance to yell and scream once a month." Although other groups may not need the therapy of sharp disagreement as much as this group did (it was then composed of stay-at-home suburban mothers), all seem to value the airing of differences much more than coming to any collective conclusion. My sense is that resolution is also low on the list of priorities among mixed-gender groups. On the other hand, the one all-male reading group meeting I attended expected concluding summations from every member. It is perhaps not a coincidence that a majority of the participants were lawyers.

Putting Academic Discourse in Its Place

The comments in the previous section highlight another quality of the book discussions in reading groups. In a successful reading group, there is no need to produce an authoritative reading of a book. This notion is almost inimical to the kind of conversation that reading group members value. As one analyst of reader reception (Tompkins 1980, 211) says, in academic settings, literature provides students with "the occasion for acquiring literary competence," whereas "if the reader is a professor, it is the occasion for advancing his professional career when he publishes a new interpretation." Academic readings, then, highlight the display of rigorous and inventive analyses of a text within a context of hierarchical relationships and scholarly instrumentalism. The context for reading groups, at least ideally, is that of voluntary participation in an enjoyable leisure activity. Discussants are not held accountable for their textual interpretations in the same way as are "professional readers" and their students. At the core of a satisfying reading group discussion is the display of diverse literary and personal responses. Multivocality is what challenges individual members' preheld notions and allows them the possibility of new epiphanies about both literature and life. Conversely, the exclusiveness and authoritarian dynamics that silence diverse perceptions in some reading groups can lead to a self-ratifying smugness that discourages new insights.

The primacy of a many-voiced and fundamentally "interested" conversation for book group members also explains why their comments often frame academic analysis as either artificial or labored. At a September 1985 meeting, a CliffsNotes question about the meaning of the river in *Huckleberry Finn*, for example, led the Leisure Learning Group to uproarious reminiscences about the tribulations of searching for symbols in English literature classes and everyone's favorite trick for getting A's. One member said that the ocean was his favorite symbol: "It could mean death, sex, rebirth—you could do anything with the ocean."

This characterization of literary analysis as an arcane, demanding, and even manipulative game may seem particularly ironic given reading group members' willingness to accept authoritative literary judgment about the relative worth of books, but it can be explained by the difference in reading contexts. At a meeting of My Book Group in October 1983, for instance, one woman, who had borrowed a classic from another group member, commented that the book's owner had underlined all references to windows. The owner responded dismissively, "Oh, that was for a class. I wrote a paper on what windows might signify, but when I looked at it before the meeting, it seemed very old, you know, sort of contrived."

Whereas critics examine books as crafted texts to understand their inner workings and to justify evaluation, reading group members tend to press books into service for the meanings they transmit and the conversations they can generate. In so doing, participants recognize that they are reading differently than they would for a class. For instance, during a discussion of a Latin American novel, a member of My Book Group said that if she had to answer an essay question on the book she would write about the church. When another member said, "But you don't have to," she replied that she had spent years reading "with essay questions in view" (meeting, April 1983).

The fact that formal textual analysis often feels out of place in reading group discussions should not be taken as meaning either that it is always irrelevant or that book group discussants are unable to produce this kind of reading. For instance, when one member of my group linked a broken roadside sign for a "[F]unfair" to the intricately elaborated moral message of a British novel, everyone in the group delightedly joined in an extensive structural analysis of the novel. The group was equally intrigued by the possibility that the main characters in Lygia Telle's 1982 novel *The Girl in the Photograph* might all be aspects of one protagonist. In these cases, insights that would have been at home in a university classroom seemed intrinsically interesting to the other group members, so at issue here is neither lack of literary competence nor some kind of total refusal to entertain an "academic" level of textual appropriation.

On the other hand, ease with formal literary analysis is not usually privileged in reading group discussions the way it is in the classroom. Sometimes, as mentioned in the last chapter, it is actually threatening to participants, although given their high level of education, reading groups usually appreciate a member who has a gift for literary analysis. My group, for example, regarded the member who most often generated formal textual insights as having literary talent and expertise but tended to see this as a special personal resource she brought to the group, like another member's wry humor. Again, this points up the primary importance of the group's conversation, for which a range of personal and intellectual qualities, talents, and skills becomes not merely relevant but essential.

An Impure Aesthetic: Literature Subject to Personal Values

As mentioned earlier, literature has a paradoxical relationship to reading groups. On the one hand, books warrant and legitimize the very existence of such groups and the serious, literate "selves" of readers and discussants. Literature inspires respect and dedicated effort and promises a payoff in cultural capital and personal insight. This helps explain the groups' tendency to follow the dictates of literary authority as they choose what to read. On the other hand, when participants appropriate books as the ground for discussion, they subject their reading experiences to their personal values with a curious disregard for authoritative critical opinion.

For example, some groups refuse to entertain for discussion any books that deal with certain subjects, such as the group that will not read about incest. Others resent novels that expose them to negativity or the seamy side of life, especially if they find no countervailing voice. In the first instance, they feel that they have not been morally instructed. As a member of the Leisure Learning Group said of Flannery O'Connor's *A Good Man Is Hard to Find,* "I have to admire her insight into depravity, but I find her very one-sided. She never talks about the positive side of people. There's depravity and then God's salvation, but no other human alternative" (meeting, 26 November 1986). In the second instance, they complain that they have not found a book elevating or that they felt it exposed them to unrelieved bleakness. The Bookworms had this problem with William Kennedy's *Ironweed,* because he dealt with low-life criminals and the gritty underbelly of urban life. Such readers tacitly assume that certain subjects are inherently more "improving" than others, which again subjugates form to content or art to life. It would be easy to dismiss this response as naive, but it is more fruitful to see it as a clue to a different way of appropriating literature than is common in the academy. This use of literature can be construed as ideologically limited, because it remains grounded in upper-middle-class American "structures of feeling." But it also shows that reading groups often resist the dominant view that literature should be judged on the basis of formal aesthetic value.

This stance seems only partially explained by the familiar category of middlebrow, for the category is drawn from the domain of aesthetics or taste, whereas what is interesting about such readers' cultural behavior is precisely their subordination of aesthetics to nonaesthetic systems of value. A Bourdieuian analysis of class fractions and cultural capital can account for some aspects of this phenomenon. Many of the readers have a strong sense of cultural entitlement that derives from their own position of educational and social privilege, so they can easily reject the pronouncements of the academy, which is to them just another fraction of the sociocultural elite.

But even if Bourdieuian terms can be used to explain this kind of attitude, he, like "brow" theorists, tends to analyze those who are less "pure" in their aesthetics as ranking lower on the hierarchy of cultural capital (Bourdieu 1984, 3–96). This kind of ranking system fails to capture the practices and social position of reading groups, however, because their uses of literature also involve the link between cultural consumption, social experience, and personal change, which has been undertheorized in the study of audience reception as well as cultural sociology.

The reading attitude described above may also spring, in part, from a generalized understanding among American reading group members that great literature should provide a quasi-religious spiritual regeneration or serve as a repository of moral virtues. Such an understanding would certainly serve the interests of this constituency by further legitimizing their activity. It is also important to consider the nature of their conversation, because the intersubjective authority that emerges from discussion has the capacity to empower people's critical judgments.

Through conversation, groups can find the consensual authority to reevaluate books or to reconsider the criteria for literary worth. The collective discourse of the reading groups I observed in Houston tends to center on experiential and moral issues. So the categories of literary judgment that develop in reading groups are grounded in what participants have found to be worth talking about, just as the makeup of each group is premised on some degree of shared values.

For example, in a heated discussion in October 1987 about Vladimir Nabokov's *Lolita,* the Leisure Learning Group agreed early on that Nabokov "wrote beautifully," but they considered this tangential to the question of whether he was a "great writer." They spent much time debating whether his portrayal of Humbert Humbert was merely a rationalization of Nabokov's own sexual predilections. I interpreted this discussion as meaning that a "great" novel must move beyond special pleading or a narrowly self-serving representation of the moral universe. Finally, they began to describe their own reading experiences. One mentioned feeling "seduced" by the text. Others reported being torn between disgust (and the desire to put the book down) and a begrudging understanding of the protagonist. Eventually, they agreed that Nabokov was great because "he could make you see what it was like to be inside someone like that." This discussion both confirmed critical judgment of Nabokov and reframed the criteria for judgment by privileging the sphere of moral vision and the ability to create moral empathy in a reluctant audience. More strikingly, during a meeting in February 1988, this same group once asserted their collective authority over the entire canonization process. In talking about what kinds of books each was going to suggest at the next meeting, one member said: "I think we should pick at least one classic. Consistently the classics do inspire the best discussion." Another replied: "Maybe we should be the ones who decide if a book's a classic. If it generates a good discussion, it's a classic."

Realism and the Centrality of Characters

When readers find the imagined worlds of a novel to be believable, the book in question often elicits the kind of connections that lead to a satisfying discussion. Characters whom readers can identify with and learn from appear to be most central to this process, so believable settings and plots serve mainly to ground the characters more fully in "reality."

Readers often signal the ease or difficulty of their entry into novelistic settings in pictorial terms. As one participant said about Flannery O'Connor at a Leisure Learning Group meeting in November 1986: "I loved her because she really paints a portrait of the South." Conversely, in a meeting of My Book Group in May 1983, at which the group was discussing the Latin American novel *Girl in the Photograph,* a discussant said, "I reacted like I was reading about Egypt or somewhere children are being prostituted. I couldn't picture it." Later in the discussion, another member commented: "That didn't seem thin to me. I had that convent. I got a picture of the courtyard and the stairs and the plants." Similarly, at a March 1984 meeting of My Book Group at which Anne Tyler's *Dinner at the Homesick Restaurant* was discussed, one participant remarked: "This isn't central, but I could see what Mrs. Scarlatti's restaurant was, and what Ezra did with the restaurant, but I wasn't sure who was there eating." Realism, then, depends on what readers can imagine. In this view, the successful novelist has used words to make a world "come alive," which implies a mimetic understanding of literature.

This understanding of literature as an imitation or representation of reality emerged in the Renaissance, according to Jane Tompkins's historical account (1980, 207–14) of literary response, and since the 1980s it has been under sharp attack in literary and philosophical circles. Its association with the rise and development of the novel as a literary form may underlie people's preference for novels that can bring scenes and characters "alive." Reading group discussants sometimes seem to have a positivistic understanding of words as a neutral or transparent veil over objective reality. Although they may doubt a writer's authority in some areas, they tend to accept the "facts" a novelist writes about as true. For example, in a meeting of My Book Group, no one questioned Nathaniel Hawthorne's view of Puritan New England (meeting, 16 April 1984). Similarly, when a coed group discussed Leon Uris's book *The Haj,* they wondered about his bias only in relation to his value judgments. They never questioned that Palestinian Arabs were as Uris described them, only whether he judged their rejection of Western ideas of progress too harshly (Bookworms meeting, 8 August 1985). This resembles a reading strategy that Janice Radway (1984, 97–108) noticed among the romance readers she studied: they differentiated between characters and plots, which they knew were unreal, and geographical and historical backgrounds, whose accuracy they accepted. As Radway also points out, this reading attitude serves the ideology of instruction and self-improvement, which justifies the reading habit.

Perhaps the brevity of a reading group's efforts at placing the books it discusses in a historical, literary, or biographical context implies that the members understand the text as a natural object that somehow reflects reality. I propose, however, that something more complex is going on here. Most of these readers are fully capable of analyzing novels on the basis of a clear awareness that they are verbal constructions. This is shown by their references to college and graduate school papers about novels as well as by episodes of formal analysis during book discussions. But a dialogue between literature and experience may not be well served by attending to how novelists construct their representation of the world. First, readers may desire immersion rather than analysis to form the kinds of connections with a book that can allow it to have the weight of reality in their imagination. In a sense, the novel may have to have the ontological equivalence of the real world in order to become comparable to personal experience. Only if it "feels real" can it enter into someone's subjectivity with the power to provoke the kinds of expansive reflection these discussants desire. What I am suggesting here is that reading groups offer the possibility of inhabiting other subjectivities. Each individual brings and discusses her experience of the book, hears others' experiences of the book, and also hears related accounts of other members' personal experiences.

Second, as noted earlier, readers sometimes resist novels that transport them to a world they do not *want* to imagine. So what can become "real" for these readers is circumscribed by what people can and desire to imagine. Those limitations—as Raymond Williams, among others, has shown—relate to the limits of the readers' social situation and the perspective it engenders. Because novels assume an educated middle-class audience, reading groups find them generally easy to "get into" in a way that is not true of other literary forms, such as the epic poem. More importantly, if a diversity of perspectives is brought to bear on a novel in a reading group, this can help readers feel at home in a novel they might have found impenetrable in a solitary reading. Therefore the way books are deployed in reading group discussions can help to expand participants' ability to understand and empathize with different worlds.

Novelistic characters are central to this process, for they often engender very powerful personal responses. In fact, the consideration of characters often dominates reading group discussions. Discussions gain depth when readers respond to fictional characters almost as if they were real people, analyzing their emotional responses to them and associating outward from them to aspects of their own lives or those of kin and friends. Indeed, to be able to relate to characters in this way is what makes a novel "real" to many of these readers. "I think when you're talking about real you have to get down to talking about characters," as one discussant said (informal interview at LS's group meeting, 20 November 1985). Because this statement implies once again subjecting a text to what readers can relate to (as another reader said in the same discussion, "It's real when I see the characters acting in ways that I might act—or that I can at least see other people doing"), this reading attitude may seem limited and close-minded. But identification itself proves to be a very complex process. Because it pulls a reader into a dynamic relationship with a character who must be reckoned with almost like another person, it can lead to deep personal insights and to critical reflection about literature and the social order. This kind of response occurs in solitary reading, but group discussion magnifies the dynamism that can come from connecting to novelistic characters, because members must also come to terms with other participants' responses and the personal stories they elicit. Here, characters become a prism for the interrogation of self, other selves, and society beyond the text.

Responses to characters show complex processes of self-definition at work as individuals explore their reactions and those of other members. On the simplest level, the women in reading groups relate to characters through identification or self-recognition. Talking about a book she had not enjoyed very much, one member said she had not felt she was like any of the characters, and continued, "You know, when I read something, I'm looking for me and my experience" (My Book Group meeting, 4 June 1984). Without that initial level of familiarity, books remain opaque and uninteresting for some readers. Moreover, women will often negotiate a novel by sorting out whom they feel closest to in it. For example, one member's key to Gail Godwin's novel *A Mother and Two Daughters* was her feeling that she was "more like the proper daughter than like the rebel" (My Book Group meeting, 31 October 1983). Mapping members' relationships to the characters was also central to My Book Group's discussion of Ntozake Shange's *sassafras, cypress, and indigo:* two members said they "saw themselves" in the mother, two others in Sassafras, and so on (meeting, 6 June 1984).

Emotional proximity and distance from characters, then, form a crucial axis for moving through novels, and "identification" often means not just recognition but closeness. This closeness can occur even when someone disapproves of a character. As one member of My Book Group said of a character in *The Girl in the Photograph*, "I found myself closest to the one who wanted to listen to music, yet I found her despicable. Of the three, she was the one I could most change places with." Later in the discussion, it emerged that this member despised "her" character because of the character's political apathy and then wondered whether she herself should be more politically involved (meeting, 5 April 1983). In this case, personal identification spurred critical self-reflection about social activism.

The spark of recognition and insight that reading group members evoke when they discuss identification entails a momentary loss of barriers between self and fictional "other" that can reintegrate aspects of the reader's self in almost therapeutic fashion. One man in the Leisure Learning Group, for example, refound his younger self in a Flannery O'Connor story: "All of a sudden I remembered myself when I was five years old—well, it wasn't quite the same, but I remembered wanting to die so I could go to Heaven" (meeting, 26 November 1986). Women may be especially prone to merge psychological boundaries in this fashion. In a typical example, one woman reader encountering Jane Austen's *Emma* was able to accept her own envy of others' accomplishments because of empathic identification. Mentioning Emma's jealousy and reluctance to admit her limitations, she said: "I think one of my favorite points is where she comes home and throws herself down at the piano for an hour and a half—faithfully—and that's it. I see myself doing that. It's just such a human thing to do. You think, *I* could do that; all I have to do is practice. It made me think, that's my life!" (LS's group meeting, 20 November 1985).

Discussants often associate characters with other people and situations in their lives and use those associations to explore the meaning of their own life situations. In such cases, identification can also have quasi-therapeutic consequences. For instance, the mother in *sassafras, cypress, and indigo* reminded several women in My Book Group of their mothers, and one, in particular, used that recognition to come to terms with what she had perceived as her mother's failings in the past and the pain it had caused during her own adolescence. As she said, referring initially to the fictional character: "She had no idea what was going on; she was just relying on her own experience. And that's what I appreciated about it, that here was my mother telling me these things that were real unnecessary, and really didn't apply, but I can't blame her, or say my mother's ignorant, or old-fashioned or anything, 'cause that's the only thing she has to draw on—her own experience" (meeting, 6 April 1984).

Women in reading groups also use character evaluation to question their own values. For example, because most members of My Book Group stayed at home when their children were young, they generally disapproved of heroines who are mothers and yet have careers. Margaret Drabble's novel *The Realms of Gold* led to a debate about that issue focused on the heroine, a successful archaeologist. By defending the novel's main character, one woman, who had to work to support her children, first articulated and then successfully challenged the group's underlying assumption that good mothering requires all-encompassing attention and devotion to children. Thus the same readerly stance that seems circumscribed because of its tendency to treat characters as "real people" with whom readers can relate can also provide the transformative power of deep connection.

The use of novelistic characters as foils for the discussion of values does not require total identification. Readers in groups, and sometimes entire groups, isolate certain aspects of a fictional character's behavior or personality for reflection. If the character as a whole seems believable to them, readers can relate almost pragmatically to certain traits. As one woman in My Book Group said in conversation with me in September 1986, "Who[m] we can't identify with we can learn from." In a moving instance of this process, one woman talked about how Thackeray's characters, especially Becky Sharp in *Vanity Fair*, helped her form her dream to leave McKinney, Texas: "Reading Thackeray is like sitting next to a witty man at a dinner party. That's why I liked it so much when I first read it, because I came from a small North Texas town where one didn't encounter that kind of wit. I'm sure that's my romance with the book. I never got to sit next to a witty man at the parties, so I read Thackeray instead" (meeting, 20 January 1986).

There was much she did *not* admire about Becky Sharp, but Becky's ironic distance and dry humor came to symbolize a way of life that this reader aspired to and eventually created for herself. In this case the author also inspired identification by assuming the status of a character himself.

Probably the most powerful example of this process was provided by a group I encountered before I began systematic research on this topic. The founders were women who had all been in the same sorority at the University of Texas and who all were then at home raising children. In the 1970s they decided that one of the social/literary movements "in the air"—a phenomenon they felt they should understand—was the women's movement. So they began to read "feminist novels" such as Erica Jong's *Fear of Flying* and Marilyn French's *The Women's Room*. Discussing these books, members would often isolate certain traits from fictional characters for fascinated examination. That examination, which also included examining other members' emotional responses to those traits, helped each woman expand and clarify her own aspirations. For instance, several members hated Jong's heroine for her "narcissism and superficiality" but were intrigued with her idea that women might want a Zipless Fuck (sex without emotional involvement), and they admired her search for "selfhood." Similarly, many members of the group took French to task for excessive anger and simplistic negative stereotyping of the husband in *The Women's Room*, yet they felt inspired by the heroine's decision to return to school and forge a demanding and creative career for herself. In fact, one by one, the group members used these books and the insight and support of their group discussions to negotiate a passage for themselves out of a housebound existence and back into the world of professional employment (interview with the University of Texas group, November 1980).

Such discussions often directly challenge authoritative literary opinion, even if critically enshrined classics such as Nathaniel Hawthorne's *The Scarlet Letter* provide the focus for a session. In dealing with that book, My Book Group unanimously disagreed with a critical introduction to an edition read by several members that urged a balanced appraisal of the human qualities represented by Hester and Dimmesdale. The group enthusiastically declared Dimmesdale "a wimp," mocked his fears, and doubted whether he had had enough passion really to father a child. Hester's only major flaw, according to the group, lay in "playing the martyr too much" (meeting, 16 April 1984).

Discussions of character provide an especially powerful basis for challenging critical authority because groups are confident in their expertise in "reading" and judging character in the world beyond books. A way of discussing books that encourages an ontological parallel between literary and real "personalities" gives groups a certain authority as readers. Their knowledge about literary characters can have the same certainty as their experiential knowledge about other people. The division of labor by gender may make it particularly easy for women to engage in critical thinking through characters, but I noticed similar processes at work in the Leisure Learning Group I observed. Several members of the group agreed that Ernest Hemingway "wrote really well" but said he was not a great writer because he was too "macho." This meant not only that *For Whom the Bell Tolls* "was really only about men" but that the men themselves were not three-dimensional human beings (meeting, 29 October 1986). Here, group members deployed their social values (one should not be macho) in conjunction with more literary standards of judgment (male and female characters should be more than one-dimensional) to critique Hemingway's status as a writer.

Discussants in these groups usually enjoy hearing a plurality of views about characters, because members' responses serve as windows into the personalities of other participants and this contributes to the sharing of group discussions. This means, however, that groups do not usually achieve a wholly collective response to books or become transformed themselves into long-lasting interpretive or textual communities. Moreover, because groups remain committed to middle-class individualism, both in regard to textual response and in general, they only approach systemic issues rarely and indirectly. But when they challenge critical opinion or an aspect of the broader status quo, they often do so on the basis of consensual appraisals of character that give the groups a collective authority of their own.

Fashioning Subjectivity

In many of their conversations about and around books, the white middle-class women in these book groups are exploring the relationship between roles and social categories acknowledged to be larger than individuals (mother, worker, citizen, woman, white person) and the sense of themselves that emerges in dialogue with the book and other discussants. In so doing, these women both discover their desires and articulate new possibilities for being, so these discussions are as productive as they are reflective. In expressing their own positions in regard to the broader historical currents of their time, women in reading groups are using literature and each other to stake out new subjective terrain.

Precisely how this happens differs from group to group and from discussion to discussion. Despite broad similarities in race and class, reading group members are differently situated in the world, bring different histories and beliefs to the discussions, and are dealing with different life issues. From meeting to meeting and group to group, discussants are also reading different books and using books differently. The discussions are always gendered, but the point of definition is different. Social categories such as class, race, and sexual orientation are also at issue, but usually in a less conscious way. In this section, I describe and analyze some of these variations.

Romance

The startling thing about both of the two romance reading groups I observed in Houston is that neither really discussed individual books.[2] Linda Griffin, who observed one of these groups for a year, notes that at some meetings the group never even mentioned the book selected for discussion. The following conversation, drawn from her dissertation, exemplifies this truncated dynamic while providing a clue to one of the group's major functions:

> JENNY The only one worth reading was Jennifer Cruise. And I mean that was funny. Nothing really that—
>
> [*Everyone in the group is looking through their Coronet book bags, pulling out paperback books, and although Jenny has brought up the reading selection for that month's meeting, Jennifer Cruise's* Anyone but You, *no one makes a comment about it.*]
>
> LIZ Did you read those two books, Rene? I did. That *True Bliss* was good. Did you read that?
>
> BETH Does anyone want to borrow this one? [*She pulls a book from her Coronet book bag.*]

RENE What did you [*addressing the group*] think of Barbara Delinsky's book? I loved that one. [*She starts to say something more.*]

CLEO Oh, my God! Hey girls, look at the abs on this one! [*Looking
at the cover of one of the books the members are passing around, she is un-
aware of Rene's comment about the Delinsky book.*] (1999, 159–60)

It was the same in the center-city romance reading group I attended.
The books (the in-town group chose three each month) rarely inspired
more than a brief positive or negative remark, if that. Yet both the books and
the meetings were clearly valuable to members.

Meeting in the shadow of the literary hierarchy, such gatherings help
to build communities of romance readers who support romance reading
materially, socially, and ideologically. Meetings also endorse a particular way
of reading, validate the pleasures to be found in reading a socially stigmatized genre, and often uphold the values that the books represent to these
readers.

The fact that both the suburban and the in-town romance groups
meet in bookstores made sense to me when I saw how important recommending and exchanging books were to the members. Women usually
brought several books to the meeting, eager to lend them to other members. They also enthusiastically recommended other titles and authors they
particularly liked or books that had received high recommendations from
Romantic Times. As they spoke, the women would often stand and cruise the
shelves to find the books they were referring to. In the suburban group,
some members mused over the bookshelves during much of the meeting,
listening to others speak, then finding a title to suggest, or following up on
someone else's recommendation and picking out a book to buy. At the end
of the meeting, almost everyone would head for the shelves to find titles
they wanted, or they would put in an order with the bookstore staff person
meeting with the group.

Exchanging books supports members' romance reading both socially
and materially. Because a majority of romance readers read between three
and five books a week, exchanging books within a group lessens a real
financial burden. It also gives members access to good reading material, because in this context exchanging books implies a positive recommendation.

The social importance of exchanging books is shown by the informal
rules that Griffin (1999, 207–9) observed governing the process in the
group she attended: first, members only passed on good books; second,
there was a norm of reciprocity; and third, everyone wrote the owners'
names in the books and returned them when they were finished.[3] Both recommending and exchanging books bound members together in a community of trust that also served to validate their taste and celebrate their simi-

larity to each other, which in turn helped make the group both meaningful and cohesive for participants.

Meeting in a group also provides ideological support for its members, all of whom are conscious of the stigma attached to romance reading. Members of the in-town group discussed several times whether or not to be "out" about their reading, with one quite pointed conversation sparked by a member's indecision about buying one of the opaque plastic book covers displayed on the bookstore's counter. Several group members were so impassioned about "owning" their romance reading that the woman eventually decided against buying a cover.

More dramatically, the suburban group dealt with an insult to their genre by a symbolic inversion of the dominant hierarchy of literary value. One group member saw a sign in a bookstore that said, "Romance novels are like bubblegum for the brain." Mona recounted her ensuing confrontation with the shopkeeper:

> M O N A   I said, "You know, romances are no better or worse or anything else, than horror stories. Why would you put a sign like this up?" . . . And I thought, what does this say about me? You know, we don't do that to male-oriented things. Even the research doesn't go into that. But we certainly do go into the romance readers and what are their shortcomings that they would be hooked on romance.

> R E N E   Don't you think to a certain extent that has to do [with] the male population and the rest of the reading population with the negative attitude toward romances?

> M O N A   Of course. (Griffin 1999, 250)

As Griffin recounts (254), at the next meeting several women returned to the topic of "bubblegum for the brain" and decided that they were going to declare that bubblegum represented something positive to them. From that point on, Mary brought a bowl of bubblegum to every meeting. It sat on the table with the coffee urn, a concrete symbol of their open and collective challenge to the stigma of reading romances.

The suburban group also advocated a way of reading that challenged the intellectualism of literary analysis. Griffin (1999, 166–67) described an instance of this attitude, drawn from a discussion that began when she said that the twins in Elaine Coffman's *If You Love Me* acted much older than their fictional age of two. One member immediately accused her of "losing something of the pleasure reading." Cleo chimed in, saying, "You can't analyze historical romance novels." Beth agreed: "No, 'cause this stuff is coming out of someone's head and their heart, you know, and it's coming out of them, and they're putting it on paper, and if it appeals to you then you know, if it speaks to you in some way, and if it doesn't you know—."

LINDA You put it down?

MARY Or you finish it.

CLEO Or you can fast forward.

MARY Or you can get another one.

Demonstrating their resistance to analysis and their tactics for avoiding criticism of even bad novels, these readers also articulate clearly that they are searching for books that speak to the emotions, not the intellect. They defend authors from criticism by stating that the books come from their hearts. Indeed, these readers identify with romance writers as "kindred souls," call them by their first names, and compare their own growth as readers with romance authors' ambition as writers (Griffin 1999, 168). Seeking a mode of reading that gives effortless access to a moving fictional experience, they describe the pleasures of "gliding" through the books, or just "skimming" them, and they account for their "love affair" with romances by asserting that they find in them something that "engages their hearts" or even lets them "cry over it a little bit" (294, 253, 344). Most of them so desire a happy ending that they read the end first, and they defend themselves against the pain of an unsatisfactory resolution by keeping their emotional distance as they read: "If I do read a book that hurts, I want to know in advance that it's gonna hurt and then I don't let myself get into it so deeply that my heart is hurt" (354).

Group members also support each other in reading for escape, a mode of reading that is one reason romances are so stigmatized. Members in the suburban group recognize that they are seeking escape and feel entirely justified in this wish because of the difficulties that they face in everyday life. As one member says:

> I don't want to read a book that has a painful ending. That is escape. You know, all of us live our lives in very real, I do, in very realistic ways. I recognize there are things I'm never going to do. There are things I look back on with wonder and joy. But to read something to escape and be kind of rewarded—to read something that is going to end with people getting together, I mean that is important to me. (Griffin 1999, 296)

Nonetheless, the suburban women also find romance novels deeply true, because for them the novels affirm the significance of loving and nurturing relationships in general and of heterosexual love in particular. This set of values or way of being in the world is the very bedrock of their subjectivity, and both their reading and their meetings validate its paramount importance.

In their view, building a permanent heterosexual relationship that can successfully survive conflict is central to the genre, and this value is reiterated every time they read a romance. This is what satisfies, reassures, and makes them feel good at the end of a book. "I like to see a man and a woman work through their problems, you know, and then wind up together." On this basis, they sharply differentiate between romances and erotica, which they characterize as being about "just getting it on" (Griffin 1999, 344, 350, 355).

A romantic attachment between a man and a woman is the linchpin for a broader ideology that celebrates love and nurture as the central organizing force for human life. Members stressed this worldview over and over again in their discussions, as in this exchange:

> BETH When you go through anybody's life and you start from, if you start from when they're a teenager, their whole life revolves around their love life. You know, when you follow their life, you're following their relationships and their love—
>
> CLEO Yeah, that's all we have. (Griffin 1999, 354–55)

Members of the group valued romance novels so highly because they felt the books demonstrated the supreme significance of loving relationships in general. Analogously, they found their meetings meaningful because they could support each other not only for their reading but also for the values it represented to them. As with many mainstream groups, this sense of shared values made the romance reading groups feel very special to their members. As Cleo said,

> CLEO You trust these people you are talking about with your feelings and your thoughts because you know you share those things. We almost reason together.
>
> MONA And they're not sitting here possibly sneering at you.
>
> CLEO And everyone's opinion is respected. We're all equal here. (Griffin 1999, 302)

Despite protestations of equality, this group, like most mainstream reading groups, was all white. They had decided not to invite a black woman to join and generally held stereotypes about black culture being in a state of moral decay (Griffin 1999, 312). Within this exclusive but safe circle, the group endorsed personal change and growth for the heroines of romances and also for each other.

The group did empower its members. As one of the romance "experts," Mona began to be less insecure about her intelligence and about reading romances. Beth came out of a depression caused by her son's accidental death, and all of the members grew more clear and confident about their values as they spoke about them within the group.

What are we to make of this empowerment? The subjectivity they developed is conservative, heterosexual, domestic, and white supremacist. One could characterize it as a simple rejection of liberal Enlightenment ideas in favor of the values held dear by an earlier generation of Southern white women. Yet this is a new, postfeminist permutation of traditionalism insofar as these readers see male domination as an important factor in the denigration of their genre and its values. Earlier, we saw Mona claiming that people generally did not disparage male-oriented books as they did romances. In another discussion, when someone remarked that the male mainstream writers avoid romance, Rose responded, "Maybe men should read a little more romance!" (Griffin 1999, 252–53). Their traditional ethos integrates a consciousness of gender inequities, a central element of feminist analysis. The romance group members articulate a late-twentieth-century reformulation of women's nature—a subject position that embraces conservatism but also challenges male domination and pure marketplace values.

In the case of the suburban romance group, members were elaborating an ideology rooted in their social situation. Although a few of the six to eight regular members (who ranged in age from thirty-five to seventy-four) had taken some college courses, only one held a college degree. Only two were employed outside the home: one was a flight attendant, and one worked in her father's office. All were married, and all but one had children—most of whom were grown (Griffin 1999, 128). Two of the women were also members of the Daughters of the American Revolution, a conservative organization. This group differed in education and social class from many of the mainstream groups I visited. Most of the members had enacted a traditional division of labor within their families, and some clearly held preexisting conservative views.

The linkage between reading romances and elaborating a conservatively gendered subject position was loose to nonexistent in the in-town group. Participants' past and present social experiences also differed from those of the suburban group, although like them, the in-town group ranged widely in age and was all white. The in-town group was better educated, however, and less unified in relation to work, marriage, and children. Out of a group of six regulars, all but one of the women had completed college, and three held postgraduate degrees. One member was a lawyer turned bookstore owner, one was a college professor, one was an elementary school teacher, and one had retired. The youngest participant was a clerical worker who was trying to gain the credentials and experience to become a private detective. The members' family situations also varied: almost all were married, but it was a second marriage for two of the women, and only half the married members had children. In this group, participants encouraged each other in reading and valuing romances, but I never heard anyone champion either heterosexuality or love as a preeminent value, as Griffin reports for the suburban group, nor did I ever hear black culture denigrated. Rather, the in-town group seemed to function mainly as a "recommendation center," to use Griffin's term, as well as a support group for the romance genre and its readers.

From these cases, one could hypothesize that people's formative social experiences, which Pierre Bourdieu (1984, 169–225) calls their "habitus," carry great weight in determining the cultural values they clarify and develop in their conversations about books. This idea comes as no surprise to sociologists, but it goes against the grain of those who do not understand the variability and social embeddedness of reading practices. It also calls into question the idea that a book has certain ideas, perspectives, or values locked inside the text, to be directly recovered—and always in the same way—when a person reads that book.

I Felt Like I Had Been Made Totally Invisible: Readers Inc. Engages the Issue of Women in the Public World

In a meeting on 22 October 1984, one member's personal concern captures a reading group's attention, turning them away from the book to reflect on women's voice in a "male-inflected" public world. The book—Billy Lee Brammer's *The Gay Place*, a 1978 novel about Texas politics— occupies only nineteen minutes of a two-hour meeting. The women use the remainder of the time for experientially based analysis, a kind of discourse developed over years of interpreting lives through books. Usually, reading groups also illuminate the text as they explore their associations with it. In this instance, however, the question of women's public presence has so much emotional salience—and ironically, a book about the public world of politics has so little pull—that it engages the group as a forum for social commentary rather than as a reading group per se. Although unrelated to the evening's book, both the issue of gender and the ambiance of openness are intimately connected to the usual cultural "work" of the group and the relationships that have grown from their literary practices.

The meeting begins with Katherine's emotional account of feeling silenced in a literary theory group she attended at Methodist College. According to her, a senior professor named Mark Brown made a point, then she said something, and then a new faculty member brushed off her remark to respond to Brown. Katherine continues,

> I was furious. Now—and I could see why he'd done it. It was like Mark Brown was the exalted senior and Martin was the new guy on the block and correctly perceived that Mark was the much more ap-

propriate power source to establish himself against. But I felt like I had been made totally invisible and I sat there during the group thinking, "Well, forget this group then. I mean is this going to be the kind of group where I can't talk?"

Aside from commiserating with Katherine, the book group members advised her to recognize that the other group might not be hospitable:

KATHERINE But I want to be effective in this group. I mean I don't care, I don't care if I never convince them about my point of view. For one thing, I want to learn from the group if there's anything to learn, which I'm not clear there is. But secondly, I want to learn how to talk that kind of talk.

JOANNE Are you sure?

KATHERINE I'm not sure.

Katherine's ambivalence about whether or not she wants to master a certain kind of academic discourse points up a striking contrast between her literary theory group and her reading group. Both deal with books, reading, and ideas, but one is predominantly male, located in the field of high academic theory, and closely tied to intellectual display, even professional success, whereas the other is female and located in the field of "general reading" and nonacademic, leisure-time reflection. Abstract theoretical discourse is the norm in one ("that kind of talk"), whereas the reading group speaks more subjectively. Both groups are at home with analysis and disputation, but the reading group is more personally framed. In it, women discuss gender differences not from a Cartesian or scientific distance but through their own embodied experience as gendered beings. The ambivalence about theoretical discourse comes, I would speculate, from the fact that "theory talk" as it is presently constituted usually requires leaving behind those embodied experiences. Leaving the body behind calls into question women's claim that as women they bring to theoretical discussions different views of the world that may be valuable precisely because of their differences.

Katherine expresses this dilemma most clearly in her attitude toward what academics of the 1980s called (pro or con) the Western tradition. Here, she explains one reason why she did not verbally respond to Seymour's brush-off:

I don't feel like it's my tradition. That's part of it. There's Plato and there's Galileo and I don't know, a whole lineage of men—and these guys feel like they're part of that tradition. And I'm not there. I don't know where I am. Somewhere off, elsewhere. I don't feel like it's my

Western tradition. I don't feel like I can claim those fathers or stand up against those fathers. It's not the same kind of relationship. And I think that's creative that it's not that same sort of relationship. We bring in something from a female perspective that's different.

The overarching question for the book group's evening discussion then becomes how to reconcile women's perceived differences from men with a desire to be equally effective as men at speaking or being heard in public. The group explores this issue in settings from an Ivy League university's Parents' Weekend to a theological discussion, a political conversation at work, and a church discussion about the Sanctuary Movement. In each variation on this basic theme, the members bring implicit theories into play to account for women's difficulties finding a public voice. For example, Sarah Grace raises the issue of women's difficulty speaking authoritatively in groups of men:

> SARAH GRACE I've been noticing with what authority they [men] speak. And for years I thought well, this is appropriate because they know what they're talking about and I don't. [*Group laughter.*] And at this stage I've realized that at least half of them don't know anymore than I do.
>
> JOANNE Well some of it's just physical and the deeper voice and things that we associate [with authority].
>
> PEGGY But it is also a speech pattern. It really is a linguistic pattern.
>
> JOANNE Like the question mark at the end.

This line of explanation sounds similar to theoretical discussions about the interactional correlates of gender inequality current in the 1980s. For example, Nancy Henley's famous essay "The Politics of Touch" (1973) initiated a line of inquiry about power, gender, and nonverbal behavior. Henley, Barrie Thorne, and Robin Lakoff (Lakoff 1975; Thorne and Henley 1975; Thorne, Kramarae, and Henley 1983) also published scholarly books on differences in linguistic usage between men and women several years before Deborah Tannen's 1990 best-seller *You Just Don't Understand* brought those ideas popular currency. All of these ideas imply the importance of socialization in accounting for gender differences, a point Sandra stresses in answer to Joanne by describing how her sons were taught in Little League to handle their shame at their mistakes "right out there in front of everybody" without crying or running off the field, whereas girls are not put in similar situations.

The next variation the group considers is the question of women's humor, raised by Sandra's experiences listening to the all-male and all-female singing groups at an Ivy League university's Parents' Weekend, which showed, according to her, that "the girls just couldn't be funny." Joanne and Peggy explain this by saying that girls have enough trouble just asserting equality without "throw[ing] it all away" by being self-deprecating or looking foolish in order to get laughs. Sarah Grace disagrees, raising the issue of male acceptance—clearly important in a heterosexual group such as this one, which also assumes the existence of a generally heteronormative social order:

> Women are not supposed to be funny. Did I tell you all about referring to God as female on an elevator with three Mormons? [*Loud laughter.*] My colleague, Bruce was just about to pop, knowing what a faux pas I'd made. And my boss was trying to disappear. [What happened was that] they were making some comment about Houston's big rains—maybe, "We should build a boat or something, it's been raining a lot, look like God's going to do us in." And I said, "Oh, She wouldn't do that." And there was just this hush. We just all faced the front of the elevator and folded our hands. Unfortunately, we were coming down fifty stories. [*Group dissolves in laughter.*]

Sarah Grace may have been in no danger of being shut off for fear of male disapproval, but humor is a mask that allows expression of serious differences under the guise of fun. Expressing those differences directly to men appears to be much more difficult for the members of this all-women group. Again, it is Sarah Grace who raises this topic by saying she was eager for the group to convene because she "needed some bleeding-heart liberals after this weekend." Describing a Friday night dinner with a very conservative couple, then a Sunday evening church meeting about the Sanctuary Movement that was taken over by another conservative couple, and finally a Monday morning discussion of the Mondale/Reagan debates with her boss that he turned into "a forty-five-minute diatribe about what's wrong with the liberals," she confesses she was "just about to cry just from the sheer . . ." Collecting herself, she says: "I guess what's bothering me is that I can't handle them in a political discussion. Somehow I am letting these people do all the talking. I cannot take them on verbally. I don't even want to change their minds, I just want to defend myself."

The group agrees that the issue is "having the control to be articulate," even in an argument that "has a strong emotional content," when, as Sarah Grace says, "what makes me so angry is that what I really want to do is cry." On those terms, success, as Sandra says, is having "really argued with someone on something you have real deep feelings about and come out feeling like—there, I did it."

Voice is a multifaceted issue for this group of readers. It encompasses issues from responding to dismissal in an academic debate to feeling disconnected from our culture's major intellectual traditions. It also includes being socialized to accept male authority (whether directly or subtly expressed) and to seek male approval. The women also discuss not being socialized to be independent enough ("out there") to take public failure or conflict in stride. And finally, they talk about how to overcome a tendency toward self-silencing so they can be articulate in political discussions and how to dissociate their ideas from their emotions so they can "speak their mind" about issues that they care deeply about.

In general, members of the group experience this lack of voice as a problem especially salient to their participation in public. The group is avowedly liberal politically, and both their dilemmas and their explanations for why women have these problems fit into the liberal feminist framework. This view stresses women's rights to equality on the basis of an equal capacity to reason and understands cognitive or emotional differences between women and men as stemming from socialization rather than biology. Most women in this group would not have called themselves feminists, but their desire to enter the public world on an equal footing with men enacts the liberal feminist project of integrating women into the public world and achieving equality of opportunity and salary.

Nonetheless, the group remains haunted by the question of difference. Socialization seems too thin a concept to account for the differences they perceive between men and women. Moreover, women's biology does matter in thinking about equality. Aside from possible sex differences in cognitive or emotional functioning, biology is the basis for a socially mediated division of labor by sex that tends in our culture to give women more family responsibilities than are given to men. This difference means that women's participation in the public world is often more variable and less single-minded than men's. Even at a time when the male breadwinner/female housewife model fits fewer and fewer American families, men can fulfill their major family responsibilities by working outside the home. This is less true for women, as is shown in studies that track the differential in time spent by women and men in child care and other domestic work.

Soon after Katherine's admission that she doesn't feel part of the Western tradition, the women of Readers Inc. discuss their sense that women and men have different natures. Sarah Grace responds: "I think women don't hook into these big pictures. I know I don't." She exemplifies this idea by describing an almost all-male theology discussion group she attends that dealt with one member's grief over a friend's death by talking about "things from the galaxy to—just everything was universal to the extreme." The grieving friend felt comforted, but she said it was "the weirdest thing I have ever seen in my entire life. I think that women talk about me and us and the people we know and interrelating relationships." Group members generally agree that although women are at home with abstractions, men use both large, impersonal concepts (such as the galaxy) and "the very tiny particulars" (such as what artillery the armies used in the Civil War) to "keep things from getting too close." There is also speculation that men may find something relational in "the big picture" that women cannot. As Katherine says: "I put my troubles into perspective by thinking of other people who have other problems. But I usually don't think of the galaxy and spin myself far away from where I am."

This interchange taps into a similar set of ideas developed more systematically by Nancy Chodorow in her book *The Reproduction of Mothering* (1978). Chodorow claims that because women mother, girls and boys develop very different patterns of unconscious psychological identification, which lead to different personality structures. Boys must reject the mother (their first object of identification) and turn to an often distant father. Among other consequences, this trajectory gives men very clear (if somewhat insecure) ego boundaries, based on distancing themselves from identifying with their mothers and anything feminine, and a sense of masculinity that must be continually reasserted because it is founded on a relatively abstract identification with their fathers. Girls, on the other hand, are secure in their gender identification, but because they don't have to reject identification with their mother, they have relatively permeable ego boundaries and a sense of self-in-relationship. This thumbnail sketch does not do her theory justice, but, in a sense, neither did most of the scholars who imported her ideas into fields as disparate as the study of moral reasoning (Carol Gilligan's *In a Different Voice* [1982]), linguistics (Deborah Tannen's *You Just Don't Understand* [1990]), and literary studies (too numerous to mention).

The similarities between Chodorow's characterization of women's nature and those of Readers Inc. are fascinating, however they arose. If, for example, the reading group were echoing popularized versions of Chodorow's theory, it would mean that this academic theory entered the "cultural tool kit" of upper-middle-class women in just seven years. This rapid dissemination implies that women were reaching for certain kinds of ideas to explain their situation. On the other hand, if Readers Inc. invented the idea of women as relational beings on their own, that implies that Chodorow the intellectual was elaborating and systematizing a line of thinking that upper-middle-class women were developing less theoretically to construct a "self" congruent with their changing circumstances in the late twentieth century.

How might such ideas be useful? For one thing, they allow for change (given that women need not necessarily be the primary parent), but they acknowledge that sex-differentiated personality structures are deeply embedded in unconscious patterns of relationships. This explains differences between men and women at a deeper level than "socialization" and is one way of accounting for the slow pace of change in gender relations. The idea of women as "selves-in-relation" can also acknowledge difference without admitting inferiority and can be used to justify (although this was not Chodorow's intent) women's closer involvement with the family. One of the questions Chodorow addresses, without resorting to a "maternal instinct," is why women want to mother. Cobbling together liberal feminist ideas of equality in the public world of work and citizenship with this kind of theory of gender difference underwrites a "self" who can work and aspire to success but whose involvement in a more "relational" or familial position in the household is entirely understandable, especially during a period of intense parenting. The kind of synthesis Readers Inc. was implicitly making of liberal feminism and "difference" theories resonates well with the increasingly common pattern of women entering the paid workforce while maintaining a relatively traditional domestic division of labor.

The subjectivity being constructed in this way also resonates well with upper-middle-class white women's social situation. Such women have enough education to enter professional fields, where work is apt to be financially rewarding as well as relatively interesting. With these prospects, they might well be (as they have been historically) more dedicated to occupational equality than are women who work in less privileged situations because of race and/or class disadvantages. Upper-middle-class women might also be less attached to an idealized and naturalized conception of motherhood, whereas for women with less social privilege, motherhood often represents a basis for power and respect. Similarly, seeing men and women as two differentiated but internally homogeneous categories (which is how scholars often appropriated Chodorow's ideas) writes off differences between women. This framework allows upper-middle-class white women to assume that they are the social norm. Such a stance is very similar to that of nineteenth-century white clubwomen, who assumed they spoke for all women.

This construction of the female subject or self fits into academic debates of the period and resonates with upper-middle-class white women's experiences and desires. Perhaps even more important, this topic shows dramatically that although women had achieved formal equality as students, workers, and citizens in the latter twentieth century, they still encountered barriers to equal participation in the world beyond the family. Informal patterns of interaction, often quite subtle, tended to silence their voices, undercut their authority, or render their presence invisible. Listening in to a conversation about these issues in a reading group shows the cultural practices by which women creatively negotiated these dilemmas and why reading groups are still an important resource for women today.

Readers Inc. on William Wharton's Dad

The meeting in May 1984 of Readers Inc. served as something more than an occasion for airing issues that impinged on middle-class white women in the latter twentieth century. Discussants returned to the book *Dad* again and again, yet they grounded their discussion in moments of connection to their own experience. The meeting demonstrates how strong the pull of literature as "equipment for living" can be within a group such as this one. It also shows women in the group actively asserting that their own dilemmas of selfhood are the subjects they want to pursue with the book.

This assertion occurred most dramatically when, from a book centered on a father-son relationship, the group repeatedly plucked opportunities for exploring what they experienced and desired as mothers, as daughters, as mothers of daughters, and as individuals in friction with these roles. At the beginning of the discussion, Audrey, who had selected the book, asked, "What did you think about the mother?" This provoked so much discussion that she twice attempted to refocus the discussion on the male characters and their relationship. Each time the attempt failed. The first time she said: "Well, no one has mentioned this man going in and nurturing these parents and doing all the work. That was the thing that struck me about the book. Sarah Grace responded shortly: "I liked him and I didn't think anything about that. I just thought he was a modern man."

The second time Audrey raised the question of the protagonist's nurturing qualities, one member agreed that she "liked a nurturing male," but other participants again found fault with him. Sarah Grace said: "But he only nurtured other males." Joanne even went so far as to imply that only a woman could have written a book about nurturing: "I think William Wharton's a woman!" This reduced the group to laughter and shifted the discussion.

The pattern of wresting mother-daughter discussions from a book about fathers and sons was so obvious that the group became reflective about it.

> KATHERINE The book is about fathers and sons and so in response we're talking about mothers and daughters, which is our relationship that's like the father-son relationship. I mean—it's the mirror opposite. Why aren't we talking about fathers? Or about men? Why are we talking about mothers?

> JOANNE I like the book a lot. But when I started thinking about it, it was real disturbing to me the way the mother was portrayed. The father is too good and not responsible for the situation, and the son is too good. I mean the way these people got to be so good was by making somebody bad.

> KATHERINE So you see it as a flaw in the novel, then?

> JOANNE Well, not if it's a man's novel. But if I'm going to read it I'm going to respond to it. There isn't any way that I can respond to

it, though, except through myself. I mean I can't jump out of me to respond to this.

Two aspects of Joanne's analysis are particularly telling. The first is the acknowledgment that a different critical response by gender is acceptable, perhaps even inevitable: "A flaw?" "Not if it's a man's novel." This implies that a book's value is dependent on the social location of its interlocutor, a rejection of the idea that literary evaluation should be objective. It also implies that one appropriate function of readerly response is to work toward the creation of personal meaning through a book, which may involve filling in textual gaps or refocusing the interaction between book and reader on questions not central to the written text. For the women in this group, such questions—and they were pressing—involved a web of familial relationships differently gendered than those Wharton described.

Strikingly, whether in relation to the book, to their own lives, or to the social world, women in the group expressed ambivalence about the mother-daughter relationship as well as about the social role of the mother. The group was also conflicted about the prospects for change either in family relationships or in general. Their discussion shows how complex and sometimes fraught it could be for women to renegotiate familial relationships in the late twentieth century.

As they describe their relationships with their mothers, they convey a sense of distance from the older generation and a feeling of separation from the women who mothered them:

SANDRA I think I understand my mother in ways I didn't when I lived with her or even as a younger woman, and appreciate things in her and so on, but there's also—she can get to me in ways that no other adult can or will. I just don't think we get past all that.

AUDREY Wouldn't it be more comfortable if you could get along with her?

SARAH GRACE No, I think it would be fake because I think, if Mother and I got there, we would acknowledge we didn't really have that much in common and we'd probably not pursue our friendship. I think that what we have in common is that I'm her daughter. And we really appreciate each other and sometimes like each other.

On the other hand, when they speak as mothers, the members of the group feel very closely identified with their daughters. They worry about their daughters' expectations: "So far, my sense of Karen is that they think they're going to do it all." "That's what I hear from all the young women I meet." Nonetheless, they can see themselves in their daughters so clearly that it is almost as if this relationship helps them embrace the changes they otherwise experience as overwhelming or enables them to cast their own hopes into the future with these young women. For instance, Sarah Grace talks about a wonderful trip she took with her daughter, while Sandra and Joanne see their idealistic younger selves mirrored in their daughters. Note the importance of books in this process:

> SANDRA When I first went to college we had to write an autobiography. Mine sounds very like Karen, just happy, happy. And we made a tape when my dad turned forty. I was a senior year in high school, and everything was so keen! [*Laughter.*] And Karen came in the other day and—she was reading *Fear and Trembling*—and she said Kierkegaard's so keen! [*More laughter.*]

> JOANNE I gave Emily a book that I had read my first year at UT— Tolstoy's *What Men Live By*. It's all full of love and universal brotherhood and stuff, and I loved it then and I haven't read it since then— she loved it. It made me think that we really were quite a bit alike.

A consideration of motherhood wove through the meeting. Each woman was struggling to define the boundaries between cultural representations of that role and what they individually experienced as real, essential, or inevitable about motherhood. In discussion, each woman staked out a slightly different position on the contested terrain of gender relations in the latter twentieth century. All of the group members, for example, felt uncomfortable about the cultural freight of Mother's Day:

> JOANNE I just don't like it when they put "Mother" on this pedestal and then throw rocks at her.

> SARAH GRACE I was kind of grossed out by Mother's Day this year. I felt assaulted by it.

> AUDREY Yeah. I just wanted to forget it [Mother's Day] yesterday. But I've felt that for quite a while. I recall years ago thinking that I wanted to not be remembered as a mother so much. Maybe because of the way I've seen so many mothers remembered. You know: "She was standing over a hot stove." "She would give me what for if I didn't toe the line." I would prefer to be remembered as a woman. I like mothering my kids, but not being remembered as a mother.

Sarah Grace, in particular, found it irksome when stereotypes about nurturing women, wives, and motherhood were reproduced in social interaction. This appeared to be an especially sensitive issue for her, although other women supported her perceptions and attempted to find solutions for her sense of being trapped in a limiting social role. Recalling some recent alumni activities she had attended, she said,

I'm recognizing now that I was doing all the nurturing of the men that sat around me at these various happenings. And almost never does a man turn to me at something like that and say, "What do you do, and let me build up your ego," or do any of this kind of nurturing. It was strictly a—I talked to him about his work and he asked me about my children. . . . And for some reason that I can't explain it never works when I just decide to go ahead and share what I'm doing whether they ask me or not—That I can't pull off for whatever reason.

Audrey comments, "I do it once in a while, but they just tend to ignore what I'm saying and keep right on talking."

Eventually, Sarah Grace mentions a humorous strategy:

A man I was talking with at a cocktail party said, "Well, I know you're somebody's wife, but I don't know who it is." And I said, "Well, then it probably doesn't make any difference, does it?" And he became very curious and spent the next forty-five minutes trying to figure out who on earth I was, and I wasn't about to tell him. At least it was entertaining.

Audrey and Sandra have very different responses to her statement. Considering how to initiate change, Audrey says, "So that's what you have to do next time," while Sandra urges a more historical and accommodating understanding: "This is just a transitional phase, and there are awkwardnesses—every social situation is transitional now with as fast as changes happen."

The difference between their responses is indicative of the deeply dissimilar ways Audrey and Sandra experience both motherhood and daughterhood. Audrey clearly feels confined by the mothering role: "That's the role we're pushed into so much of the time—we have to be disciplining, we have to be watching, we have to be saying no, no, we have to be watchful all the time." On the other hand, Sandra sees some aspects of parenthood as inevitable:

I think there's something unavoidable that we take on when we become a mother or a father that has within it both the basic glory of being a human and the basic tragedy of being a human. I don't think we can ever not be a parent to our children. I don't think our parents are ever not a parent to us, which will always be the dividing line and I don't think we can get around it.

In the discussion, the boundaries between cultural representations and "real life" become blurred at times. For instance, here is Sarah Grace making a rapid segue from the fictional mother in Wharton's novel to women's actual behavior: "The mother is the typical, controlling, manipulating bitch who really loves everybody, and she plays a role that I think females play all the time, and it just concerns me. I'd really like for us to look at that." When Joanne asserts that Wharton's portrayal of women is "a betrayal of women," Sarah Grace responds: "Well, I think that unfortunately life bears this out more than 60 to 70 percent of the time. And my question is how is it that men can generally manage to pull off their idiosyncrasies as charming, as Dad did? Why is it that women become the bitches?"

Seemingly accepting her claims about reality, the group proffers two major explanations. One is material, the other interactional:

SARAH GRACE It may be that bitches come from insecurity and lack of economic power. Maybe being a bitch is a way of control. That's how women get to it. They don't have control any other way than by moods.

JOANNE No one would confront her [the character in Wharton's novel] and say, "Hey, what are you doing?"

SANDRA My mother-in-law would kind of rattle on about things, and we all knew it, and we all made fun of it, including John's Dad. Well, his Dad just wouldn't acknowledge it. He'd just pick up his paper and go on reading. He was never unkind. And now her conversation is not very meaningful. No one ever called for her to make sense. They were patronizing, I think, and just rolled their eyes and let her go on. I think they participated in letting her look foolish.

When the discussion shifts to wifehood and what one might call the issue of masculine authority, the women in the group recount their gradual negotiation of more power within their marriages. Again, they mention the importance of earned income, but they also identify the legitimating ideology for masculine authority as scientific rationality. Reason, coupled with male self-confidence and female deference, appears to have successfully undergirded masculine authority in these marriages for a time. But gradually the women began to perceive the self-interest behind their husbands' deployment of "reason." With that comes demystification and a tendency to understand rationality itself as a potentially self-serving tool for those in power.

This larger issue is discussed in concrete situations that are symptomatic of how priorities are adjudicated in marriage. For instance, Sandra says about the trip she and her daughter Karen took to look at colleges: "John thinks it was the height of foolishness. That's one of the ways he couches it. Dishwashers use too much water and microwaves radiate. Whatever it was—often that I was the one who most wanted—there were all kinds of scientific reasons [against it]. And then as soon as he starts having to wash dishes, it's suddenly entirely rational to have a dishwasher."

After supportive comments from others, she resumes:

> When I bought the piano, I said "I've done it," and he said, "Are you going to practice?" I said, "I'm not telling!" I could have said, "Well, obviously I think I'm going to but I'm not going to sign up a practice schedule. I may just look at it—I'm also paying for it, so—I want it!"

> SARAH GRACE We were in kitchen the other day. And Steven leans back and says he's going to throw away most of this stuff—we just don't need it, and he started ticking things off, and I said, "Okay, for every piece [of dishware], you may throw away one book." And he said, "Oh, we'll just find room for all of it."

> SANDRA But I think we're all kind of blinded, the things we really want seem reasonable. But I had thought and thought, and rationalized, and shut off, and whatever for years now about this piano. And having an independent paycheck makes a lot of difference." [*General assent.*]

This discussion centers on change within marriage. But like motherhood, the theme of change weaves through this meeting on many levels. Sandra, for example, identifies a social sea change in work and family that she feels she has missed by a few years:

> Sarah Grace and I have noticed that we know hardly any women our age and above who have in any significant way challenged their husbands' career path and had much ambition for themselves outside the domestic range. Most every woman of a certain level of intelligence and achievement within five years younger than us had at least dealt significantly with the problem, whatever conclusion she drew. Some of the people our age have done it, after work, after children. But it didn't form a compromise with their husband's ascent in his career.

Their responses to this perceived change show a double consciousness. On the one hand, they note what they see as problematic effects, such as the burden that choice can put on motherhood if it is measured against the rewards of a busy career life. Audrey talks about a group of career women with whom she was on a panel who were all, she sensed, "in misery" about parenting, "really feeling that it was such a crisis." For once Sandra agrees with her, saying, "It puts such a burden on the poor child. All of a sudden this poor innocent bit of flesh has to be so rewarding and it just isn't." This leads Joanne to express her genuine nostalgia for motherhood as she experienced it: "Every six months I dream that I have a little baby." Even such nostalgia can register as slightly ambivalent, as when Sarah Grace describes her own baby dreams: "Sometimes I'd dream I'd forget it. I'd go off. I'd forget I had a child, and I'd leave it on the sidewalk."

Toward the end of the meeting, the group steps back to reflect on social change more generally. Audrey says:

> I was thinking about that [change] this weekend. I was listening to sixties music. Thinking about what I thought then—how all these great changes were going to take place, and that everything was going to be great. I was real optimistic. Watergate and all those things happened and now we're into this, whatever *this* is, and it's just going to keep right on going. We are going through a lot of changes, fast.

Sandra comments that she is an "optimistic cynic" who expects day-to-day life to be happy but not the world in general. Sarah Grace replies, "I'm just the opposite. I expect some days to be bad, but the world's wonderful."

> SANDRA Well, I have a historical sense. I appreciate the sense of being in some train of humankind. I like to discover that this is a truth that humans have. I feel a connection that way. I recognize I don't really expect either Armageddon or a Messiah.

> JOANNE Well, that's all very rational, but it's not real to me, the way that sitting here with you is real.

This comment sums up something very meaningful about book groups like Readers Inc. and the ways they serve women who are navigating through a bewildering array of emergent possibilities and constraints for constructing new ways of being in the world. Reading groups can provide a grounding among both textual and personal companions that enables participants to confront the wider changes they perceive around them and their own personal wishes, fears, dreams, and regrets. Articulating these responses to world, books, and each other, they are inventing new forms of subjectivity. In a sense, all of us create ourselves as we stand on the threshold of the future, but at their most successful, reading groups provide a deliberative space that encourages reflective awareness of this process.

The Challenge of Sameness and Difference

Focusing on characters as if they were ontologically equivalent to living persons is not the only mode in which they are discussed by reading groups, although this mode seems especially central to the conversations among women's book group members. Other modes of access to characters and novels show members appropriating books in a complex dialogue between difference and similarity. Readers enjoy finding something they can recognize or feel close to (and sometimes this recognition provides them a self-reflective insight, much like seeing oneself through a mirror), but they also enjoy exploring what is strange or different, which they can also learn from. There is an intriguing parallel between the composition of reading groups and what readers need in order to appropriate a book: a series of exchanges between sameness and difference. This structure is revealed most clearly in book discussions that touch on areas in which difference seems most challenging to these late-twentieth-century readers: race and the classics.

Dealing with the Classics

Reframing the classics in experiential terms paradoxically gives reading group members the grounds to judge them vis-à-vis their own individual reading experience—an authority magnified by the consensual authority of the group if everybody finds a book disappointing. Thus, in a discussion of Charles Dickens's *Nicholas Nickleby,* Readers Inc. members agreed that although the book was certainly interesting, it had "little pull." As one participant said, "You could enjoy it but easily put it down." People quickly dismissed the plot, agreeing that the language and the "gallery of characters" were the main pleasures of the book. Then, after some desultory discussion of the characters, the group moved into a much more passionate discussion of the problems of being a professional woman, specifically, of how to express or conceal being a mother at the workplace (meeting, October 1987). This book had clearly not impressed the group.

Several times I witnessed a group dynamic that emerges when most of the group is very critical, even dismissive, of a classic but one or two members disagree. In these cases, the book's advocates attract all the majority's frustration and sharp criticisms, and in response they take on the mantle of champions of the literary heritage. In such meetings there is no guarantee that the classic and its spokeswoman will emerge victorious, despite the advocate's deployment of traditional evaluative judgments in the debate. The most dramatic instance of this occurred at a meeting in which Jane Austen's *Mansfield Park* elicited merciless criticism. After Rachel's introduction, Jane began a direct attack on the novel, saying she thought it was "really boring and the heroine was really a prig." Charity expanded, saying, "Boring, boring, boring. It's a seminar about right and wrong." Others attacked the heroine's passivity, and most agreed they found it boring ("Were you bored?" "I read about one third of it, and I was so bored I couldn't stand it!"). At my end of the table people began chatting about how they hadn't finished it and how repetitive it was, someone saying, "It was like reading one Miss Manners column after another Miss Manners column. I just don't like that style."Then a very respected member of the group began to speak for Austen, retreating in the face of earlier criticism to the last line of defense: her writing.

> R O S E I think that her writing is absolutely superb. I really do. I feel that she can convey so much in just a few words.

> N A O M I Oh! If only she would! [*The whole group laughs uproariously.*]

> R O S E I'm sorry. I think her language is marvelous. Look, the first three sentences of this book present a picture of these three sisters right away. How they got into the circumstances they're in.

> N A O M I I did read the first three sentences. The first three sentences are a *whole page!* [*More laughter.*]

Someone says privately to me in a quiet voice, "I thought the book was very good," but the group as a whole has dissolved into mirth. Then Rachel and Rose gather their forces again, Rachel saying in an aggrieved tone, "That book is a timely book today because it's classical, okay? I mean it's talking about things that we are experiencing today." Rose chimes in, "The thing is that we can't pick a book that everyone is going to like, but we ought to at least, I think, make an effort to finish it. Because how can we have a discussion if we haven't finished the book?" But Jane (the initial and most vociferous critic) responds: "I just want to say one thing about that. I could have finished this, but I needed another month!" More mirth follows, which effectively ends the discussion (MR's group meeting, 8 June 1990).

This is a striking demonstration of the egalitarian nature of reading groups. Here, the respect for classics in general, in addition to the respect for Rose, who was much loved and recognized as very well read, was inadequate to turn the tide that left Jane Austen's reputation in tatters. Despite meetings such as this, the investment most reading groups have in legitimate culture ensures that the category of "classic" remains untarnished and continues to guide selection and accord seriousness to those who accept its generalized value.

Scholarly authority has little weight to unseat readers' own experientially based judgments of individual classics, and advocates must employ a series of persuasive strategies to change people's minds. Most of these have the effect of bringing the book closer to the dismissive readers. For instance, defenders will sometimes link the book to the author's life, trying to make the author into a sympathetic character so that the group will not be able to derogate his or her work. Thus, in a discussion of *Middlemarch* in My Book Group, two of us spent considerable time sketching in a portrait of George Eliot that might appeal to the rest of the group (meeting, November 1990). We mentioned her relatively lowly background and determination to get an education, her rejection of the harsh Protestantism of her youth, her dif-

ficulties in finding personal happiness even as she met with success as a literary essayist in London, and the romantic story of her relationship with George Henry Lewes, not forgetting the social ostracism they faced. Looking back over the transcript, it seems a picture designed to appeal to this group of educated and socially mobile women, some of whom had grown up in fundamentalist Texas homes but had become more liberal over time, and most of whom had returned to the workforce after a period of intensive motherhood to pursue professional careers. Although I am not sure how permanently we changed individual members' critical evaluation of *Middlemarch,* the group began to discuss the book and its author much more sympathetically.

Another common strategy for a classic's champions is to attempt to move the majority by speaking about how important the book or author has been in their lives. In a meeting of My Book Group, whose members had mostly not enjoyed Jane Austen's *Persuasion,* I became a champion and employed this strategy at several points in the conversation (meeting, 18 February 1991). Participants argued that the book was not as large or complex as *Pride and Prejudice* ("It doesn't even have a wedding in it, she's in such a hurry to end it"). I responded by discussing how helpful it had been to me in dealing with my situation when I was still single and growing older, and I praised its Zen minimalism. They criticized the book because of the irrelevance of the world of leisured gentry to our contemporary society, and I replied by saying that I used to read Austen as a means of coping with going back to the college town I grew up in. She had made me understand the ways a small, insular community remains the same in nature despite vast historical changes. They expressed dismay at the "thinness" of the novel. I spoke at length about the way Austen's precision in accounting for subtle emotional transformations had helped me understand my own intense and private feelings about people in my life:

> E L What's so wonderful to me is the way she talks about the tiny incidents that show her feelings toward him and his feeling toward her. I just think that's stunningly done. The tiny, tiny incidents—shifts in feeling and tone. And of course you can tell that she, the heroine, was hanging on every tiny, tiny thing.

> S U S A N Their lives are built on tiny, tiny things! [*All laugh at this.*]

> E L But [refusing to give up] it's just done so beautifully. I can't think of anybody for many, many decades who's that good at that. I mean that's sort of like a Beethoven string quartet. She's getting into a register that people haven't gotten into before—and aren't going to get into for some time. [*No further laughter, and the discussion shifts ground.*]
> (Meeting, 18 February 1991)

In all these ploys, I was, in a sense, daring them to dislike a novel that had meant so much to one of the other members of the group. That tactic, combined with judicious comparisons with other high-culture phenomena (Beethoven and Zen), may not have changed people's minds, but it persuaded them to hear my case.

Jane Austen provides an interesting exemplification of the complex processes by which groups negotiate books that have been valorized by tradition. Her works proved difficult for three groups I observed because of both the formality and the elegance of the language and because of the very different ways people are portrayed as living in her novels. Both stylistically and substantively, these books were so different from what these book group members were used to that the books proved inaccessible even to willing readers. Substantively, readers found it hard to relate to a social world in which the protagonists were not gainfully employed, where the people who did the work (such as servants) were invisible, and where parents seemed to have only a limited involvement with their children.

In the discussion about Austen's *Mansfield Park* mentioned earlier, one participant commented on the heroine, "Fanny was like the old-time movies when you saw the girl strapped to the conveyor belt and not a wrong curl in her hair—you know, she was Miss Perfect, Miss Morality, Miss Honor—and she was a stereotypical figure of purity"; another said the book would have been good forty years ago, "before television." Here, references to the mass media seem to signify a desire for both a faster pace and grittier realism. Usually, however, such comments made implicit comparisons with contemporary upper-middle-class reality. In a discussion of *Persuasion* at a meeting of Readers Inc., on 18 February 1991, one member, irritated by what she saw as "the lack of everyday life," asked bluntly, "Who did the wash?" Later, she demanded, "What did the heroine's father do all day?" Another member responded, "Well nothing." And a third chimed in, "But that's Regency England. There's a whole class of people who do not work." The original commenter replied, with some irritation, "I find it just incredible that the country prospers!"

Later in the same discussion, two members reflected on what it had meant to them when, in reading Austen's *Pride and Prejudice,* they first confronted the idea that "there really were just whole groups of people who never worked."

> MARY BETH I was so naive that I thought I would achieve it someday! [*The group laughs.*] But, when you're twelve or thirteen or whenever I read it, the world is full of possibilities. Maybe you'll do everything. And that would certainly be one of the phases.

> KAREN Yes, that you could have an estate, a beautiful estate, that you could just walk on.

MARY BETH   I think that it was so romantic that I didn't need to deal with the technicalities. I just assumed that life would come on a silver tray with whipping cream and that swarthy handsome men would come in and waltz with me.

KAREN   Yes, but you know my world was so small that it didn't occur to me that there could be that much money. Nor the privilege or class—again, because of American views. Everybody I knew worked at something. It was just sort of mind-boggling. But, you know, I realize that I didn't think that I would achieve it. [*Looking at Mary Beth*] I didn't go so far as you.

HELEN   Well, I think she writes nicely. [*Much laughter.*]

MARY BETH   [*ironically*]: May we quote you?

Confronting the world of the British landed gentry was a culture shock to both Mary Beth and Karen. The cultural horizons of Karen's "small world" expanded in response. This supports the claim that people learn from novels, that books broaden our sense of possibilities. Mary Beth reports another register of response. For her, the depiction of the leisured gentry became personified by and fused with Elizabeth Bennett's romance with Darcy. Both entered her psyche as vague, animating dreams that may have begun in adolescence but that still appear to have some hold over her. This marks a complex moment of cultural appropriation. Austen portrays a world very strange to these twentieth-century women who grew up in small Texas towns, and yet she draws characters and relationships that foster deep identification. In Mary Beth's case, at least, those characters carry with them an ideal of wealth and leisure, as well as of romance, that has a lasting psychological resonance. In this sense, Austen's discourse, especially as a "classic," appears to have constitutive power in relation to the reader's subjectivity, once its strangeness has been familiarized through character and the already familiar structure of romance.

Listening to readers come to terms with the strangeness of Austen's language was also fascinating. Many felt put off by what one group characterized as her "wordiness." Several discussants of *Mansfield Park* felt so impatient with this quality they were compelled to reject the book altogether. Those readers of Austen who tried to overcome their feelings of linguistic distance from her novels seemed to search the text so they could reframe that distance in terms they felt familiar with. One discussant of *Emma,* for example, missed a "physical picture" in Austen's writing, but she said, "You have a very mental picture of how they're going to behave—What they're going to be talking about. It was easy to imagine. It was more connected to radio rather than watching a movie or TV. It's more like listening to a radio with voices coming through, and you're listening to them talk." She used the radio to bring Austen's style closer to herself, while another discussant in that group favorably compared Austen's work with contemporary mass media, remarking that it gave her "a nice change of pace." She continued, "I got hooked on *Dynasty* a couple of weeks ago. And it's all smut. And then you go to the movies and it's all cursing or dirty language or something. It's so nice to read some kind of gentle little—It's a love story. There's nothing really nasty in what anybody does" (LS's group meeting, 20 November 1985).

Although a critic might blanch at this characterization of *Emma,* it clearly brought this reader a welcome relief. This difference in tone may serve an important function in undercutting some of the worst features of mass culture. Certainly there is something moving about the following comment, also from the same meeting, about why one reader loves Austen:

> I took one of those courses, Great Authors of the so-and-so century—And I usually hated them, but okay, they're great works, okay, we'll read them. But I read *Pride and Prejudice* and I really liked it. They thought I was just nuts, you know, reading this for recreation. But I just felt she's so—it's not a soap opera; it's not that messy, but there's all this intertwining, and you know what's going on, but everybody else doesn't and there's this gentle irony. It's never mean, so you can laugh at the situation, which in any other case would be really bad. It's the general tone of the book, I guess.

More than anything else, what pulled readers past the linguistic difficulties they encountered in Austen's works were the characterizations. Even the group that found *Mansfield Park* unbearably boring delighted in the descriptions of Mrs. Fanny's manipulative and self-serving aunt. And the group that struggled some with *Emma* agreed with the comment: "She is wordy. Extremely wordy. But then you do get to know the people. She's very good on characterizations." This suggests that for these groups, reflection on characters may be their most powerful reason for connecting to difficult novels. Further, if the "structure of feeling" that enables connection between Austen and contemporary American women readers relates to character, it is in the representation of characters and their lives that "classic" novels may be most influential in shaping modern sensibility. Here, in other words, may be the most powerful and enduring aspect of the literary tradition.

Yet negotiating these novels was not easy for readers. The foreignness of Jane Austen's world led to criticisms of her limitations as a novelist and, more often, to criticisms of the upper classes of her time. To me, these discussions also pointed up limitations of contemporary readers' perspectives—an inability or refusal to imagine other ways of living than their own. Indeed, these attempts to understand Austen show the complexity of negotiating tradition even among women who are in many ways its most dutiful heirs. Scholars do not often think that the reception of legitimate culture is so difficult, because they think of it as "our" culture, which tends to erase its distance from present-day lived reality. Such difficulty, coupled with readers' efforts to reframe and render the distant aspects of the classics on more familiar terms, shows the cultural labor that audiences as well as educators must perform to keep the classics alive.

Dealing with Race

If the classics challenge reading groups because of differences in language and historical period, then novels dealing with race present white women's reading groups with the challenge of confronting America's most divisive contemporary social issue. Reviewing transcripts of meetings and interviews centered on books by or about African Americans raises questions about the limitations of people's ability to enter into such books and identify or empathize with their subjects, who represent a troubling "Other" for their white readers. When readers achieve engagement, reading and discussing these books can facilitate remarkable critical insights.

The transcript of Readers Inc.'s discussion of Toni Morrison's *Beloved* on 27 March 1989 provides an example of how difficult it can be for white readers even to "get into" a serious portrayal of slavery and its legacy among blacks. When the discussion turned to the book, the first comments introduced the theme of the book's difficulty, both stylistically and emotionally. One member said that she was not finished with the book: "I needed a year!" Another admitted that although she had finished it, she wasn't sure had what happened. Her remark was greeted by laughter, and another member responded, "Yeah, finishing the book and knowing what happened are two different things."

Next, a member confessed: "I found the whole book so depressing. I really did. I mean, I just . . . you know, it was a good book to read for that reason, I guess, but it was so awful . . . I just found it so depressing." Another responded, "It was hard reading." A third chimed in: "I didn't like it. . . . I had never thought about slavery—as being that awful. I thought of it as being hard work, but probably above everybody else. I mean, morally, you know . . . and their faith . . . " A fourth continued, "I thought it was unrelieved." People developed this theme, one woman saying she had put it down and "I just thought, I can't read anymore," while another said, "I could only read a couple or three chapters at a time. You can't go to bed thinking about it all—I had dreams about this stuff. I just . . . I don't know. I'm sure it was probably worse than this."

Not only was it hard for people to read, but for some the pain of reading encouraged dismissal. As one member said, "I mean, it could really be said in a way that could just put you off and you would just say you don't have anything to do with that. It's not my deal and I don't want to hear about it." Another chimed in, "That's true. There's been several plays in the past two years that I've come away from saying, 'I acknowledge that's true and I'm very sorry about it but I feel no need to go through that experience.' Again, I don't feel that anybody's better off from my having been through that, but that was not why I—it hasn't been—I mean how did the rest of you feel?"

Other members respond by bringing up aspects of cruelty toward blacks as represented in the book (bits in people's mouths; people being molested), and that part of the conversation ends with a curiously abstract affirmation of the characters' courage, "their humanity in the face of that." The rest of the discussion has a disjointed character. The conversation flits over historical details and briefly mentions a few characters, with occasional detours away from the book (for instance, a discussion of superstition and planting gardens), two comments about "redemption" that echo in their brevity the earlier affirmation of characters' courage, and isolated remarks about how people had framed the book in order to "handle" it. One woman thought of it as almost about another culture: "In some ways it was our culture because it was happening here and so on and in other ways it's like reading about another culture. And it reminded me of Latin America—the spirits." Another found relief in treating it purely aesthetically: "I just thought the language was so beautiful. I don't think I descended into the valley of despair the way you all did. I'm wondering if it's because I just sort of read it almost as poetry."

As a whole, the transcript reveals a reading task that, for most members, was so "depressing" that it elicited only discouragement. Several participants never found a home in this book and could not really respond to the characters or the situation with empathy. It elicited stunned horror, despair, and gestures of distance. Only the final remark makes a case for deeper engagement, and it is cast in the same abstract way that courage and redemption surface in the text, almost as if members are marking the appropriate humanistic insights readers should have.

Susan sums up her feelings about the book by saying it was all "just awful. The way that the people have to live. You know they only see each other once a day, and married people see each other only once a day when it's not dark. They work so many hours a day. Have whoever's babies they're supposed to have and they—it's just so awful. It's just for me the whole situation." Mary Beth responds tartly: "Then, it's good that you have to confront it." At that point, someone brings up "next month," everyone laughs with relief, and the conversation turns to Annie Dillard (next month's selection), families, and recipes.

If this discussion marks a failure to engage, others show participants making more successful efforts to deal with racial difference and using the issue of race to criticize present-day social stereotypes or social arrangements. In one case, the literary convention that characters ought to be complex and many-dimensional led a group to criticize both a canonized author and racial clichés. This conversation took place during a meeting of the Leisure Learning Group on 11 September 1985 to discuss *Huckleberry Finn,* and it was centered, as is often the case, on evaluations of the novel's characters. Jim's character provoked a heated debate that has echoes of Wayne Booth's account of University of Chicago faculty members' discussion of the same book. Everyone agreed that Jim lacked depth and complexity because of the author's racism, but some maintained that in spite of racism the portrayal was "realistic" for the time because of the oppression blacks had suffered under slavery. To make their point, they contextualized the book with much more sophistication than is usual among reading groups, who generally do so only briefly. The majority, who prevailed, granted that blacks had not had many opportunities for learning but felt that Twain did not allow Jim to be the "whole character" he could have been because of Twain's own prejudices. "He's *good,*" one member said, "but he's too simple-minded and stereotypic—too much like a child—and almost *too* good." Here a character provided the leverage for a discussion that moved beyond the level of personality to take up questions of how prejudice distorts people's vision of one other and of how to ameliorate racist stereotypes and the social structure that engenders them.

My Book Group's discussion of Ntozake Shange's *sassafras, cypress, and indigo* provides a more extended example of the way a group's reflections on race, as a result of characters in a novel, can lead to a critical appraisal of the social order. Despite reservations about the book's "hostility" toward whites and about individual characters' erotic choices—Sassafras tolerated battering from a lover, and Cypress became a lesbian—all members endorsed the author enthusiastically for having created women they characterized as "nurturing," "sensuous," "creative," and "powerful." As one member said, "Being female was truly celebrated without any of the 'Be carefuls.'" Several women found aspects of themselves in these characters and their relationships. Moreover, the book details visionary rituals for marking a girl's menarche; the group responded by describing their own unhappy experiences of their first periods and expressing a desire to experiment with some of the "very earthy" potions and the magnolia bath Ntozake Shange describes. When one member suggested, "Maybe we can have a female purification ritual next time," others chimed in with "A menses celebration!" and "A celebration of the womb!" (meeting, 4 June 1984). This theme surfaced again and again throughout the three-hour meeting. Although very different from academic critical discourse, this discussion gave voice to some of the pain women suffer as a result of our society's denigration of female sexuality, and it affirmed values and social practices that might challenge the traditional dichotomy between spirituality and the (female) flesh and celebrate an embodied womanhood.

Although the book is about black women, these discussants really only made use of insights from the novel that spoke to their own social situation as white women. So it could be said that the book served to help their own cultural reflection on gender, whereas race faded away as a subject for consideration. This marks a complex appropriative move that was, in a sense, self-serving, even though Shange's novel certainly spurred a sharp social critique.

Occasionally, some readers in all-white groups have such deep and complex experiences with books by black authors that they change even deeply held attitudes related to race. This happened to one woman who read *Beloved*. I interviewed Jeri informally in April 1999 when she mentioned at the end of another group we belonged to that she was so busy she might not be coming back; all she had time for was work, her family, and her reading group, "always a number one priority." When another person standing nearby asked her why it was so important to her, Jeri responded, "Because books can change your life!" She then said that *Beloved* had done that for her:

> I mean, I was never one who thought blacks had a problem, or [who] approved of affirmative action or anything like that. I figured that was then, and this is now, and I've certainly never done anything to oppress anyone. Then I read *Beloved*. And I mean it was hard. But it really made me see what it felt like to be owned by somebody else; it really made me stand in people's shoes, and understand how something like that could last for generations. It really changed my life. I think very differently now.

Literature does have the power to allow some white readers a quasi-experiential expansion of empathy or identification across the racial divide, but it is a fragile power, for it rests on the reader's desire and ability to make an intersubjective bridge as she reads. And although some books and discussions can enhance the possibility of engagement, there is always a countervailing tendency: that white groups will ratify the sense that this is not "our" issue or that they will be able to incorporate only those insights that are closest to home. Moreover, even an individual's deeply felt change may—given the structural conditions of our social world—bear little fruit in the form of actions. On the other hand, even insights "borrowed" from writings about blacks can be useful for reflection among white readers that is, if limited, still genuinely critical. And, given the obduracy of racist attitudes, it is remarkable that novels can do even this much in making the racial Other less strange.

Conclusion

It can be argued that reading groups affect their members' solitary reading because people often read different books for their groups than they would on their own. Sometimes members claim to read books differently as well, citing more attention both to the text and to their own reactions to it. But discussing their reading among trusted coparticipants engenders a particular kind of reflection that can have transformative potential either for individuals or for the group as a whole. Such conversations allow participants to clarify their own insights and opinions and also to integrate the various perspectives other readers bring to bear on the book.

Through this integrative process, individuals—and sometimes the group as a whole—can reach new understandings, whether about life or about the text at hand. The discussion itself, then, can be a creative process, for it elicits a certain kind of value-oriented textual interpretation and encourages (through difference and disputation) a clearer articulation of partially formulated perceptions and implicit assumptions, whether about a specific book or about personal experience. This process is particularly enlightening for participants (and perhaps most innovative) when groups can forge a new consensus from the diversity of opinions represented in discussion. The discussion of Shange's novel and the issue of gender mentioned earlier are examples of this process.

Group composition, members' previous social values, participants' ease in dealing with challenging books, even processes of book selection are all factors in determining whether reading groups become settings that enable this kind of critical and creative reflection to occur. Also, the general quality of the group dynamics can encourage an atmosphere of trust that seems crucial for the sometimes tentative and exploratory openness—toward new ideas, about one's own feelings—that characterizes critical reflection in reading groups. On the other hand, informal processes of social control can be extremely effective in silencing or stigmatizing members so as to enforce conformity. Joking and a lack of responsiveness appear to be most often used as enforcement mechanisms. Recall, for example, the member of My Book Group who was greeted with total and sustained silence when she proposed discussing a book by Shirley MacLaine.

Such examples show groups falling short of attaining the "ideal speech situation" described by Jürgen Habermas (1979) in which an egalitarian group process enables people to reflect on underlying cultural assumptions. Indeed most groups do not usually achieve that ideal because of power relations both within the groups and within the world that frames their activities—for example, most are middle to upper middle class and share the partialities of their social group. Also, most accept distinctions between the spheres of literature, society, and politics that inhibit some varieties of critical thinking, although those same distinctions underwrite the existence of reading groups as sites of cultural reflectiveness. However, an almost Habermasian Enlightenment ideal is at play in most groups' understanding of what makes a "good discussion," and those good discussions are remarkable for the ways they mobilize texts in the service of multileveled and often creative reflection. This reflection bridges the world of books and the world of individual and social experience—which some academics conceptualize as a text for purposes of analysis—but presents possibilities for action that cannot be reduced to either reading or writing.

The process of "living" stories other than one's own—whether in books or through hearing other people discuss their lives through books— may be crucial for confronting times of individual or social change, in part because it is then that such "equipment for living" is especially needed. Julie Cruikshank (1990) makes this point in her discussion of modern Native American Yukon women's refusal to abandon traditional storytelling during a time of irrevocable cultural change. Carolyn Heilbrun's discussion of reading about other women's lives in *Writing a Woman's Life* (1988) shows that contemporary uses of literature among other women can be similarly motivated. Women's reading groups may be especially valuable resources for women navigating a social world that is both demanding and volatile. As one reading group founder said of her all-women group, "Some people read to escape from life; we read to deal with life" (interview with JS, 18 September 1997). And in living out the importance of ideas, in striving for self-understanding as well as for personal and social criticism, these groups, however limited—as we all are—by their own social situations and ideological perspectives, show that it is possible to work through some of those biases by collective reflection about books.

SEVEN

Reading Groups and the Challenge of Mass Communication and Marketing

Reading groups came into being with the rise of the first mass medium of communication—the printed book. The groups of lay readers that Natalie Davis (1975, 214) describes in her cultural history of sixteenth-century France were able to discuss books together because they had access to printed books written in the vernacular. Before that time, only clerics versed in Latin and other classical languages could join each other in conversation about a text to share their insights and opinions. At their inception, reading groups represented a cultural community enabled by the most revolutionary form of communication of the age. They were at the cutting edge of culture.

Four hundred years later, a host of innovations in the technology and social organization of communication have overtaken reading groups. They now share an extremely complex universe of communication with other more mass-oriented media and their audiences. Even the book trade has become more highly centralized and consolidated than early printer-publishers could ever have imagined. What effects will such new developments have on reading groups? And what concerns do these developments raise in regard to reading groups and, more generally, audiences for literature? In exploring these questions, I point to three innovations—book superstores and the bookstore chains, television book clubs, and the online literary world—that might be especially fruitful areas for future research.

The growth of "large-format" bookstores and chains such as Barnes and Noble has brought mass marketing techniques to book distribution. Aside from consolidating what has traditionally been a fragmented world of very small retail outlets (with as yet undetermined effects on the audience for books), these stores have consciously integrated the sponsoring and "hosting" of reading groups into their book-marketing strategies.

Television has traditionally been discussed as a threat to reading. But in 1996 Oprah Winfrey marshaled the considerable resources of her talk show to "get America reading again." From its inception, Oprah's Book of the Month Club assured huge sales for every author she chose and has inspired the formation of reading groups nationwide. Her Internet site provided even more opportunities for book discussion as well as advice for forming and running face-to-face groups. Less dramatically, some television channels devote airtime to live book discussions. And at the network level, Arts and Entertainment Network (A&E) has begun an online book discussion club.

The growth of the Internet has had both direct and indirect effects on reading groups. For instance, online book groups on every conceivable subject, genre, and author have arisen with great rapidity. The Internet has also become a tremendous resource for reading group members as well as for readers in general. Traditional publishers circulate online discussion questions for reading group members, Web sites have sprung up to serve reading groups, and online publishing and book marketing make more titles easily available to readers.

These developments signify that contemporary reading groups exist in a complex cultural array that includes both new media and new channels of communication (even for books) that have as yet undetermined influence over the audience for books and the prospects for communities of readers. This territory is so new that any analysis must be provisional, so here I simply describe each innovation briefly and raise questions for future scholarship. I focus on how these changes might affect reading and book discussion as a group activity, although more general questions about audiences for books and literary culture as a whole are also relevant. Do these developments restrict or broaden the community of readers? And more specifically, do they change the sense of community among reading group members? Do they change the relationship of readers to cultural authority or affect the sense of distinction that has surrounded reading as a cultural activity? Does the increasing integration of the book into a mass-oriented matrix of communication appear to narrow either the universe of readers or the range of books in circulation? Or might it offer crosscutting possibilities of democratization? These are big questions with important implications for the literary endeavor in general.

Chain Bookstores and Reading Groups

The growth of large bookstore chains transformed book marketing during the final decades of the twentieth century. Chain stores now claim approximately 25 percent of the entire market for books, followed by book clubs, with about 20 percent of the market. Since the mid-1990s, independent bookstores and small chains, which in the past were the premiere outlet for books, have only accounted for between 15 percent and 17 percent of the retail market. Even among the chains, there is clear dominance by the largest two companies, with Barnes and Noble and the Borders group accounting for almost 30 percent of the total chain-store market share (Lazich 2000, 1541). This is extraordinary consolidation for the book trade, which historically has been one of the most fragmented merchandising markets in the country.

When compared with other industries, book publishing and distribution are small in scale and very diversified. It is arguable that people really only need a few types of toothpaste from which to choose, but books are unlike many other commodities in that they are the material repository of ideas, individual voices, and imaginative diversity. Not even the most aggressive paperback publishers (who often propound the "books are like toothpaste" view when arguing with less commercially oriented publishers) would publicly claim that our culture needs only a couple of ideas or three or four distinctive literary voices. From these differences between books and other marketed products springs the worry about chain bookstores. Critics fear that they may be part of a process that consolidates the content as well as the distribution of books, thus narrowing the range of ideas and suppressing creative expressions that appeal only to small numbers of people. The debate surrounding this concern covers not only distribution but also the consolidation of publishing and issues related to book warehousing, wholesaling, and pricing and to the longevity of publishers' backlists. It is a complex set of issues that cannot be given full justice here, nor is it central to questions about reading groups.[1] The debate has been so influential, though, that it has tended to dominate discussions of the large book chains and marginalize other issues more related to audiences for books.

For instance, the impact of chain bookstores on reading is mixed. From the viewpoint of readers, book superstores can be an improvement over smaller independent bookstores. The chains (which use demographic information to map the book-buying public) tend to be conveniently located for readers, which is very important in supporting book purchasing and even reading as a routine. In Houston, for example, most literary and specialized bookstores (such as mystery and science fiction genre stores or scientific and medical bookstores) are located in the central city. Chain stores have opened in the upscale areas "inside the Loop," but they have also quickly established a presence in all the prosperous new suburbs.

Large-format bookstores, whether independents or chain stores, are also convenient in another sense: they are open long hours, and they are arranged to be both comfortable and anonymous. Because of economies of scale, they are able to stock a larger number of titles and a broader range of books than most independent stores can afford to. Readers can pursue several genres and interests from a seat in a cozily situated armchair, often with refreshments from an in-house café. It may be true that all topics are not as deeply represented, nor is assistance as educated as that offered by smaller literary bookstores, but the superstores do offer employment to "bookish" people as well as computerized backup should a customer's tastes go beyond the offerings on the shelves.

In relation to reading groups, chain bookstores have a varied record. Barnes and Noble, for instance, has community relations managers who are responsible for organizing book groups as well as other literary events. The Borders group has not made the same organization-wide commitment to book groups. Individual chain stores also vary in their hospitality to reading groups.

Some innovations often attributed to chains—such as the rise of the in-store reading group—actually were fostered by the rise of the independent book superstore (such as Powell's in Portland, Oregon, and the Tattered Cover in Denver, Colorado). Of course, even before the rise of these huge stores, booksellers encouraged reading groups. Many independent bookstores work with reading groups, offering help in planning a yearlong program or suggesting monthly selections. Even small stores often provide a place for groups to gather in discussion. One tiny used bookstore around the corner from my house in Houston, for example, hosts a general-fiction group and a romance group. The proprietor offers free coffee and homemade sweets for the women who discuss books around a table in front of the almost labyrinthine forest of shelves that crowds the rest of the store. So chain stores can be said to be doing what bookstores have traditionally done in the way of nurturing reading groups. But they have offered their resources more publicly, formally, and bureaucratically than have smaller independent stores.

The idea of formalizing and publicizing a bookstore's close relationship to book groups appears to have been enabled by the size of the superstores. Their spacious floor plans, organized to provide semiprivate reading nooks, make it easy for them to accommodate even quite large groups of people. Similarly, such stores operate with more capital than smaller independents, which may make it easier for one person on their comparatively large staffs to devote some of his or her time to building relationships with book clubs. Such relationships are advantageous in the short run because, once in the store, book group members often browse for other titles before or after their meeting. More significant may be the long-term benefits that accrue to bookstores from encouraging active readership in general, for in so doing they are developing a consumer base for their very survival. Bookstores' self-interest unites with the socially approved goal of encouraging broad-based literacy. This gives everyone involved, in the songwriter Tom Lehrer's words, a sense of "doing well by doing good." Indeed, the desire to share a genuine passion for books and reading often powerfully motivates bookstore owners and staff to reach out to potential readers, giving them a sense that they are just doing what naturally occurs to them, given the resources of a very large store.

This sense of a gradual and natural evolution toward new relations with book groups suffused the interviews I conducted with Virginia Valentine, who is the book club coordinator for the Tattered Cover and something of a phenomenon in the field. Valentine is unquestionably a person of enormous energy (she herself says she talks "like a gattling gun") with a deep love of literature. Yet she is also right in saying, as she did during an interview in September 2000, that "It was being in the right place at the right time." About twenty years ago, when she took a job at the Tattered Cover, the innovative mega-bookstore in Denver, her predecessor at the store "handed" her a group for which she was to review several books. She told me about it when I interviewed her in March 2000:

> I never thought twice about it and did it. This was in the very early eighties. Around that time book clubs started in earnest, and they would come to me since I was in the fiction department, and they would ask for recommendations, and I would do it. I can't remember quite how it started, but I would invite the book clubs into the store. I would then give recommendations that consisted of reviews of, say, twenty books. That's how it all began. I remember one time in the later eighties—I had fifty clubs that had scheduled me for that particular year.

Joyce Meskis, owner of the Tattered Cover and nationally recognized as a dynamic innovator in the world of books, has encouraged outreach to reading groups in every possible way. So, from a confluence of cultural, institutional, and personal factors evolved a set of practices that elaborated the connection between bookstores and reading groups. Three seem particularly important.

First, Valentine compiles an annual list of contemporary literature that might be of interest to reading groups. The Tattered Cover issues "Virginia's List" in print and online. Both are free and circulate not only in Denver but also around the country. In May 2000, the list was twenty-two single-spaced pages long. It contained descriptions of seventy books, mentioned major awards won by the various volumes, and discussed authors' earlier works. So it is a substantial offering for interested individuals and groups.

Second, Valentine also organizes an in-store seminar late each January. As noted in a flyer issued in January 2000, the seminar introduces "members of book clubs and individuals interested in literary discussion" to authors, publishers, and other like-minded individuals. The seminar first met on the last Saturday of January 1995 and, despite horrendous weather, drew 120 people. In January 2000 the theme was "How to make a book." This event has attracted articulate and reflective publishers as well as authors from the very literary to the very popular. During the March 2000 interview, Valentine said that the meeting accomplished two things:

> It enabled people to spend a day talking to the authors and publishers. Of course, the authors addressed them, but then they were allowed to ask any questions they wanted to about the books, whatever. They could also get together informally and swap ideas about book clubs, and then people who didn't have book clubs could get together—and some of the participants recruited new members for their book clubs. It's an informal way for them to network.

Last but not least, Valentine serves as a personal connection and resource for about four hundred book groups and for individuals who want to join a group. For individuals, she can suggest two open groups that meet in the Tattered Cover as well as the January seminar. For groups she will review an individual title or a group of books, help locate a facilitator for discussions, suggest specific selections for a category they are interested in, such as biography, or supply background information on titles and tell groups how to research books for themselves. The store also provides a place for many groups to gather, whether in a semiprivate corner on the floor or in the store's restaurant. Taken together, these practices constitute an innovative paradigm of the relationship between bookstore and reading group, a relationship that has since been formalized and bureaucratized by Barnes and Noble, the largest of the bookstore chains.

There is a shift in discourse about reading groups as we move from independent superstore to nationwide bookstore chain. The tone is more commercial; the issues are less literary than organizational. This shift leads to two important questions that require further research: How do reading groups themselves feel about these different "reading contexts"? And have the chains encouraged a substantive change in either the audience for books or the cultural meaning of reading?

According to Tom Tolworthy, who was president of Barnes and Noble when I interviewed him in June 2000, the company initiated their community relations program in 1991, "at the time of the rollout of our large-format bookstores," and it was "seen as store staffing to begin with." Later he described the conceptual underpinnings of the program this way:

> Our community relations program is solely based on the idea that our bookstores are community bookstores, and as such, have a responsibility to those communities to connect with them on many levels: as a resource, as a community partner, as a public space for community events, and to open the world of books and authors

through our events calendar. From this idea has grown our whole program for Community Relations Managers and the events we run. Simply stated, this is our grand plan. No policy needed. It works by virtue of its own value to the store, booksellers, and community. (E-mail message, 8 June 2000)

There is no doubt that Barnes and Noble benefits commercially from the program, nor that there are national policies (as communicated in the Community Relations Encyclopedia, that is, the job manual) specifying how to implement the program. Nonetheless, much of what makes the program effective also works to encourage reading. For example, several of Houston's community relations managers mentioned that one of their missions was "to encourage a love of reading," which enabled them to think about their long-term goals in a broad way.

Over time, implementation of this general mission has also become more focused on books. As Tolworthy said,

At some point in the early development of our bookstores you found things like singles nights or chess-club championships at our cafés being well attended, but not necessarily being community activist programs for a bookstore. We've refined and further refined what our mission was from a community relations standpoint over the years and really targeted the idea of developing in-store events that would be in keeping with what a good community-oriented bookstore would do, as opposed to just being some exterior entertainment. (Interview, June 2000)

Finally, it appears that Barnes and Noble has introduced a good deal of decentralization, allowing considerable leeway for individual personnel. In Tolworthy's words,

The goals for the store are developed at the store. Based on a global set of criteria that's established in the manual, what are the best kinds of events for that store? Given the Houston market, the rodeo down there, which may not be considered a literary event in itself, certainly is a large part of the Houston community. We actually try to do events in the stores that are somewhat literary that coincide with that event. Where in New York, the store that we have in the Bronx does events with the Bronx Zoo. It doesn't work unless you do it that way. I can't run it from New York. It's not only something like the Houston rodeo which plays probably in all the stores, whether it's in Sugarland or on Westheimer or up in the Woodlands. At the next level, in each of those stores, there are specific events that are in the Woodlands that they're probably not holding at the Alabama Theater and they're certainly not holding down in Sugarland. (Interview, June 2000)

It is beyond this book's focus on grassroots reading groups to investigate fully the issues of centralization and commercialization raised by the entrance of the bookstore chains into the world of reading groups. Further research is needed, for example, to discover how many reading groups have begun under the auspices of the chains and how these groups (as well as long-standing groups that now meet in the stores) feel about the chains' role. Also, it would be important to discover in which ways such groups are different from grassroots groups, and whether special reading constituencies or kinds of reading have been encouraged or discouraged by the chains. Because in this work I have focused on Houston, I have briefly interviewed several of Houston's community relations managers (CRMs) to see from their point of view how the national program has played out in local stores.

CRMs are the staff members of Barnes and Noble stores charged with outreach to book groups as well as with the organization of events such as book signings, poetry readings, and children's story hours. Outreach means both encouraging existing groups to meet at the stores and initiating ideas for reading groups. The first strategy appears to be very successful. For example, Alethia Nelson, when interviewed by me in February 2000, mentioned two African American women's groups that meet at the Galleria Barnes and Noble store—Professional Black Women's Enterprise and Essence of Reading. Both existed before they decided to come to the store for their meetings.

When the CRMs initiate groups, as management encourages them to do, the success of the group depends on how well the CRM has "read" community interest. Sometimes local demographics work against them. For example, Julia Fraser of the Barnes and Noble store in Sugarland—a commuter suburb with many young families—told me during interviews in February and March 2000 that she has struggled to form adult book groups, although she can "get hordes of children out without even breaking a sweat." Similarly, Claudia Arce, who had recently left her position as CRM for the Champions (another Houston suburb) Barnes and Noble, had no success with a Great Books of the Twentieth Century group she initiated, despite professions of enthusiasm from customers. She told me about her experience when I interviewed her in February 2000: "I would tell people about it when they were talking with me, and they said, 'Oh, that's great. Nobody ever has reading groups for classics. That's terrific. When is it?' Everybody was real excited about it but nobody came. It's like PBS: it's great that it's there, but you don't necessarily watch it."

On the other hand, both Gina Cook of the Woodlands store and Arce of Champions had great success developing mother–daughter book groups. Both were aware of the idea from features in the mainstream press, and both thought it might fly among the young suburban families surrounding their stores. Arce also clearly conceptualized it in relation to empowerment, as she told me in February 2000: "I had recently read Mary Bray's *Reviving Ophelia*. Although the mothers and I never really said it or discussed it, we kind of knew that it was a reading group, but it was also a group to empower the girls and help them through that really awkward period." She described how she would pick books with "a strong female lead [who] was someone who was a little bit different than what is considered the norm." She also mentioned a subtle collusion between herself as facilitator and the mothers to take "care to draw out the younger, quieter girls. We had the outgoing, 'I want to talk about everything' girls, which was great that they had a place to speak their mind. But we also were careful to ask some of the quieter girls what they thought and what their favorite part was to draw them in. It was the event that I was the proudest of at that store."

Almost every CRM I spoke with mentioned several flourishing book groups they had initiated, from women's groups, mystery groups, African American groups, and Civil War groups to science fiction groups and even (briefly) an Animorphs group. Generally, they credited both company policies and higher-level management with supportive leadership that stressed a general mission to encourage reading.

CRMs sometimes mentioned policies that could be constraining or confusing as well as enabling. For example, when Barnes and Noble began to concentrate on reading groups in the mid-1990s, many in-store reading groups received a discount that came with the recommendation of a title by the CRM. Now groups must commit in advance to buying a certain number of copies (communicated to store personnel) to get the discount. But Tolworthy himself said in our June 2000 interview that "The decentralization of the process and a lot of folklore led to a lot of different ideas about what the policy really was." At least one Houston-area CRM worked around this confusion by deciding on the next month's selection early and urging participants to find the book at local libraries if they couldn't afford to buy it. She didn't announce this to management, but then again, they never inquired. Similarly, one CRM found herself at odds with management over a group that started strongly and then went through a period of thin attendance. The manual for CRMs apparently advises letting groups go if they fail to attract people, and she said that her in-store management had urged her to disband this group. She was convinced that the slump in attendance was just part of the group's development, and eventually she was proved right.

Other policies work to form book groups with distinctive characteristics. Barnes and Noble, for example, insists that all groups that meet in their stores and that want to be listed on store calendars must be open to new members. CRMs say this is not a problem, because many groups are happy to have new members, but it would be useful to interview group members about the issue. Barnes and Noble also seems to understand reading groups as functioning best with a stable facilitator, whether an employee or a customer. This is not the case with many grassroots groups, but the notion was mentioned by Tolworthy and was repeated often enough to me by CRMs that it seemed be part of the organization's collective wisdom. Arce, when interviewed in February 2000, conceptualized her work selecting books and facilitating discussion as relieving groups of a burden. She also thought that in-store facilitators, combined with the relative informality of meeting in the store, might have made reading groups "more relaxed and less formal and less intellectual—less academic. It has become more accessible to people."

By providing a framework for reading groups, corporate policies and practices may have allowed this cultural form to spread out into constituencies that don't "naturally" know how to form and run a book group. This remains a question that requires further research, as does the more interesting question of whether the involvement of the chains for commercial purposes has affected either the composition or the reading practices of book groups. At this point, however, it is fair to say that the explicit support of reading groups by chain bookstores and independent book superstores appears to be one factor in the groups' rising popularity. It may also be subtly changing the cultural meaning of books and reading.

Television and Reading Groups

The collective wisdom about television is that it discourages reading. Like questions about book superstores, the issue is too complex to cover here. But whether generally true or not, this formulation certainly oversimplifies the relationship between reading and television. Here, I focus on some of the ways that television has encouraged reading and reading groups.

Early television mined books for adaptations of novels and plays; in that regard, it was a derivative medium. Sometimes book-based television programs would conclude with a recommendation to find the book at your local bookstore or with an advertisement of a particular edition of the book. Presumably such programs, with or without explicit mention of books, encouraged some people to read, but whether they simply suggested new directions for established readers or actually introduced newcomers to leisure reading is unclear.

Television programmers now elaborate the tie-in with the use of the Internet for book discussions. This format has loosened the connection between television adaptations and literature, for the book discussions do not always feature books that networks have televised. In 1999, for example, A&E's book club director, a newly created position, invited a colleague of mine to serve as a host and literary resource for their first online book discussion. The discussion focused on a book A&E had not adapted for television. The director interviewed my colleague, Helena Michie, about Thomas Hardy's *Tess of the D'Ubervilles,* their featured book, and about her research interests. Michie then served as an online expert for a week, posting daily questions about the book and answering questions or responding to comments from other discussion participants. She reported that there was not a great deal of discussion, perhaps because it was the first officially sponsored discussion with an "expert" (personal communication, 14 June 2000).

Television has capitalized on the recent resurgence of interest in book clubs by televising some book discussion groups. In Houston one can watch book discussions on C-SPAN2 almost all Sunday. This is not exciting fare. It partakes of the "talking heads" genre, which builds on television's weaknesses, not its strengths. To my mind such programming has none of the fascination of more focused discussion panels and none of the pleasures of actually participating in book discussions. Still, it must interest some members of the audience or the experiment would be dropped for low ratings.

By far the most dramatic interaction between television and literature in recent years was Oprah Winfrey's Book Club. During its six-year existence, Oprah's Book Club became a cultural phenomenon of such note that when she announced that she would end it as a regular feature of her weekly television show, her statement became headline news (Publisher's Weekly.com, 5 April 2002). Her show represented a genuine departure from the televisual book tie-in and even from the simple televised book discussion, although the format featured a discussion segment. Oprah's Book Club can only be understood in the context of her remarkable history as a talk show innovator. Beginning in 1984 with a local Chicago morning show, Winfrey transformed the talk show format by constructing a mass-oriented yet extremely intimate relationship with her audience and by eschewing experts in favor of issue-oriented personal stories from panelists and the audience. Twelve years later, this innovation enabled her to garner audience participation in what can be described as a grand experiment in reading.

By 1986, the *Oprah Winfrey Show* went into national syndication and became the standard for all such programs, rising meteorically to the top of the talk show ratings, a position it has continued to maintain for fourteen years (Abt and Mustazza 1997, 64–66). During that time, Winfrey also built a media empire; her personal worth is valued at well over $200 million. She has produced her own show, some successful television miniseries, and a cinematic adaptation of Toni Morrison's *Beloved,* and she played starring roles in the movies based on both *Beloved* and *The Color Purple.* Winfrey has also become a noted philanthropist and has used her celebrity status to speak out publicly and campaign politically on issues such as child abuse. By now she is not just a television innovator but a cultural phenomenon. Nonetheless, by the mid-1990s Winfrey's ratings were slipping, which intensified her own personal sense that the show needed to be reconceptualized.

Thus Winfrey returned to the strategy she had applied so well at the beginning of her talk show career: she centered her show on the mutual identification between herself and her audience. In her words, she decided to "go with her gut." Reflecting on her own personal journey and what most passionately engaged her, she shifted the show's emphasis toward empowerment and social issues. She also announced that she would begin Oprah's Book Club and "get America reading again" (*Cincinnati Enquirer,* 18 November 1996).

Despite fears about ratings (in previous years Winfrey had used her show to suggest both holiday and summer reading, and those shows had traditionally lost viewers), the experiment was a resounding success. Winfrey figured as a fairy godmother to the authors she selected: every book featured on her show—whether by a Nobel Prize winner or an obscure first-time novelist—sold hundreds of thousands of copies. Publishers and booksellers greeted her book club with enthusiasm not only because of the increased revenue but because of the excitement she generated around books and reading. They perceived her as attracting people to reading literary fiction who had never before been engaged.

The literary establishment generally concurred with this positive response, although there have been some ambivalent and even negative reactions. Most of these concerns centered on Winfrey's role as tastemaker. She herself differs on almost every possible dimension from traditional literati: she is an African American woman raised in poverty, who left Morehouse College before finishing a degree, and she has made her career in a medium most literary pundits view with condescension and mistrust. She selected books without deference to—indeed independently of—the traditional literary canon. Instead, her own visceral connection to each book guided her selections, just as her desire to open her audience to reading was fueled by a passionate love of the books that have offered her insight, solace, and new horizons since her difficult childhood. This is perhaps what galled her critics most: she picked her book club fare according to her own idiosyncratic vision of which books mattered and approached them (at least for her viewers) experientially, with as little regard for academic literary analysis as for traditional literary authority.

Winfrey's detractors worried that she might have been dominating publishing, exploiting "easy issues," even recommending easy books and approaching them on the least difficult level. One critic, Gavin McNett

(1999), neatly summing up this position, argued that her selections were designed "to play on base sentiment, to reaffirm popular wisdom, to tell readers what they expect to hear . . . to help them learn what they already know . . . and to reinforce what they think is right and wrong in the world." Some of this rhetoric surely comes from a Bourdieuian turf war over cultural capital, a conflict about who has the right to judge, but it raises interesting questions about how Winfrey might have been culturally repositioning literature and reading.

What has been the effect on readers and book clubs? This, after all, is the constituency Winfrey was primarily concerned about when she began the club. My discussion here is of necessity based on somewhat impressionistic data, for no one, including Winfrey's Harpo Productions, knows how the generality of American readers have responded.

There are some clear indications that Oprah's Book Club had significant effects on many readers. The sales figures of Winfrey's selections alone are one indication of that. She herself also became a cultural icon for the broader reading public. Online book clubs often referred to her, for example. People would say that a book they were discussing would or would not be the kind of book Winfrey might feature on her show. Or moderators would bemoan the fact that when Oprah picked a book, thousands were talking about it, whereas only six messages had been posted about their own monthly selection. One short-lived online book club, in fact, defined itself as NotOprah'sBookClub: the list's owner wanted to discuss erotica and other fare Oprah tended to ban from her show. Her selections also became a reference point in general conversations about books. I have heard people denigrate the books she chose for being too focused on abuse or empowerment, whereas others commented favorably on individual titles she had chosen or said that they used her selections as a guide for their personal reading.

Oprah Winfrey herself and her organization also cited examples of people writing in to say that they had picked up a book for the first time in years, or that Winfrey had opened a whole new world of reading for them. The televised Oprah's Book Club solicited letters in which readers described the impact that each month's book had on their lives. It seems clear that Oprah's Book Club engaged many people with literature for the first time in their lives, and it reawakened many others to the pleasures of reading. The program also galvanized people who might already have been book readers to read more "literary" novels than they had before. Given the predominantly female nature of Winfrey's audience, most of these people were probably women. Women certainly dominated the book-related discussions on Oprah's Web site, and she usually picked books that either were written by women authors or were centered on female protagonists.

Oprah's Book Club affected book clubs in impressive ways. Her selections made a useful list for ongoing and for new book clubs. In fact, Valentine of the Tattered Cover says she saw several Denver-area book clubs begin by relying exclusively on Oprah's books, then branch out to other literary fiction as they gained confidence and a sense of their group's special interests. Winfrey also inspired women, in particular, to start their own face-to-face book clubs. This might have been part of a cultural fad, as some have claimed, but it might also have been the case that Winfrey succeeded in opening literary discussion to new constituencies. Her message seems to have had a strong resonance for African American women. This was not a new constituency—African American women's book clubs date back to at least the 1830s—but Winfrey's example, and her choice of several minority authors, might have been empowering to a new generation of African American women.

Through her Web site, Winfrey also encouraged book discussion. There was a section on how to build your own book club, including discussion of some common problems that book clubs face, such as members who dominate the conversation. There was also additional information about each monthly selection. For the June 2000 book, Sue Miller's *While I Was Gone,* there were links to the pages "About *While I Was Gone*" (a short description of the book) and "About Sue Miller" (an autobiographical essay about the author's personal and authorial development). The page also linked to an excerpt from the novel, an "Exclusive Essay" (in which Miller discussed writers who influenced her work), "Discussion Questions for Your Book Club" (e.g., "How do themes of memory and forgetfulness reverberate in the novel as a whole? What relationship, if any, does memory have to morality?"), and "Discuss This Book with Others in Our Oprah.com Community" (Oprah.com, June 2000). The online discussion contained 207 postings about the book, from May 26 to June 23, when Oprah aired her televised discussion. There were many replies to previous postings about the book—indicating intra-group communication—and several women responded to one posting from a woman who was hoping to find the book at low cost or for free. So in some fashion, this message board was serving as the "community" of literary discourse that Winfrey claimed it to be.

For many readers, then, Oprah's Book Club was tremendously influential. Winfrey mobilized the art and craft of television (and the Internet) in the service of reading and book discussion. She did so by offering the books as *her* books, books *she* loved, and thus books that became transmuted by identification with her own identity. Interestingly, the most frequent question I encountered about the Oprah Book Club was whether Winfrey herself picked the books. No one seems to know the answer to this. Oprah has claimed that she did, and that to succeed, the book club needed this "purity" of connection. On the day I watched the *Oprah Winfrey Show* (23 June

2000), she spoke in detail about her reading experience of Sue Miller's *While I Was Gone* and the summer's selection, Barbara Kingsolver's *The Poisonwood Bible*. Next she addressed doubters by saying, "I go through the year, and every book I recommend is a book that I have read and personally loved, so for people who think that somebody's reading them for me: not!" To me, the fascinated attention this issue elicited is a strong indication that books became somehow different when she selected them for her audience. How did she purvey the Oprah-ness of these books, and how did this influence the cultural construction of books and reading? As one way to consider this question, I analyzed, with a colleague's help,[2] how books and reading were presented on the show itself, using as my example the show on Miller's book presented on 23 June 2000, when Oprah also announced the summer selection.

One of the first things I noticed about books and reading on the show is how little time was actually spent lingering on the book itself. The first ten-minute segment of the show barely mentioned the book at all, except as an occasion for a discussion about love affairs, how to define them, and when to confess them. Oprah involved her audience in a many-leveled dialogue about this experiential topic, reading letters from three women, discussing an online poll and inviting members of the studio audience to participate, and asking specific guests by name to contribute to the discussion. This segment worked to accomplish at least two things: to make the issue alive to people and to forge an identification between Oprah and the audience's emotional lives and opinions, which could then be mobilized as interest in the book. Initially, the book was constructed entirely in terms of this emotional issue.

In fact, the panel discussion on *While I Was Gone* lasted only ten minutes. The book discussion was nested within layers of material that certainly referred to the book but tended to show how reading could take you out of the book, transporting you somewhere else, whether to the Congo (*The Poisonwood Bible*) or into yourself. The book functioned, then, as a launching pad to somewhere else. In compensation, the visual message of the show repeatedly emphasized the book and the activity of reading, as if a constant reminder were necessary that this was, indeed, a show about a book. The show's logo: Book / OPRAH / Club was transposed on top of a book. Book jackets of both Miller's and Barbara Kingsolver's book appeared in the backdrop behind Oprah. And in the two segments about books affecting women's lives, as well as in a short segment in which Miller talked about writing *While I Was Gone,* the women were all shown with the book in their laps, reading and musing over the text. Yet even visually, these images of reading gave way almost immediately to images of the women contemplatively walking through nature or gazing into space.

The show seemed to be intended to overcome assumed barriers to reading, an assumed mistrust of books. (I say "assumed," because the studio audience, at least, seemed full of readers, and certainly other indicators point to large numbers of Oprah's viewers being involved with books.) The dialogue binding Winfrey and the book to audience concerns was one mechanism for accomplishing this goal.

Another was the elaboration of Oprah's personal connection to these books. Winfrey made it very clear that she picked all of her book club's books: in a sense she framed them as her gift to her audience. She also made it clear that she had worked hard to give this gift. At the beginning of the show, she said: "I've been all year trying to figure out what is going to be the summer book, reading, reading, reading, till I was exhausted reading. I have now found the perfect summer book—for you, all for you, 'cause I've already read it!" Later, while recommending *The Poisonwood Bible,* she said, "I read this book in three days, and it was exhausting to me to try to do it in three days. I really wish I'd had the time to take the time to read it in a leisurely form. So I'm telling you, take your time with it." Not only was she wearing herself out for her audience, but she was also giving them the luxury of having time to really enjoy it, time she did not have for herself. Most literally, at the end of the show, she gave away stacks of free copies of her summer selection, *The Poisonwood Bible,* to the studio audience's cries of delight.

Perhaps most forcefully, the show constructed the book as having almost magical power. This stood in some tension with more formal, analytic modes of approaching a text. Indeed, Winfrey seemed to define herself against more academic modes of textual appropriation, as in the moment when she said to Miller: "If we were reading this in English class, our English teacher would be talking about the levels of confession for everybody. And I'd be like; did she know that that was supposed to be part of the theme of the book? Jo?" Oprah was asking, I think, about the author's intention (although Miller answered the question about the character's consciousness). But she posed the question by distancing herself from the academy. Even the taped segment in which Miller talked about her intentions in writing *While I Was Gone* is framed like a story rather than an analysis. She is visualized just like the women who were changed by her book—reading, gazing into the distance, and walking, all with a lush musical accompaniment. Miller did respond to one reader who found it hard to like the protagonist. She described how difficult it was to write in the first person—in a sense "being" a person who made her impatient because of the character's lack of self-knowledge—but this was almost the only moment an analytic textual issue surfaced.

The book was shown as having a remarkable power to, in the phrase with which Winfrey solicited readers' letters, "impact" your world. Books were referred to as impacting, transporting, scaring, pulling you in, making a difference, and "taking you further than you've ever imagined possible in your mind." It was as if they had to be imagined as having extraordinary agency or power to overcome people's reluctance to engage with them. As Winfrey said about *The Poisonwood Bible:* "You can't deny it. You just can't deny it."

Two segments about women whose lives changed dramatically because they read *While I Was Gone* dramatized the power of books. To take one example, Crystal said she first picked up *While I Was Gone* when Oprah recommended it, and she thought of her own situation and being tempted by intimacy with an old friend. She had been feeling "kind of lost and floating like she states in the opening part of her book. . . . My husband has always been very supportive, but emotionally, we've been disconnected." The visuals showed her reading, walking by a river, musing over family photographs, driving her van into her driveway, staring out the window, and talking to the camera as she wept gently. "When I finished the book I cried. . . . What I realized was that I love my husband. I realized that my husband is a good man and that I've sold him short for a long time—that maybe I have to stop and look inside, and I'm doing that. I think this show is making me do that." From the audience, she and her husband affirmed that now they're working on their relationship together and talking more with each other.

Oprah's response to this showed a remarkable ambivalence about the nature of books. She said to Crystal: "It's just a novel! I wanted you to read it. I didn't know it would unravel all of that, but that's the power of a book." It's as if she had to underscore the power of books in order to persuade people to actually pick them up. Yet on the other hand she said: "It's just a novel!" Or earlier: "It's just a book! I wanted you to read it and think about some things!" At these points, Winfrey almost identified with the cultural denigration of novels (How can you be so moved by just a book?) or perhaps with concerns about the power of books (Your life came apart; books can be dangerous!).

Certainly Winfrey was making a case for books and reading. Here, books took you into yourself and offered you a healing insight about your life. Not coincidentally, I think, both featured readers found new hope for their marriages. This sent the message that although books can be unsettling, they also bring the reader safely back into the fold of normalcy. At other moments in the show, it was shown that books transport you to new and unimaginable realms of experience.

The case Winfrey made, both visually and through the voices of real readers, was experiential rather than analytic. Books offered moral instruction, the potential for seeing oneself anew or for exploring faraway worlds imaginatively, and the possibility of becoming part of an Oprah-centered community of readers. This cultural construction of books and reading stands independent of the contemporary academy. It also tends to linger at a reading level characterized mainly by identification and encourages a direct dialogue between the book and readers' emotional concerns. The show offered thematic discussion that moved to consider, in the case of *While I Was Gone,* forgiveness, consciousness, memory, and the place of the past. Yet in the main, it constructed the text as a transparent veil (a figure echoed in many of the visual representations of semitransparent pages on the show) through which readers could access another world or another level of understanding of their own inner lives. This resembles one common strategy of appropriating books among many reading groups. But Winfrey was not simply another member of a grassroots book club. As founder of Oprah's Book Club, she was responsible for choosing books and for shaping the ways other readers appropriated them. She wielded the power of a cultural celebrity, and, as such, she was teaching both what to read and how to read. In that sense, I agree with critics who worry that she might have been approaching books on the easiest level and using them to reinforce the status quo. On the other hand, Winfrey offered an alternative to more academic literary canons and analyses, and that might have opened up some cultural space for readers—space for them to forge their own ways of relating to the books they read. Questions such as these point to the need for further investigation of how Oprah's Book Club did, in fact, affect different constituencies of readers.

Online Book Clubs

Conversation about books occurs on the Internet in a variety of different settings. For example, Amazon.com encourages readers to comment on books for the company's own commercial purposes. For similar reasons, authors and publishers have designed user-friendly Web sites that also provide forums for discussion. Broadly defined or multipurpose Web sites often offer locations for literary talk. For example, Oprah's Web site offered a variety of links to online visitors, including one that enabled users to discuss on the Internet the books she featured on her monthly book club program. There are also more purely literary sites that host many-stranded discussions about books and reading. For instance, Readers Paradise Forum (which has some connection to Amazon.com, as indicated by a link prominently featured on their Web page) urges visitors to post messages on any topic related to books and reading. When I last visited the site, there were postings on a number of books and authors, from R. D. Blackmore's 1908 novel *Lorna Doone* and John Berendt's *Midnight in the Garden of Good and Evil* to work by Richard Brautigan. There were also requests for book recommendations. One person expressed a desire to hear about newly published thrillers, and another person wanted suggestions of good science fiction and fantasy titles to get her out of a reading slump. Someone also posted two queries that led to general discussions about reading: "When did you discover your passion for reading?" and "What book has changed your life?" Internet locations such as this encourage readers to feel part of a large and friendly literary community. It would be important to research these sites and investigate, for example, why and by whom each was founded, how each is funded, and what the social characteristics are of the users of each site.

Perhaps because I am used to reading groups that discuss one book at a time, I have defined online reading groups rather narrowly as groups that participate in similar—although computer-mediated—conversations. Groups with this format follow many of the same procedures as face-to-face groups do, with slight modifications. For instance, most select a book to discuss every month by declaring that the list will be open for suggestions until a certain date. At the end of that time, the moderator asks for a vote (often setting up a site for an online survey) and announces what the month's selection will be. At another appointed date, the list is open for comments on that month's title.

For this discussion, I drew on data from all the groups that identified themselves as reading or book clubs at Onelist.com (now eGroups), one of the sites that provide services for user groups. In all, my research assistant and I found twenty groups. Seven of these were general interest fiction or non-fiction groups, and six were genre groups (including three that read horror books, one that read true crime fiction, one that read romance, and one that read medical books). Three of the groups were organized around religion, with two fundamentalist Christian groups and a New Age group. Two were organized around professions (Teenbooks and LATAR, LibrariansAnd-TeachersAsReaders) and attracted significant numbers of educators and librarians. Two others read books related to non-Western culture: Global-books and a group that read Asian literature. This population appeared to be, if not a strictly representative sample, at least quite characteristic of the larger universe of such groups. The following discussion is based on postings from these groups and online "interviews" conducted with group moderators.

For some groups, online activity is an extension of face-to-face meetings. In other words, there are book groups that meet in the real world but have Web pages and user groups for online communication. This means that they are open to participation by members who cannot meet with them physically. Two examples from the eGroups I am acquainted with are Glob-albookgroup and NewAgeLiteraryGuild.[3] The Globalbookgroup reads mainly multicultural books and meets once a month at a bookstore in the greater Atlanta area, but they also have an online component so that people can send e-mail messages about the books. Some of the messages come from the people who meet at the bookstore, but people who live far away also participate by correspondence. The NewAgeLiteraryGuild works in much the same way. They are an outgrowth of the Pagan / Wicca / New Age community in Portland, Oregon. They meet there to discuss books and also to correspond online about events of local interest. Some members of the list, who have similar literary interests, live far from Portland and only participate in the online discussions. My assumption is that the list is open to purely online members because Pagans and New Agers define themselves as a spiritual movement and wish to reach out to the Pagans and New Agers who do not live near other like-minded people and who are searching for ways to connect to the broader New Age community.

Some online reading groups manage to re-create a feeling of face-to-face discussions by arranging "live" or real-time chat sessions on the computer. Moderators or webmasters set up a site especially for this purpose, establish a regular meeting time, and welcome all participants. Or there may be a special meeting, which moderators arrange as a "visit" from a particular author, who is then present to host a discussion of his / her books and answer questions from readers. M. J. Rose, an author whose 1998 book *Lip Service* was first published online, and who is an expert in online literary activities, told me that she found this both interesting and enjoyable because of the feedback it gave her about audience response (phone interview, 15 July 2000). She also had been an invited "guest" of online reading groups for several days, which meant that she would check in several times a day to answer any questions about her work. Not only does this provide authors with a sense of connection with their audience, but it is a publicity tool that helps generate interest in their books. So, once again, commercialism and communication work in tandem.

Most online reading groups, however, appear to be simple e-mail lists. Someone who wants to converse about books online will set up a list through an organization such as eGroups, and then the list is open for members to join. Members arrive both through browsing the Web and through word of mouth, for people who are members of online reading groups often casually pass on literary Web site information to each other, just as members of face-to-face groups let each other know about literary events or resources. Sometimes new online groups take a while to attract a viable number of new members for good discussions. This problem is exacerbated by the fact that many who subscribe are not very active participants.

In general, the founders of such groups are also group moderators. They "own" the list and serve as the liaison with eGroups as well as take responsibility for running the list. Usually this includes setting up a welcome message for new subscribers, making the rules for suggesting and choosing books, and setting times for voting and discussing books. It may also include surveying members, whether about book choices or other group decisions, and vetting the incoming messages to keep advertisements and other inappropriate postings (spam) off the list. The heavy responsibilities of online moderators make their role different from that of many facilitators of face-to-face groups, so I discuss them in more detail later.

One of my colleagues speculated that these hardworking moderators must be very lonely people to engage in this activity, but that is not the impression their messages give. Some of them appear to be women who are not employed outside the home—a situation that encourages many women to join face-to-face groups—but whatever their circumstances, most moderators seem to be outgoing and friendly people. They are distinguished only by the fact that, unlike many people, they have chosen to fulfill their needs online, and they are used to reaching out via computer for many reasons. Often their networks and friendships either originate online or are sustained by online correspondence. For example, Jill, one of the online reading group moderators I corresponded with, said that online she had met more than one hundred people with whom she then became acquainted (e-mail interview, 21 April 2000). In her words, "I truly consider these people my friends. I've traveled more than I ever did before I got online too—to get together with online friends." She describes a process of feeling "more free to be open and honest with each other. There's a sense of anonymity at first, as well as safety in distance. Then you find that you are really getting to know people well. Once you get to that point, it can become a most fulfilling friendship, especially for those of us who find it difficult to maintain 'real life' friendships because of time and scheduling conflicts."

Similarities with Face-to-Face Groups

Like face-to-face groups, online reading groups bring together people who are united by reading interests but who are otherwise somewhat different, certainly in terms of geographical location but also in terms of age, occupation (except among groups united by profession, such as the group Librarians and Teachers as Readers), and life situation. In fact, members appear to be less socially similar than those belonging to face-to-face groups, because online groups do not emerge from daily interaction (among neighbors or acquaintances) or organizational linkages. It is difficult to determine race or class composition of groups, however, because people do not need to reveal their race online, and because not enough people reveal their occupations to enable a reliable categorization of members by class. Internet participation ensures a common ground in very basic computer literacy, but that is widespread in the United States. Internet access is somewhat more restricted, because it is differentially distributed in society in a way that favors people with more monetary and educational resources. Also, members must be well enough educated to feel competent to write comments about books.

The same moderator who discussed online friendships also informed me that in her experience both online and when meeting online acquaintances face to face, she has seen "mostly people who would, I believe, fall into the lower middle class, more than I would expect that fall directly into the lower class, and somewhat more people who can afford housekeepers than those in the lower class" (e-mail interview, 21 April 2000). Such categorizations were, according to her, based on what she knew of people's income and education as well as on cues from dress and conversation.

On the whole, online reading groups do not appear to be upper class. One group I subscribed to was joined by an author who talked about his life in an impressive, even intimidating fashion. He mentioned an international career and authorship of several books. This elicited a warm but envious response from the moderator and curious but friendly welcomes from other members. His only comments after introducing himself related to the generally low level of the group's discussion. I suspected, in fact, that he had joined this group—and perhaps several others—to tout his most recent book. His presence was certainly off-putting, judging from the unresponsiveness of the group to his criticisms.

One of the striking and unexpected similarities I found between online and face-to-face reading groups was the intimacy that emerges, especially in groups that are active and long lasting. I had naively thought that writing might constrain the emotional expressiveness that characterizes many face-to-face interactions, but I rapidly discovered tremendous emotional expressiveness in the postings. Users have developed conventions to signal emotions from smiling faces, :) or :-), and frowns, :(or :-(, to BIG CAPS (usually in book groups big caps signify emphasis rather than anger), many exclamation points (as in "Glad to have you with us!!!!"), or emotional abbreviations such as lol (laughing out loud). Messages are peppered with emotions, sometimes so much so that the reader feels exhausted by the level of intensity.

Similarly, I had expected that the "open" nature of the groups, including the large numbers of uninvolved lurkers as well as the lack of immediate response that characterizes e-mail messaging, would discourage intimate personal disclosure, but nothing could be farther from the truth. Members of the larger or quieter online groups did not reveal much personal information, but more active and long-standing groups appear to encourage a dynamic of trust similar to the predominantly closed face-to-face groups. For example, an aspiring writer who became involved with the RealCrime group became a father during the time I received their digests. He was very excited about the baby's birth, and others responded by sharing their own experiences, congratulating him, teasing with him about parenthood, and generally celebrating the event. In an e-mail, he quite movingly expressed his feelings that this group had in fact become his truest friends because of the openness, shared interests, and supportiveness he had found in the group. This leads me to speculate that, for some people, it may be easier to reveal themselves online than in person, a speculation that seems affirmed by Jill's remarks earlier about online friendships. After all, because this is a virtual and geographically dispersed group, self-disclosure is in some ways less risky or less consequential than it would be among peers one sees every day. Online "presence" is also not marked by annoying physical habits. In this sense, online groups may amplify the feelings of safety in distance (both because one is speaking through a book and because in most reading groups not all members are close friends) that often prevail in face-to-face reading groups.

Differences from Face-to-Face Groups

One obvious difference between online groups and other reading groups is that online members are often extremely geographically dispersed. In this, they hark back to early corresponding societies, such as the radical groups of nineteenth-century Britain, which sometimes also shared reading programs. Online book groups I have observed draw members from all regions of the United States, Canada, the United Kingdom, Australia, and New Zealand as well as attracting English speakers located across the globe. This gives them a cosmopolitan feeling, although in general they are within the cultural borders of the old British Empire. Cross-nationality figures most often in discussions about the difficulty of getting books. (This problem also affects members who are far from large libraries or well-stocked bookstores.) Because eGroups is centered in the United States, Americans often suggest a book, only to have members abroad express dismay when they cannot find it. In some cases, they will offer to read other books by the same author or ask that the group delay discussing a title until they can find it. Sometimes people offer to send them copies, but the mails are a problem for really far-flung members, so groups often reschedule discussions, think of different books, or open the discussion to two titles rather than one in order to accommodate those who are at a loss.

All of the online reading groups discussed here also remain open to new members. Face-to-face groups, on the other hand, usually have very clear boundaries. After their formation, they tend to be closed to new members, except at specific times when they feel the need to recruit new members because of departures from the group or a desire to expand. Online moderators who have experience with many groups over time have informed me that there are many closed online groups, including some that evolve into closed groups and others that were initiated as private discussions. Further research is needed to explore this issue more fully. Certainly, those eGroups I subscribed to were open by definition.

In the previous section, I discussed the fact that this lack of boundaries does not appear to discourage people from rather intimate self-revelation, although experienced moderators assure me that closed groups can become even more intimate. Openness to newcomers, on the other hand, gives rise to a great deal of repetitious discussion of group rules and procedures. Newcomers introduce themselves, sometimes referring to their age, family, location, occupation, and reading interests, express enthusiasm for the group and the books, and then ask how things are run. (In fact, one can find this out directly on the eGroups Web site.) Consequently, moderators find themselves explaining basic procedures over and over again. Active members also spend a fair amount of effort welcoming newcomers, which may become discouraging over time, since many newcomers revert to inactivity after posting just a few messages. But these issues are not limited to online groups; I have witnessed the same problem in face-to-face groups that include more than one or two new members on a regular basis.

Yet another procedural difference between online groups and their face-to-face counterparts is that moderators tend to bear most of the responsibility for initiating or enlivening book discussions. True, other online members often ask questions or explore an aspect of the book. More often than not, however, the moderator fulfills functions that are usually rotated among members of face-to-face groups: challenging participants with questions or suggesting issues for discussion.

I found two substantive differences between the online groups and the more traditional reading groups I observed: there seemed to be less interpreting or analyzing of individual titles and less evidence that participants' comments were building on and amplifying comments that preceded them. One contributing factor is that online comments are scattered over the course of several days or even weeks, thus inhibiting the interconnectedness and intensity of most face-to-face discussions. Another factor is that crafting a lengthy e-mail requires time and care, which can feel a bit like writing a paper. Perhaps this was the case only with the groups I observed during the short time that I observed them. Some comments indicated that there are other online literary "gatherings" that discuss books more deeply. A few moderators also mentioned wonderful discussions in their groups that I had not witnessed. Even if the online format does make it more rare to encounter deep literary discussions (which I cannot claim with certainty), online discussions seemed to feature many references to other books and other literary Web sites, as I mentioned earlier.

More specific to online interaction are conventions used during the book discussion itself. For example, because people are reading on slightly different schedules, not everyone finishes the current book, even during the period during which the group is open to discuss it. To deal with this, moderators and experienced members urge others to put "Spoiler" in the subject line of the message and then to scroll down far enough so that the message about the book (which may give away plot details) will not appear on the screen when that message is first opened. Recipients can then file the message away until they are finished reading the book, so their pleasure is not spoiled. Likewise, most online groups I observed select books by voting on individual selections, because that handles the lack of direct interaction that characterizes online groups.

More often than is the case for face-to-face reading groups, groups of online readers are organized around special interests or professional identities. These are usually signaled by the group's name in order to attract Web browsers. Among the groups whose messages I read was one called Real-Crime, a group interested in reading books about real-life crimes. This group (like the romance, horror, and vampire groups on eGroups) shared a reading interest, which the group nurtured by recommending titles to each other as well as by discussing some of the negative reactions they encountered from booksellers, family members, and friends because of their fascination with this genre. M. J. Rose informed me that there were also many online groups of science fiction and fantasy readers, who, like the Real-Crime group, might not easily find friends or neighbors to share their literary interests and who might, as well, be a population especially at home on the Internet (interview, 15 July 2000).

As I read messages, it became clear that I had missed certain online reading groups that were organized entirely around the literature of specific authors, such as Stephen King or Jane Austen. It would be interesting to know how long such author-centered groups tend to last, and whether subscribers drift in and out, subscribe for a long period of time, or belong to several online literary groups, only some of which are limited to one writer's work. One moderator says that author-centered groups, especially if the authors are popular (e.g., Stephen King), are large, active, and long lasting. Others she knows of are quieter and smaller. This moderator is very experienced; she has been online for six years, has moderated five groups, and now belongs to twenty. According to her, members' online interests are sometimes limited to one writer, but sometimes they branch out into closely related interests (Stephen King fans tend to be interested in other horror books, for example), and often they are more broad-ranging, both within literature and beyond.

Other groups are united by more than reading interests. The Apostolic group, a mixed-gender book group on eGroups that ended during the period when I received postings, tended to read fiction published by Christian houses or books such as the Left Behind series about the Rapture and the end of days that appeal to many fundamentalist or evangelical Christian readers. But messages from this group made it clear that this reading interest was only one aspect of a deeply held set of common beliefs and practices. All had a personal relationship with God and were familiar with topics such as home schooling. Another very active eGroup of Christian women has a similar global orientation. The New Age group, while espousing very different beliefs, also shares more than purely literary concerns.

Professional identities serve as a powerful binding force for some online reading groups. One of the largest and most active groups among those I subscribed to was composed mainly of teachers and librarians, and discussed books for adolescent readers (they were called Teenbooks). Another similar eGroup was the LATAR (LibrariansAndTeachersAsReaders) literary forum. Like the Teenbooks group, they were all dedicated and "professional" readers. Both groups had passionate and varied book interests to discuss and also occasionally spoke of work problems and public issues (such as censorship) that impinged on their educative mission. During the time I observed them, for instance, conservative Christians were attacking the Harry Potter books because of their positive portrayal of magic, witchcraft, and sorcery. Generally, these educators were outraged at what they saw as a misguided attack on both free speech and freedom of the imagination. Professions less connected to literature were not represented among the groups I observed.

When I mentioned the "special interest" quality of online reading groups to Rose, she commented that this is true of many online lists (interview, 15 July 2000). Often, people can pursue general interests—whether literary or not—in more traditional ways, and they only take to the Internet if they cannot find the people or resources they need. Perhaps for this reason, the more general online reading groups I subscribed to were noteworthy for their extroverted and energetic moderators. It seemed as if the moderator's personality was particularly important for keeping members engaged, given that there was no unusual reading interest or particular social identity (aside from that of reader) being supported by these lists. I suspect that the friendships and fun of participating in such general reading groups are more necessary to hold the interest of their members than is the case with online groups that share specialized literary tastes.

This ties in to the unique nature of participation in online reading groups. On the one hand, participation is extremely easy. Space and time, which constrain face-to-face participation, are nonissues on the Internet. Book group members associate with readers from all over the world just by turning on a computer at home or at work, and they can read postings and comment at their convenience because there is no defined "meeting" time. Such groups are thus a tremendous resource for isolated or extremely busy readers.

It is equally easy to belong to an online group and participate only minimally or not at all. Most of the groups I observed had at most only ten or twelve active members out of a membership list of between thirty and fifty members. This is not really a problem in the main, because a smaller group can sustain a sense of community and enthusiasm for discussion. Moderators work hard to maintain this enthusiasm. They welcome new members, often initiate discussions about whether procedures should change, and ask questions to liven up discussions.

It can be discouraging for participants and especially for moderators if the "regulars" begin to flag or if hardly anyone votes when it is time to select a title. The postings I read were peppered with comments from moderators about the problem of nonparticipation. Sometimes these messages were irritated ("Have you all disappeared???"), sometimes chiding ("Why is everyone so quiet?" "Won't someone please say something about the book!"), sometimes sad ("I am wondering if I should continue with this list. It is very discouraging to have so little response."). It generally falls upon moderators to inject new energy into a quiescent group. Sometimes a despairing message from the moderator is enough in itself to get things moving again. Members appear to feel obligated to moderators because moderators take so much responsibility for the group's well-being and simply because they are friendly, nice people. Members will often respond with excuses for their silence ("I was out of town." "My computer was down." "I've been sick.") or with expressions of appreciation for the moderator and a renewed commitment to the group. Sometimes moderators will ask general questions to reengage members. Examples I have seen include questions about why members joined the book group or what they have been reading lately.

The issue of participation has clear adverse effects on moderators. Even from my examination only four months' worth of messages from twenty groups, it is clear that moderators expend much effort on this voluntary activity, making their role far more extensive than that of most face-to-face group leaders. I observed several moderators depart for a break or forever, which makes me conclude that online moderators battle a significant problem with burnout.

The difficulty of sustaining group commitment also contributes to online group demise. If inventive and enthusiastic moderators' ploys do not call forth response from members, groups themselves simply fade into silence. During the short time I observed the literary eGroups, five of the twenty dissolved. I suspect that few online groups last a very long time. This would make them different from face-to-face groups, which often last from the date of their foundation to the end of members' reading lives and sometimes continue over generations. Still, the notion of online groups is too new as yet to be able to determine their usual life span.

Despite the common assumption that individuals use it mainly for information ("the information highway" captures this view), the Internet also encourages affiliation, association, and personal validation and is thus a profoundly social technology. The number and vitality of online reading groups certainly confirm this analysis. The Internet offers remarkable resources for readers who either cannot find other readers—or other readers who share their interests—in their immediate vicinity or simply want the flexibility of participating in "book talk" at home or at work. And online reading groups are only part of a burgeoning world of literature online. These developments have not yet threatened more traditional ways of publishing, marketing, or discussing books, although they may augur change. For now, however, the online world of literature appears mainly to offer broader opportunities for easy access to literature and the pleasures of sharing books with other readers.

Conclusion

The reading group has been drawn into a new matrix of communication, and the cultural consequences of this matrix, whether for reading groups or for the cultural construction of literature, are still unfolding. I would argue that the emergence of the bookstore chains and Oprah's Book Club, and the increasing use of the Internet for book discussions have opened books and reading to broader constituencies. They have also loosened the bond between the book and traditional kinds of literary authority and raised questions about the increasing commercialization and "celebritization" of the reading group.

The chains bring books closer to many people's daily routines and timetables and offer an atmosphere for browsing that is like a comfortable living room. They house existing reading groups and initiate them as well, perhaps making them more hospitable to less confident readers. Oprah Winfrey made book talk as close as the family television and imbued it with her inimitable personal style. She selected books because of their experiential meaning to her and dramatized their emotional impact for her audience. Her show provided something different from the academy's formal and analytic discourse about books. This might have been especially engaging for her core audience members, who have been characterized as predominantly lower middle class. Such people may—if Bourdieu's ideas about cultural consumption hold in this case—want art linked closely to life. Oprah's Book Club also appears to have encouraged women's reading groups and especially African American women's reading groups. Like Oprah's Web site, numerous online book groups and book discussions provide social support to readers with diverse interests while also providing Internet users a wide range of information about books and authors, presumably increasing readers' independence from more traditional sources of information and opinion about literature.

The online literary world has a populist, almost anarchic feeling. Any-

one with Internet access and a pinch of initiative can begin an online reading group or find an enthusiastic welcome from group members already out
there. There is a frontier sense of wide-open spaces on the Web, which seems
far from the top-down structure of either Oprah's Book Club or the chain
stores. Nonetheless, entrepreneurs vie for commercial payoffs in the virtual
world: authors' and publishers' Web sites publicize their books, and small
companies jostle for book-related commercial niches; the role of organizations like Amazon.com in the funding of literary Web sites needs further research. The book chains are unabashedly commercial. Tom Tolworthy
speaks the language of the marketplace, with little of the obvious love of literature that suffuses Virginia Valentine's conversation. Books have always
been commerce as well as culture, yet new forces of consolidation within
the industry may augur less varied fare or less "shelf time" for ideas. One
must ask how much and in what ways this matters for the future of books,
reading, and reading groups. The same question holds true for Oprah's role
of "celebrity-as-teacher."

In the absence of solid empirical knowledge, I am caught between
two worries. The first is a suspicion that ever-more sophisticated, ever-more
knowledgeable forms of commercialism may be penetrating and reshaping
our everyday lives for purposes not our own. This has worried critical
thinkers from Habermas to Daniel Bell, and I have similar fears. The second
is a concern about elitism, the increasingly closed and specialized nature of
the contemporary university, and the increasingly arcane nature of academic literary discourse. Another group of cultural critics, from Raymond
Williams or Richard Harbage to some cultural studies scholars (see Long
1997), makes the case that literature requires a broad social base of readers to
flourish. The fruitful nature of a close relationship between legitimate culture and more popular forms and audiences is perhaps best exemplified by
the rise of the novel, but surely over time democratization has enriched culture as well as society.

So I watch these new developments with cautious optimism, hoping
that their potential for encouraging openness and cultural innovation out-
strips the possibility that they will discourage critical thinking or simply
"dumb down" reading. One reason for optimism has to do with the re-
silience of face-to-face relations, even within the new matrix of mass communication. Although both Oprah's Book Club and the bookstore chains
have provided top-down structures for reading groups, reading groups
themselves seem able to take their resources and use them for goals that
spring from direct communication with other people. Similarly, on the Internet there appears to be a pull toward as much direct interaction as possible, whether real-time chats or actual travel to be in the presence of online
acquaintances. Human relationships, with their possibility for surprise and

217

invention, are not just a residual aftereffect of new communication technologies but a force unto themselves, much like the force driving people to tell their stories and listen to those narrated by others.

Under the new dispensation, the book may have lost some of the earlier manifestations of its sacred power. Yet it seems clear to me that in other respects, modern channels of communication have enabled the book to assume a newly powerful presence for some readers. This presence may be somewhat disconnected from its earlier acolytes and their vision, but books are still closely tied to moments of experiential insight and still show a stunning ability to make people, in discussion, feel part of a significant book-related community.

EIGHT

At the End

Looking back, it now seems to me that exactly those issues that earlier had troubled me about researching women's reading groups have made the topic fruitful. For example, take the disjuncture between women's feelings about the importance of reading groups in their lives and the groups' relative invisibility—or dismissability—to most men and historically male-dominated scholarship. What can this disjuncture tell us?

First, the disparities between middle-class women's lives and those of middle-class men remain more deeply felt and problematic for women than for men. Much of the time these disparities are not even recognized by men. One reason for this harks back to Simone de Beauvoir's explanation of why women have difficulty organizing as a group: that women are everywhere dispersed among men as friends, wives, lovers, daughters, and mothers (1952, xviii–xxi). Men who are united to women by family, race, religion, class, occupation, or region often feel (not without foundation) that they know us intimately, so it is difficult for them to imagine that our experiences could be so deeply divergent from theirs. I think of male colleagues who still respond with astonishment when they hear evidence of sexism or sexual harassment in the work environment they occupy alongside the women bearing witness.

Second, these disparities often occur along dimensions that both our common sense and academic categories characterize as personal or private. This is a problem both for the women experiencing them and for the scholarship that obscures them.

More than men, women may need the deliberative spaces to voice their concerns, to narrate the particularities of their lives, to expand their cultural repertoires in dialogue with narratives in books or from other women's lives, to name what delights or troubles them, to explore the dissociations between what matters to them and the social strictures or ideological frameworks that fail in important ways to address them. Nancy Fraser (1989, 167) has coined the interesting term "counterhegemonic publics" to refer to similar spaces. Reading groups may exemplify this concept, although it still seems to me that book groups may be compelling precisely because they ride the boundary between public and private life.

As for scholarship, much important work in the social sciences and humanities has begun to reframe academic categories so that they can include rather than marginalize women's experiences. Yet it is clear that this scholarship still has a long way to go to achieve the revolutionary impact that feminists of the 1970s hoped it would have. The sexual division of labor at home, bodily and reproductive politics, the structure of careers, sexual harassment as a workplace issue, "caring labor," systemic violence against women—all have begun to achieve legitimacy as areas of scholarly inquiry, but gender issues are still largely perceived as women's issues, as attendance at courses or academic panels about gender all too graphically testify.

As another instance of how this undisciplined topic proved productive, consider the fact that these are reading groups rather than purely social or political groups. More precisely, these are groups in which women collectively choose a book to read, read it by themselves, and gather together to discuss that book and their individual responses to it. These practices, difficult for scholars to categorize or even perceive until recently, can illuminate a great deal about reading in our society and about cultural reception more generally.

From the early stages of this research, it was remarkable to me how complex people's responses to books were. Women related to characters, authors, narrators, tone, language, imagery, and structure. They found significance in ill-realized characters, and sometimes they spent more time considering the silences or gaps in narratives than whatever had found its way to words on the page. For many women, identification proved a powerful tool to navigate books, but it was itself a complex intersubjective process of the kind that Booth's term "coduction" begins to capture.

Equally obvious were the great differences between these responses, one generated by reading for pleasure and the other by what I think of as schooled reading. Because book clubs choose mainly "good books," the Great Tradition enshrined in universities underwrites their activities, which in turn legitimates culture and their own place within it. Their reading choices demonstrate this most clearly, showing that even groups that contest the authoritative hierarchy of genres, subjects, and authors accept it as a stable feature of the cultural landscape. But as they discuss books, they act more like de Certeau's poachers on the fields of legitimate culture. They raid books for what they find interesting to discuss, and they are not afraid to find even the classics or critically acclaimed books sadly wanting. They are also stubbornly attached to reading as "equipment for living" and find many practices of academic literary criticism irrelevant for their project.

Scholars have generally not considered the variety and complexity of reading as a cultural practice, all too often assuming that their readings can stand for everyone else's, or that there is a homology between literary quality and worthwhile reading experiences. Both of these assumptions deserve to be unseated, especially among scholars who want to understand what reading means in the broader social world.

As I moved more deeply into the project and attended less to individual readings and more to the conversations, I realized that a major difference between these grassroots women's groups and others, such as gardening or craft groups, lay in their production of normative discussions. The central and defining practice of reading groups melds narratives from books and lives into a collective reflection on life as these women have experienced it, have desired it, and can imagine it. Much of this is what one might broadly call identity work. It is not just receptive or reflective but creative in the sense that through such discussion they are imagining and expressing new insights, new definitions both of their own situations in the world and of their own desires or judgments, and new understandings of who they can or want to become.

Cultural reception is an impoverished term for these practices. It obscures the productivity and creativity of these collective conversations by framing them in the linear narrative of information-transfer or meaning-transfer from author to audience. Perhaps there is something special about reading or reading groups that encourages this kind of cultural production among audiences, but recent scholarship that explores other cultural audiences suggests that reading groups are not alone in using culture to fashion subjectivities.[1]

If this is so, then it is important to understand the relationship between practices of reading and other uses of cultural products. This direction for research is a promising one, because we all intuitively recognize that culture matters to people, even that culture shapes people in both obvious and subtle ways. Attention to audiences and their practices, especially to collective associations born of people's interactions with culture, could balance that recognition by exploring the dialectic between being shaped by culture and in turn using culture to forge our selves as human subjects and to reinvent our individual or social actions.

The difficulty of classifying reading groups as either wholly public or private also suggests that such interstitial groups may be a very interesting site for investigating the relationship between the public and private aspects of social life. This problem has been vexing to social thinkers because it is much easier to perceive how people are socially determined when examining large-scale institutional forces, while at a smaller level of analysis the importance of people's creative agency becomes overwhelmingly clear. So size tends to become coupled with both methodology and epistemology, and sociologists debate how to integrate the macro and micro levels of social analysis in much the same way that physicists have debated whether to consider light as a particle or a wave.

Groups such as reading groups serve two useful functions in regard to this issue. First, they are evidence of the complexity of social relationships within everyday life, so they show that categories like "private" must be disassembled into their myriad constituent practices, groups, and networks in order to be adequately understood. Second, the way their members negotiate between private life and public concerns makes it clear that we need to understand the disjunctures and ties that relate public and private to each other. At the beginning of *The Making of the English Working Class,* E. P. Thompson (1972) claims that social class is not a static thing, for social classes define themselves, and thus *become* class groupings, only in relationship to each other. The same is true for public and private life, and it is in understanding how that relationship is constituted in its historical particularity that we can best grasp the nature of our social world and how it may change.[2]

In turn, this raises the issue of reification in social analysis. Whether scholars or not, people seem to find it easier to think with clearly defined categories that can then figure almost as objects to be manipulated in analysis. It is hard to imagine, in fact, how we could think without categories like child and adult, man and woman, minority and white, or public and private. But it is important to remember that these categories are also human creations, defined and given content by human practices of law, custom, and symbolism. These conceptual constructs sometimes take on a life of their own, obscuring aspects of life whose recognition is necessary for a full understanding of the social world. In particular, we need more processual thinking to bring to light the fact that lived social and cultural experience is always open-ended, always under construction. Historical and ethnographic methods are important here, for it is through grounding abstractions in human practices and their meaning for those who enact them that we can lay bare the ways that determinism and human agency interrelate in the fluidity of social creation.

The fact that society and culture themselves are human creations is particularly important to remember today, when our world is dominated by large and ever more powerful organizations, when social inequality has become a global problem of almost inconceivable extremity, and when commercial interests have unprecedented abilities to penetrate the inmost recesses of the self. The concerns and realities of women's reading groups may seem small when set against such vast canvases, but their practices demonstrate some of the ways that people use culture to find the deliberative spaces, the companions, and the resources with which to creatively remake themselves and their world, even if in circumstances not of their own making.

So, I send this book off to find its readers, knowing that they will engage with it in ways beyond its author's imagining and hoping that they will find in it something they can use in their own projects of reflective self-fashioning.

Preface

1. An example of this occurred early in the research, when I tried to explain the project to a senior colleague at Rice. I thought he would find it interesting because of its link to work on literary reception by Stanley Fish, who I knew my colleague was trying to attract to an endowed chair. My colleague listened with increasing bewilderment and finally asked a question I heard many times later: "But what do you mean by book discussion groups?" I answered, "Locally organized groups of readers who get together once a month to discuss a book they've chosen to read." "Oh," he said with an abrupt change of expression that signified both comprehension and dismissal, "my wife's in one of those." End of conversation. Or rather, immediate segue into questions about how to make Rice more attractive to Fish. It seems not unrelated that this colleague saw a recruiting effort that included a women's studies position for Jane Tompkins, Fish's wife and herself the author of several books discussing the social nature of literary value (1980, 1985, 1992), only in relation to Fish.

2. By the time I had finished, another bookstore that served over a dozen black women's reading groups had sprung up on the west side of Houston. As publishers began marketing books by authors of color, black book clubs began to grow in numbers. Oprah's Book Club may also have played a part in this phenomenon.

3. This research will probably be published in volume 5 of *The History of the Book in America*. The first volume is Amory and Hall 2000.

Chapter One

1. Interestingly enough, several reader-response theorists have moved beyond their early preoccupation with solitary readers, following a trajectory that seems, first, to problematize the formally autonomous text by considering the interaction between text and (individual) reader and then to recognize similar problems in an interactionist text/reader model that envisions such negotiations as similarly isolated and formally autonomous. Certainly, Iser, Bleich, and Holland have all begun to consider the broader social contexts and constraints that constitute textual realizations in actual reading practices. Iser calls for a "literary anthropology" that would research the needs for and functions of fiction, which he defines as something that "opens up new possibilities" for individuals and society. This endeavor he sees leading to a theory of culture that might mark a new kind of "enlightenment"—one less encyclopedic than self-reflective (1989, 262–84). Bleich, on the other hand, is drawn to a multifaceted investigation of literacy both within and beyond the academy, literacy defined less as skill than as a practice integrally bound up with "the community, the culture, and the process of language socialization" (1988, 75). Holland, remaining the most psychologically oriented of the three, has drawn on the language of feedback

loops to construct a model of how individuals respond to texts. He envisions a hierarchy of loops beginning with species-defined physiological loops, progressing to culturally shared "code-loops" and culturally disputed "canon-loops," and at the highest level involving "a unique identity interpreted as a theme and variations" (1991, 49). There is much to be said about each author's moves, but despite differences there are remarkable similarities. For example, all abandon the textual critic's concentration on literature in the interest of programs that could be called "cultural studies," and all have found the text/reader situation a model for thinking of other social processes and cultural relationships in interactionist and mutually causational terms. Interpenetration, doubledness, and multiperspectival understandings seem central to all their projects, implying that challenges to a traditional ontology of the text bring in their train new kinds of epistemology and associated methodological orientations.

2. Such images do not intentionally portray the "solitary reader"; they are portraits of individuals, saints, or writers of the Gospels, surrounded by the symbolic attributes of serious reading and writing. I am interpreting them as *representing* a certain understanding of reading, an ideology, if you will, much as the sex-differentiated pictures of boys and girls playing with toys on commercial packaging can be construed as representing a certain, unintended, construction of gender in the late twentieth century.

3. The cover of the original edition of Janice Radway's *Reading the Romance* is an ironic comment on this point, and the cover of the new edition (1991) is even more sensuously escapist.

4. Feminist literary theorists, in their considerations of women writers, have already traced many implications of the dichotomy between male and female authorship and between serious or high culture and ephemeral or questionable culture. The parallels between female readership and female authorship are striking. See Abel 1982, and note the cover of that volume for its representation of a related iconographic dichotomy.

5. The first volume, edited by Hugh Amory and David Hall (2000), is titled *The Colonial Book in the Atlantic World*. Four other volumes are forthcoming. See Lemert and Branaman 1997 (149–261) for shorter essays on frame analysis by Goffman, and see Rose 2001 (6) for an application of Goffman to culture and class.

6. For example, Fish's work (1980) on "interpretive communities," however contentious and nonsociological, demonstrates conclusively that textual interpretation among those Bourdieu calls "professional valuers" (1984, 4) is dependent on shifting conventions or paradigms within a hierarchical academic community. It has aroused opposition that seems only partially explicable by his "bad boy" cultural relativism (Bloom 1987; Hirsch 1987). Similarly, another strand of research into reading has investigated the social relationships among publishers, booksellers, popular and authoritative readers, and aestheticians that determine the fortunes of books vis-à-vis the literary canon (Davidson 1986, 1989; Eagleton 1983, 1984; Ohmann 1976, 1987; Smith 1988; Tompkins 1985). Again, the scholarly outcry that has greeted this work seems to a certain degree symptomatic of a desire to return literary debates to the realm of "pure" aesthetics, unsullied by commerce or other sociocultural interests. See Ellen Messer-Davidow 1997 for a fascinating discussion of some problems arising from the liberal academy's presupposition that scholarly life can be above politics.

7. For interesting discussions in this "medium as determinant" vein, see McLuhan 1962, McLuhan and Powers 1989, and Ong 1967 (esp. chap. 3) and 1982. Elizabeth Eisenstein's fascinating book *The Printing Press as an Agent of Change* (1979) has recently been

critiqued by Adrian Johns (1998) for its tendency to overlook the myriad social practices that themselves constituted printing and bookmaking as we have come to know them.

8. See Anthony Giddens's (1979, 1984) work for the elaboration of one overview of this tradition and an attempt to destabilize this categorical framework. Jürgen Habermas (1989), as well, has outlined a more interesting relationship between public and private spheres than the traditional dichotomy, although feminist critics take him to task for not pushing his critique far enough (Fraser 1989). And one could see almost all of Pierre Bourdieu's oeuvre as deconstructing this dichotomy, because for him cultural capital is as central to social structure as economic capital. Among his other books, see *Distinction* (1984).

9. Some of the sociologists whose names have been most closely linked to discussions of civil society and communitarianism are Robert Bellah, whose book *Habits of the Heart: Individualism and Commitment in American Life* (1996), like Putnam's later volume, attracted much comment outside the academy. The same team who joined with him to write *Habits of the Heart* (Richard Madsen, William M. Sullivan, Ann Swidler, and Steven M. Tipton) also coauthored with Bellah *The Good Society* (1991). Amitai Etzioni (1993, 2001) has also profoundly influenced the discussion, and his edited volume, *The Essential Communitarian Reader* (1998), is a good introduction to many other important scholars debating the issues of community, social trust, public space, and how civil society relates to democracy. Theda Skocpol's work (1992) has been central in this discussion. Also see the collection *Civic Engagement in American Democracy* (1999), which she edited with Morris Fiorina. Michael Schudson's *The Good Citizen: A History of American Civic Life* (1998) provides a nuanced history that calls for equally nuanced theoretical categories to frame our consideration of civic life.

10. Putnam's original article, "Bowling Alone: America's Declining Social Capital," appeared in the *Journal of Democracy* (1995). It was followed by another article, "The Strange Disappearance of Civic America" in the *American Prospect* (1996). The next issue of the *American Prospect* published a section titled "Controversy: Unsolved Mysteries: The Tocqueville Files," with commentaries on various aspects of Putnam's work by Michael Schudson (1996), Theda Skocpol (1996), and Richard M. Valelly (1996) as well as a response from Putnam.

11. Schudson's *The Good Citizen* (1998) is a useful corrective for the problem of ahistoricity, as is Skocpol's *Protecting Soldiers and Mothers* (1992).

Chapter Two

1. This process clearly brought cultural capital and social distinction, but its importance does not seem exhausted by the Bourdieuian notion of cultural usage.

2. For example, see *Les salons de Vienne et de Berlin* (L'auteur des hommes du jour 1861) and Wilhelmy's *Der Berliner Salon im 19. Jahrhundert* (1989), and for a lighthearted discussion of salons in Germany, Poland, Sweden, and Italy, see *Salons* by Valerian Tornius (1929).

3. The earliest women's reading associations appear to have been composed of young women who were relatively free of domestic duties. These associations probably dissolved, like that of Hannah Mather, who in 1778 started a Woman's Lodge with a group of her Boston friends "for the purpose of improving their minds," because of members' marriages and the ensuing birth of children. (Mather herself had ten.) The Woman's Lodge is discussed by Scott in "As Easily as They Breathe . . ." (1984, quotation at 262). In a small notebook at Radcliffe's Schlesinger Library, I found records of a group that met in

Charlestown, Massachusetts, between 1813 and 1816, which looks to be a similar sort of group. Exactly what went on in their meetings is impossible to discern, for except for a list of attendees, the only records extant are lengthy extracts of the books under discussion. Those books, however, are notable for their quality. They include *The Iliad,* works of history, and issues of the English literary magazine *The Spectator.* The notes do not include any exemplars of that young and suspect genre, the novel. On the other hand, the group did not aspire to classical learning, at that time the badge of serious scholarship. The books they read were all in the vernacular. Karen Blair, one of the analysts of the later-nineteenth-century literary club movement, mentions a group of women meeting in 1800 in Chelsea, Connecticut, who in addition to their charity and temperance work, founded a literary society "to enlighten the understanding and expand the ideas of its members, and to promote useful knowledge" by reading such works as *History of Columbus,* Watts's *Treatise of the Mind,* and Trumbull's *History of Connecticut"* (1980, 12; Wood 1912, 350–52; Winslow 1908, 556). This may have been a slightly older group, because married women often undertook benevolent activities, but again it is difficult to ascertain this from the historical record. Dorothy B. Porter (1936) describes free African American women's literary associations in her pathbreaking article "The Organized Educational Activities of Negro Literary Societies, 1828–1846." She mentions eight women's literary groups and one Ohio women's education society. It should be noted that in 1830 there were less than 320,000 free blacks in the United States (Porter 1936, 555, citing U.S. Bureau of the Census) and that other literary groups may have existed among that population but escaped historical notice.

    4. It was not the first. The Brontë Club of Victoria, Texas, had begun as a schoolgirls' literary club in 1855 and developed into an adult woman's club by 1885; historian John Boles (personal communication) also knows of a woman's poetry club meeting somewhere in the Texas hill country, among German immigrants, by the 1830s. But certainly the Ladies Reading Club was the flagship club for the late-century literary movement, and its programs, mailed out upon request, served as an inspiration for other clubs across the state.

    5. General Gordon served in the Crimea, put down the Taiping Rebellion in China, and was governor of the Sudan (then a province of Upper Egypt) from 1877 to 1880. He was called back in 1884 to relieve the garrison at Khartoum, because Sudan had been overrun by militant Muslim rebels. He occupied the city and helped refugees escape, but the rebels then besieged Khartoum. Gladstone's government delayed sending reinforcements, and in January 1885 after a ten-month siege, the city was overrun and Gordon was killed. Two days later, the reinforcements finally arrived (www.bartleby.com/189/401c.html; www.fordham.edu/halsall/islam/1885khartoum1.html; www.biography.com).

    6. Martin (1987, 40) points out that only about seven in one thousand young women achieved the equivalent of a high school education in even the least rigorous academies and seminaries. On the question of educational substance, schools such as Emma Willard's in Troy, New York, Catharine Beecher's in Hartford, Connecticut, and Mary Lyon's Mount Holyoke in Holyoke, Massachusetts, were, as Martin says, "notable exceptions" to the prevailing dismal standards.

    7. Oberlin College had opened its doors to women in 1837, but by 1857 only 20 women had entered the Collegiate Department, while 299 took the "ladies course" instead. Mary Sharp College in Tennessee (1851) may have been the first true college for women (Martin 1987, 42–43). Theda Skocpol (1992, 341–42) points out that American women were well educated by comparison with women in Britain and France; in partic-

ular, they were more likely to attend institutions of higher learning. It is nonetheless true that many were keenly aware of the disparity between their own opportunities for education and those of similarly situated men.

8. Martin 1987, 46, citing Croly 1898, 452.

9. Blair 1980, 13; Martin 1987, 16. "The Sanitary," as it was called, was a nationwide ladies' aid society created in 1861 with the approval of President Lincoln to provide for the benefit and comfort of the common volunteer soldier in the United States Army. A forerunner of the Red Cross, it contributed money, personnel, and material to the Army Medical Corps and established and staffed relief stations and hospitals for soldiers.

10. Wood, it should be noted, was a stalwart leader of the club movement, and her statements in other publications, especially those addressed to the movement, had a more militant tone.

11. Martin 1987, 65. Newly founded clubs often imported organizational forms from sister clubs. Julia Ward Howe's "How Can Women Best Associate," delivered at many venues across the country, also provided organizational guidelines.

12. Catherine Beecher (1800–1878) was an early proponent of women's education. She founded a female academy and wrote extensively on "home economics," which she felt should be at the center of women's education because she believed that wifehood and motherhood should be the profession for all women.

13. Houston's Ladies Reading Club also established an early national reputation as a particularly serious club.

14. Seaholm 1988, 236–37. Blair (1980) also notes that many of the discussions centered on people, speculating that it was through people, both authors and characters, that women most easily made sense out of the world. This, too, is characteristic of twentieth-century groups; it may be particularly true for women but may also signify something about human processes of meaning-making in general. Work with storytelling among Native Americans indicates that men as well as women find reflection about characters extremely useful for sorting out life choices and moral issues.

15. Seaholm 1988, 225. The Pierians took their name from Alexander Pope's famous lines: "A little learning is a dangerous thing; Drink deep or taste not the Pierian spring." The Pierian spring, located in Greece, was sacred to the Muses. Pope's lines were referred to by many of the Romantic poets, such as Keats and Shelley (Pope 1711, 215–16).

16. Blair 1980, 108–12. Josephine Ruffin, member of the New England Woman's Press Club and founder, in 1894, of the African American New Era Club, brought the race question to a head when she planned to attend the 1900 General Federation of Women's Clubs (GFWC) Biennial as a representative of both clubs and of the Massachusetts Federation. By 1902, the GFWC enacted a compromise at the Los Angeles Biennial meeting that to all intents and purposes excluded "colored clubs" from membership. For a discussion of the National Association of Colored Women and its similarities and differences from the General Federation of Women's Clubs, see Giddings 1984 (93–95).

17. Blair 1980, 39–44. In 1873, Croly's successor as president of Sorosis founded the Association for the Advancement of Women, envisioned as an elite body to educate women on issues of domestic feminism. It held enthusiastically attended annual congresses in a different city each year, where plans for possible reform initiatives were aired and topics such as "Enlightened Motherhood" or "Scholarships for Women" were explored. It was superseded by the GFWC and came to an end in 1897.

18. Seaholm claims that the Women's Christian Temperance Union was the only national women's organization in Texas before the GFWC. It began in 1873, and the National Woman's Suffrage Association appeared in 1869.

19. It should also be noted that although Texas culture clubs did not successfully organize across the state until 1897, with the help of the national federation, they had initiated three grassroots attempts to move to statewide organization. In 1894, a woman's congress gathered at the Dallas State Fair. In 1895, the Wednesday Club of Forth Worth polled other clubs about a state organization. In 1896, the Pierian Club of Dallas convened a Congress of Women's Clubs involving several north Texas clubs. None of these efforts bore lasting fruit. Statewide organization apparently needed the support of a national effort (Christian 1919, 6; Seaholm 1988, 339). After its inception, the Federation of Women's Clubs also drew on nonliterary constituencies, for example, the popular Mothers' Clubs, which are often referred to as the progenitors of modern PTOs or PTAs and which were especially interested in early childhood education and novel ideas about teaching "the whole child" or "learning by doing."

20. At its foundation, in 1897 in Waco, the Texas organization was called the Texas Federation of Literary Clubs. By 1899, members had embarked on so many reformist projects that they decided to excise "Literary" from the organization's name (Seaholm 1988, 344).

21. Conservation also appealed to Texas clubwomen for some of the same reasons. They helped the General Federation of Women's Clubs in initiatives such as boycotting hats trimmed with bird feathers and took up the fight to make Palo Duro Canyon part of the national parks system, achieving limited success when it became a state park.

22. Such voluntary social research, which often included door-to-door surveys and some statistics, was an important recruiting ground for early academic sociology.

23. Seaholm 1988, 474. This amendment also established the poll tax.

24. Before the Civil War, men of many vocations—from bookkeepers, carpenters, and druggists to mechanists, merchants, surveyors, and tinners—had participated. After 1865 its membership was largely composed of professionals: lawyers, doctors, ministers, newspapermen, and teachers. The literary clubwomen of the city were, in the main, married to men of this class, and their use of and influence over the Houston Lyceum appears to have increased with the change in its membership.

Chapter Three

1. This shift was most dramatic for middle-class women, because poorer women had often worked from necessity even at the height of the nineteenth century's cult of domesticity.

2. Statistics for percentage of labor force by gender comes from the Bureau of Statistics' *Current Population Survey* (U.S. Department of Labor 2001) annual averages.

3. Several things should probably be said here. First, the "traditional family division of labor" is itself a product of the industrial revolution, so to say that the world of paid employment is structurally "male" refers to a historical construction, not to an essence of transhistorical maleness. That is to say, even within our country's history, there have been ways of dividing work between men and women that didn't give all family responsibilities except wage earning to women and all financial burdens to men. Also, it is obvious that this arrangement gears men into the world that hurts them—by depriving them of non-wage-earning duties/opportunities within the family. It is also clear that some changes are hap-

pening in the world of paid employment: high-tech flexibility of the home/job division, flextime, job sharing, and parental leaves. But these appear to have limits, and one can certainly make the case for resistance within the world of wage labor to the flexibility that women and many men would like to see.

4. In writing this chapter, I consulted many more historical sources than I have cited. Some (Degler 1980; Evans 1989; Kerber, Kessler-Harris, and Sklar 1995; Newton, Ryan, and Walkowitz 1983; Rosenberg 1992) were relatively general histories of women. Others (Douglas 1994; Meyerowitz 1994; Solinger 1992; Stansell 2000) were more specialized social and cultural histories. A relatively large number concerned feminism and women's participation in public affairs (Cott 1987; Echols 1989; Evans 1979; Melich 1996; Rupp and Taylor 1987; Ryan 1990; Ware 1993). I consulted both historical and sociological works on marriage and the family (Cott 2000; Ehrenreich 1983; Hays 1996; May 1999; Zelizer 1985) and books on work-related issues by economists, historians, and sociologists (England and Farkas 1986; Goldin 1990; Kessler-Harris 1982; Wiener 1985). Thanks to Allison Sneider for help with the historical sources.

5. This is a very brief discussion of a complex set of issues. For further discussion, see Richard Ohmann's *English in America* (1976) and *Politics of Letters* (1987), Gerald Graff's *Professing Literature* (1987), Graff and Gibbons's edited volume *Criticism in the University* (1985), and Terry Eagleton's *The Function of Criticism* (1984).

Chapter Four

1. See Klineberg's (1996, 1–4) discussion of this issue. I mention this despite the fact that I do not pretend to a traditionally scientific notion of representativeness. Houston has always seemed to me very much a new Sunbelt city.

2. On the survey, incomes were divided into eight categories, each representing a range. In 2000 dollars, the amounts were $21,001–$42,000, $42,001–$61,000, $61,001–$83,000, $83,001–$104,000, $104,001–$139,000, $139,001–$174,000, $174,001–$208,000, and $208,000 and over.

3. This survey raises methodological issues that need discussion. I attempted to hand out the survey to ten women's reading groups, selected randomly during the outreach process that eventually yielded a population of seventy-seven women's reading groups in Harris County. Of those ten groups, four refused to complete the survey. This represents a 60 percent response rate. The total number of surveys completed is, however, very small because I encountered several problems beyond simple refusals. Two of the four refusals came from groups that had professed willingness but wanted to do the survey at the end of meetings; they then somehow ran out of time and failed to do it. All of the six groups that did complete the survey clearly did not enjoy taking time from their meetings to do so. Two consented to fill in only the short-answer part of the survey during the meeting and said they would take the open-ended questionnaire home. Then only a small number of women sent back the self-addressed and stamped envelopes to me. Eventually, I judged that attempting to distribute the questionnaires was significantly interfering with the primary research method of the book: participant observation of reading groups and interviews with members. I then decided not to continue to administer the questionnaires. Obviously, this is not an ideal way to undertake survey research, which would involve taking a larger random sample from all seventy-seven groups, I am including the information gathered, however, because although I cannot be completely confident of its representativeness, it still gives us important information about these groups. In many

ways, the six groups represent the range of reading groups in the broader population I studied, with the exception of one group, all of whose members except one were Jewish. Predominantly Jewish groups did not constitute 17 percent of the larger population. But even this group resembled other groups in every respect except religious composition. So, realizing the problems with these data, I nonetheless include them to provide a somewhat different perspective on Houston's reading groups than does my qualitative research.

4. There are younger groups. Mother-daughter groups have been popular since the nineteenth century, I have heard of both girls' and boys' book groups, and there are the institutionally more formalized Junior Great Books discussion groups, often organized at schools by parents and teachers.

5. This interview and other interviews by DeNel Sedo, assistant professor at Mount St.Vincent University, are part of her research project on reading groups, "Badges of Wisdom, Spaces for Being: A Social History of Women's Reading Groups" (2002). She has generously granted me permission to use them in this volume.

6. Far fewer (twelve) indicated that their "reading skills have improved," and just two said they "feel more ignorant than before."

7. This separation was arguably less clear in the late nineteenth century.

Chapter Five

1. I use the term *classic* here, as do reading group members, to mean a work of lasting significance or recognized worth rather than a work from the ancient Greek or Roman era.

2. In this sense, literary booksellers serve as opinion leaders (Lazarsfeld, Berelson, and Gandet 1948; Berelson and Janowitz 1984) who are in touch with the wider world of literary judgment and can also interpret it to the local audience.

3. See Janice Radway's *A Feeling for Books* (1997) for a discussion of middlebrow culture as a historical formation. She also shows that the articulation of middlebrow as a category was the accomplishment of segments of the intellectual elite. Her account theorizes variability in reading practices and is particularly sensitive to reading for pleasure.

4. In a sense, a reading group's reading boundaries and emotional tone reveal something similar to Gary Alan Fine's concept of the "idiolect," or special language and culture that small groups develop, which define them as different from otherwise similar groups (Fine 1987).

Chapter Six

1. The conceptual model underlying this assumption came from Stanley Fish's work (1980) on the variability of textual meaning and "interpretive communities." Fish is one of several twentieth-century reception theorists who have, in a sense, extended the arguments that began in the nineteenth-century hermeneutic discussions of the Bible. Those biblical scholars, to put it briefly, argued that to understand the meaning of the Bible fully and accurately, one must take into account the historical and cultural contexts in which it was written. In other words, biblical translation was a complex—and in their terms "circular"—process of determining what words, expressions, and texts meant in the time and place of their transcription, and the "word of God" could only be accurately understood under two conditions. First, the difficult historical task of investigating the Bible's textual or linguistic meaning for those people writing down the Word then had to be accomplished. Second, the hermeneutic scholar had to bring that distant meaning back

and try to determine how to relate it to our present, and quite different, cultural lexicon. Twentieth-century reception theorists—and especially Fish—have pushed this cultural relativism even further by contending that textual meanings are always constituted by their readers, for texts do not "mean" except insofar as they are read. Fish further makes the case that readers' cultural horizons, historical frames, and even personal experiences are so variable that even if the "same" text is highly valued by readers over long periods of time (i.e., is a stable part of the literary canon), readers are really experiencing very different texts. He supports his contentions by examining changes in the interpretations of canonized literary works among "interpretive communities" of literary scholars over time. For him, the interpretive community takes on the authority previously accorded to the literary text. As a sociologist, I became fascinated by how Fish's ideas might fare if one extended his investigations of literary scholars into the broader social world of ordinary readers.

2. This discussion relies on Linda Griffin's dissertation "An Analysis of Meaning Creation through the Integration of Sociology and Literature: A Critical Ethnography of a Romance Reading Group" (1999) as well as my own observations. She conducted a year of fieldwork with one suburban Houston romance group, becoming a participating "member" over the course of that year. She also interviewed all of the members in small group settings and six members individually. I sat in on one of this group's meetings and also attended several meetings of an in-town group. Griffin also attended those meetings. She has given me permission to draw extensively on her work.

3. Often they also wrote their own initials in the books they borrowed, so they could keep track of what they had read.

Chapter Seven

1. For an overview of the origins of this debate in concerns about the massification of culture, see Long 1986.

2. Thanks to Helena Michie for her generosity and interpretive skill.

3. All group names have been changed unless moderators gave permission to use actual names.

Chapter Eight

1. See Press 1991 for an early discussion of women and television. Also see my collection (Long 1997) for work by both sociologists and cultural studies scholars from other disciplines. Grossberg, Nelson, and Treichler's *Cultural Studies* (1992) is a massive interdisciplinary compilation. See my own essay "Feminism and Cultural Studies: Britain and America" (1989) for a smaller review of cultural studies scholarship on women.

2. Feminist scholars have made this point about public and private life, both as categories and empirically, more recently and with special reference to gender. See Fraser 1989 (120–30) and Fraser and Gordon 1997, as well as some of the excellent collections of essays on gender and political theory; for example, see Joan Landes's *Feminism, the Public and the Private* (1998).

BIBLIOGRAPHY

Abel, Elizabeth, ed. 1982. *Writing and Sexual Difference.* Chicago: University of Chicago Press.

Abt,Vicki, and Leonard Mustazza. 1997. *Coming after Oprah: Cultural Fallout in the Age of the TV Talk Show.* Bowling Green, Ohio: Bowling Green State University Popular Press.

Amory, Hugh, and David D. Hall, eds. 2000. *The Colonial Book in the Atlantic World.* Cambridge and New York: Cambridge University Press.

Anderson, Benedict. 1991. *Imagined Communities: Reflections on the Origin and Spread of Nationalism.* 2d ed. London and New York:Verso.

Ariès, Philippe. 1962. *Centuries of Childhood: A Social History of Family Life.* Trans. Robert Baldock. New York: Knopf.

Armstrong, Nancy. 1987. *Desire and Domestic Fiction: A Political History of the Novel.* New York and Oxford: Oxford University Press.

Armstrong, Nancy, and Leonard Tennenhouse. 1992. *The Imaginary Puritan: Literature, Intellectual Labor, and the Origins of Personal Life.* Berkeley: University of California Press.

L'auteur des hommes du jour. 1861. *Les salons de Vienne et de Berlin.* Paris: Michel Levy Freres.

Axson Club 1917–1918 Yearbook. 1918. Houston Metropolitan Archives. Houston Public Library.

Bahr, Howard. 1980. "Changes in Family Life in Middletown, 1924–77." *Public Opinion Quarterly* 44, no. 1 (spring): 35–52.

Barthes, Roland. 1975. *The Pleasure of the Text.* Trans. Richard Miller. New York: Hill and Wang.

Beauvoir, Simone de. 1952. *The Second Sex.* Trans. and ed. H. M. Parshley. New York: Knopf.

Bellah, Robert N. 1991. *Beyond Belief: Essays on Religion in a Post-Industrial World.* Berkeley: University of California Press.

Bellah, Robert Neelly, Richard Madsen, William M. Sullivan, Ann Swidler, and Steven M. Tipton. 1985. *Habits of the Heart: Individualism and Commitment in American Life.* New York: Harper and Row.

———. 1991. *The Good Society.* New York: Knopf.

Berelson, Bernard, and L. Asheim. 1949. *The Library's Public: A Report of the Public Library Inquiry.* New York: Columbia University Press.

Berelson, Bernard, and Morris Janowitz, eds. 1984. *Reader in Public Opinion and Communication.* 2d ed. New York: Free Press.

Bernstein, Basil. 1971. *Class, Codes and Control.* London: Routledge and Kegan Paul.

Blair, Karen J. 1980. *The Clubwoman as Feminist: True Womanhood Redefined, 1868–1914.* New York: Holmes and Meier Publishers.

Bleich, David. 1975. *Readings and Feelings: An Introduction to Subjective Criticism.* Urbana, Ill.: National Council of Teachers of English.

_____. 1978. *Subjective Criticism.* Baltimore: Johns Hopkins University Press.

_____. 1988. *The Double Perspective: Language, Literacy, and Social Relations.* New York: Oxford University Press.

Bloom, Allan David. 1987. *The Closing of the America Mind: How Higher Education Has Failed Democracy and Impoverished the Souls of Today's Students.* New York: Simon and Schuster.

Booth, Wayne C. 1988. *The Company We Keep: An Ethics of Fiction.* Berkeley: University of California Press.

Bourdieu, Pierre. 1979. *The Inheritors: French Students and Their Relation to Culture.* Trans. Richard Nice. Chicago: University of Chicago Press.

_____. 1984. *Distinction: A Social Critique of the Judgment of Taste.* Trans. Richard Nice. Cambridge: Harvard University Press.

_____. 1988. *Homo Academicus.* Trans. Peter Collier. Cambridge, U.K.: Polity Press in Association with Basil Blackwell.

_____. 1990a. *The Love of Art: European Art Museums and Their Public.* Trans. Caroline Beattie and Nick Merriman. Stanford, Calif.: Stanford University Press.

_____. 1990b. *Photography: A Middle-Brow Art.* Cambridge, U.K.: Polity Press.

_____. 1991. *Language and Symbolic Power.* Ed. John B. Thompson and trans. Gino Raymond and Matthew Adamson. Cambridge, U.K.: Polity Press.

_____. 1993. *The Field of Cultural Production: Essays on Art and Literature.* Ed. Randal Johnson. New York: Columbia University Press.

_____. 1996a. *The Rules of Art: Genesis and Structure of the Literary Field.* Trans. Susan Emanuel. Cambridge, U.K.: Polity Press.

_____. 1996b. *The State Nobility: Elite Schools in the Field of Power.* Trans. Lauretta C. Clough. Cambridge, U.K.: Polity Press.

_____. 1999. *The Weight of the World: Social Suffering in Contemporary Society.* Trans. Pricilla Parkhurst Ferguson. Stanford, Calif.: Stanford University Press.

Bourdieu, Pierre, and Jean-Claude Passeron. 1977. *Reproduction in Education, Society, and Culture.* Trans. Richard Nice. London and Beverly Hills, Calif.: Sage Publications.

Bourdieu, Pierre, Jean-Claude Passeron, and Monique de Saint Martin. 1994. *Academic Discourse. Linguistic Misunderstanding and Professional Power.* Trans. Richard Teese. Stanford, Calif.: Stanford University Press.

Brodkey. Linda. 1987. *Academic Writing as Social Practice.* Philadelphia: Temple University Press.

Burke, Kenneth. 1957. *The Philosophy of Literary Form: Studies in Symbolic Action.* Rev. ed. abridged by the author. New York: Vintage Books.

Butler, Judith P. 1990. *Gender Trouble: Feminism and the Subversion of Identity.* New York: Routledge.

Caplow, Theodore, and Bruce Chadwick. 1979. "Inequality and Life-Style in Middletown, 1920–1978." *Social Science Quarterly* 60, no. 3 (December): 367–86.

Certeau, Michel de. 1984. *The Practice of Everyday Life.* Trans. Steven F. Rendeall. Berkeley, Los Angeles, and London: University of California Press.

Chodorow, Nancy. 1972. "Being and Doing: A Cross-Cultural Examination of the Socialization of Males and Females." In *Woman in Sexist Society: Studies in Power and Powerlessness,* ed. Vivian Gornick and Barbara K. Moran, 259–91. New York American Library.

_____. 1978. *The Reproduction of Mothering: Psychoanalysis and the Sociology of Gender.* Berkeley: University of California Press.

Christian, Stella L., ed. 1919. *The History of the Texas Federation of Women's Clubs.* Houston: Dealy-Adey-Elgin Co., Stationers and Printers.

Cohen, Jean L., and Andrew Arato. 1992. *Civil Society and Political Theory.* Cambridge: MIT Press.

Coles, Robert. 1977. *Privileged Ones: The Well-Off and the Rich in America.* Boston: Little, Brown.

Connell, R. W. 1995. *Masculinities: Knowledge, Power, and Social Change.* Cambridge, U.K.: Polity Press.

Cott, Nancy. 1987. *The Grounding of Modern Feminism.* New Haven: Yale University Press.

_____. 2000. *Public Vows: A History of Marriage and the Nation.* Cambridge: Harvard University Press.

Cowan, Ruth Schwartz. 1983. *More Work for Mother: The Ironies of Household Technology from the Open Hearth to the Microwave.* New York: Basic Books.

Croly, J. C. 1898. *The History of the Women's Club Movement in America.* New York: H. G. Allen and Co.

Cruikshank, Julie. 1990. *Life Lived Like a Story: Life Stories of Three Yukon Native Elders.* Lincoln: University of Nebraska Press.

Csikszentmihalyi, Mihaly. 1981. *The Meaning of Things: Domestic Symbols and the Self.* Cambridge: Cambridge University Press.

Cunningham, Mary S. 1978. *The Woman's Club of El Paso.* El Paso: Texas Western Press.

Darnton, Robert. 1974. "Trade in the Taboo: The Life of a Clandestine Book Dealer in Revolutionary France." In *The Widening Circle: Essays on the Circulation of Literature in Eighteenth-Century Europe,* ed. Paul J. Korshin. Philadelphia: University of Pennsylvania Press.

_____. 1979. *The Business of Enlightenment: A Publishing History of the Encyclopédie.* Cambridge: Harvard University Press.

_____. 1982. *The Literary Underground of the Old Regime.* Cambridge: Harvard University Press.

_____. 1984. *The Great Cat Massacre and Other Episodes in French Cultural History.* New York: Basic Books.

Davidson, Cathy N. 1986. *Revolution and the Word: The Rise of the Novel in America.* New York: Oxford University Press.

_____. 1989. *Reading in America: Literature and Social History.* Baltimore: Johns Hopkins University Press.

Davis, Natalie Zemon. 1975. "Printing and the People." In *Society and Culture in Early Modern France: Eight Essays,* 189–226. Stanford, Calif.: Stanford University Press.

Degler, Carl. 1980. *At Odds: Women and the Family from the Revolution to the Present.* New York: Oxford University Press.

DiMaggio, Paul. 1982a. "Cultural Entrepreneurship in Nineteenth-Century Boston, Part I: The Creation of an Organizational Base for High Culture in America." *Media, Culture and Society* (U.K.) 4, no. 1 (winter): 33–50.

_____. 1982b. "Cultural Entrepreneurship in Nineteenth-Century Boston, Part II: The Classification and Framing of American Art." *Media, Culture and Society* (U.K.) 4, no. 4 (autumn): 303–22.

Douglas, Susan. 1994. *Where the Girls Are: Growing Up Female with the Mass Media.* New York: Times Books.

Eagleton, Terry. 1983. *Literary Theory: An Introduction.* Minneapolis: University of Minnesota Press.

———. 1984. *The Function of Criticism. From the Spectator to Post-Structuralism.* London: Verso.

Echols, Alice. 1989. *Daring to Be Bad: Radical Feminism in America, 1967–1975.* Minneapolis: University of Minnesota Press.

Ehrenreich, Barbara. 1983. *The Hearts of Men: American Dreams and the Flight from Commitment.* Garden City, N.Y.: Anchor Press.

Eisenstein, Elizabeth L. 1979. *The Printing Press as an Agent of Change: Communications and Cultural Transformation in Early Modern Europe.* Cambridge and New York: Cambridge University Press.

———. 1983. *The Printing Revolution in Early Modern Europe.* Cambridge: Cambridge University Press.

England, Paula, and George Farkas. 1986. *Households, Employment and Gender: A Social, Economic and Demographic View.* New York: Aldine Publishers.

Ennis, P. H. 1965. *Adult Book Reading in the United States: A Preliminary Report.* National Opinion Research Center Report No. 105. Chicago: National Opinion Research Center.

Etzioni, Amitai. 1993. *The Spirit of Community: Rights, Responsibilities, and the Communitarian Agenda.* New York: Crown Publishers.

———. 2001. *Next: The Road to the Good Society.* New York: Basic Books.

———, ed. 1998. *The Essential Communitarian Reader.* Lanham, Md.: Rowman and Littlefield.

Evans, Sara. 1979. *Personal Politics: The Roots of Women's Liberation in the Civil Rights Movement and the New Left.* New York: Knopf.

———. 1989. *Born for Liberty: A History of Women in America.* New York: Free Press.

Fetterley, Judith. 1978. *The Resisting Reader: A Feminist Approach to American Fiction.* Bloomington: Indiana University Press.

Fine, Gary Alan. 1987. *With the Boys: Little League Baseball and Preadolescent Culture.* Chicago: University of Chicago Press.

Fish, Stanley. 1980. *Is There a Text in This Class? The Authority of Interpretive Communities.* Cambridge: Harvard University Press.

Forbes, E. W., ed. 1991. *E. W. Forbes Directory: Greater Houston Texas and Gulf Coast Edition.* Houston: E. W. Forbes.

Frank, Henriette G., and Amalie H. Jerome. 1916. *Annals of the Chicago Woman's Club.* Chicago: Chicago Woman's Club.

Fraser, Nancy. 1989. *Unruly Practices: Power, Discourse and Gender in Contemporary Social Theory.* Minneapolis: University of Minnesota Press.

Fraser, Nancy, and Linda Gordon. 1997. "A Genealogy of 'Dependency': Tracing a Keyword of the U.S. Welfare State." In *Justice Interruptus: Critical Reflections on the "Post-Socialist" Condition,* ed. Nancy Fraser. New York and London: Routledge. First published in *Signs* 19, no. 2 (1994): 309–36.

Freud, Sigmund. 1900. *The Interpretation of Dreams.* New York: Macmillan.

Friedan, Betty. 1974 [1963]. *The Feminine Mystique.* New York: Dell.

Gans, Herbert J. 1975. *Popular Culture and High Culture: An Analysis and Evaluation of Taste.* New York: Basic Books.

Gere, Anne Ruggles. 1997. *Intimate Practices: Literacy and Cultural Work in U.S. Women's Clubs, 1880–1920*. Urbana: University of Illinois Press.

Gere, Anne Ruggles, and Sarah Robbins. 1996. "Gendered Literacy in Black and White: Turn-of-the-Century African-American and European-American Club Women's Printed Texts." *Signs* 21, no. 3 (spring): 643–78.

Giddings, Paula. 1984. *When and Where I Enter: The Impact of Black Women on Race and Sex in America*. New York: William Morrow and Company.

Gilligan, Carol. 1982. *In a Different Voice: A Psychological Theory and Women's Development*. Cambridge: Harvard University Press.

Goffman, Erving. 1959. *The Presentation of Self in Everyday Life*. Woodstock, N.Y.: Overlook Press.

————. 1974. *Frame Analysis: An Essay on the Organization of Experience*. Cambridge: Harvard University Press.

Goldin, Claudia. 1990. *Understanding the Gender Gap: An Economic History of American Women*. New York: Oxford University Press.

Graff, Gerald. 1987. *Professing Literature: An Institutional History*. Chicago: University of Chicago Press.

Graff, Gerald, and Reginald Gibbons, eds. 1985. *Criticism in the University*. Evanston, Ill.: Northwestern University Press.

Granger, Mrs. A. O. 1906. "The Effect of Club Work in the South." *Annals of the American Academy of Political and Social Sciences* 28, no. 2: 245–57.

Griffin, Linda. 1999. "An Analysis of Meaning Creation through the Integration of Sociology and Literature: A Critical Ethnography of a Romance Reading Group." Ph.D. dissertation, University of Houston.

Griswold, Wendy. 1994. *Cultures and Societies in a Changing World*. Thousand Oaks, Calif.: Pine George Press.

Grossberg, Lawrence, Cary Nelson, and Paula Treichler. 1992. *Cultural Studies*. New York and London: Routledge.

Habermas, Jürgen. 1979. *Communication and the Evolution of Society*. Trans. Thomas McCarthy. Boston: Beacon Press.

————. 1987. *The Theory of Communicative Action*. Vol. 2. Trans. Thomas McCarthy. Boston: Beacon Press.

————. 1989. *The Structural Transformation of the Public Sphere: An Inquiry into a Category of Bourgeois Society*. Trans. Thomas Burger with the assistance of Frederick Lawrence. Cambridge: MIT Press.

Hatch, Orin Walker. 1963. "The Development of the Houston Lyceum and the Houston Public Library." Master's thesis, University of Houston.

————. 1965. *Lyceum to Library: A Chapter in the Cultural History of Houston*. Publication series 9, no. 1. Houston: Texas Gulf Coast Historical Association.

Hays, Sharon. 1996. *The Cultural Contradictions of Motherhood*. New Haven: Yale University Press.

Heilbrun, Carolyn G. 1988. *Writing a Woman's Life*. New York: W. W. Norton.

Henley, Nancy. 1973. "The Politics of Touch." In *Radical Psychology*, ed. P. Brown, 421–33. New York: Harper.

Hirsch, Eric Donald, Jr. 1987. *Cultural Literacy: What Every American Needs to Know*. Boston: Houghton Mifflin.

Hobsbawm, Eric, and Terence Ranger, eds. 1983. *The Invention of Tradition.* Cambridge: Cambridge University Press.

Holland, Norman Norwood. 1968. *The Dynamics of Literary Response.* New York: Oxford University Press.

———. 1975. *5 Readers Reading.* New Haven: Yale University Press.

———. 1991. *The Critical I.* New York: Columbia University Press.

Hochschild, Arlie. 1989. *The Second Shift: Working Parents and the Revolution at Home.* New York: Viking.

Houston City Directory. 1895–96. Galveston: Morrison and Fourmy.

Houston 1000 Directory, 1990–1991. 1991. Houston: Corporate Directories of America.

Howe, Julia Ward. 1874. "How Can Women Best Associate?" In *Papers and Letters Presented at the First Woman's Congress of the Association for the Advancement of Woman, 1873.* New York: Association for the Advancement of Woman.

Howie, Linsey M. 1998. "Speaking Subjects: A Reading of Women's Book Groups." Ph.D. dissertation, La Trobe University, Bundoora, Australia.

Ingarden, Roman. 1973. *The Literary Work of Art: An Investigation on the Borderlines of Ontology, Logic, and Theory of Literature. With an Appendix on the Functions of Language in Theater.* Trans. George G. Grabowicz. Evanston, Ill.: Northwestern University Press.

Iser, Wolfgang. 1978. *The Act of Reading: A Theory of Aesthetic Response.* Baltimore: Johns Hopkins University Press.

———. 1989. *Prospecting: From Reader Response to Literary Anthropology.* Baltimore: Johns Hopkins University Press.

———. 1993. *The Fictive and the Imaginary: Charting Literary Anthropology.* Baltimore: Johns Hopkins University Press.

Jacobsohn, Rachel. 1994. *The Reading Group Handbook: Everything You Need to Know, from Choosing Members to Leading Discussion.* New York: Hyperion.

Johns, Adrian. 1998. *The Nature of the Book: Print and Knowledge in the Making.* Chicago: University of Chicago Press.

Kerber, Linda, Alice Kessler-Harris, and Kathryn Kish Sklar, eds. 1995. *U.S. History as Women's History: New Feminist Essays.* Chapel Hill: University of North Carolina Press.

Kessler-Harris, Alice. 1982. *Out to Work: A History of Wage-Earning Women in the United States.* New York: Oxford University Press.

Klineberg, Stephen L. 1996. *Houston's Ethnic Communities, Third Edition: Updated and Expanded to Include the First-Ever Survey of the Asian Communities.* Houston: Rice University Publications.

Kondo, Dorinne. 1990. *Crafting Selves: Gender, Power, and Discourses of Identity in a Japanese Workplace.* Chicago: University of Chicago Press.

Ladies Reading Club. 1888. Meeting minutes for 7 February and 6 March. Ladies Reading Club Collection, box 1, folder 1. Houston Metropolitan Archives. Houston Public Library.

Lakoff, Robin Tolmach. 1975. *Language and Woman's Place.* New York: Harper and Row.

Lamont, Michèle. 1992. *Money, Morals, and Manners: The Culture of the French and American Upper Middle Class.* Chicago: University of Chicago Press.

Landes, Joan B., ed. 1998. *Feminism, the Public and the Private.* Oxford and New York: Oxford University Press.

Lasch, Christopher. 1977. *Haven in a Heartless World: The Family Besieged.* New York: Basic Books.

_____. 1978. *The Culture of Narcissism: American Life in an Age of Diminishing Expectations.* New York: W. W. Norton.

Lazarsfeld, Paul, Bernard Berelson, and Hazel Gandet. 1948. *The People's Choice: How the Voter Makes up His Mind in a Presidential Election.* New York: Columbia University Press.

Lazich, Robert S. 2000. *Market Share Reporter.* Detroit: Gale Research.

LeGuin, Ursula. 1975. *The Wind's Twelve Quarters.* New York: Bantam.

Lemert, Charles, and Ann Branaman, eds. 1997. *The Goffman Reader.* Malden, Mass., and Oxford: Blackwell.

Levine, Lawrence W. 1988. *Highbrow/Lowbrow: The Emergence of Cultural Hierarchy in America.* Cambridge: Harvard University Press.

Long, Elizabeth. 1986. "Women, Reading, and Cultural Authority: Some Implications of the Audience Perspective in Cultural Studies." *American Quarterly* 38, no. 4 (fall): 591–611.

_____. 1988. "Reading at the Grassroots: Local Book Discussion Groups, Social Interaction, and Cultural Change." Manuscript. Rice University.

_____. 1989. "Feminism and Cultural Studies: Britain and America." *Critical Studies in Mass Communication* 6, no. 4 (December): 427–35.

_____, ed. 1997. *From Sociology to Cultural Studies: New Perspectives.* Malden, Mass., and Oxford: Blackwell Publishers.

Looscan, Adele Briscoe. 1890. "Annual Report for the Ladies Reading Club." Ladies Reading Club Collection. Houston Metropolitan Archives. Houston Public Library.

_____. 1921. Text of speech (read 29 November 1921). Ladies Reading Club Collection, box 2, folder 9. Houston Metropolitan Archives. Houston Public Library.

_____. N.d. "Club Life and Women's Review." Ladies Reading Club Collection, box 11. Houston Metropolitan Archives. Houston Public Library.

MacKnight, Kate Cassatt. 1906. "Report of the Civic Committee." *Annals of the American Academy of Political and Social Sciences* 28, no. 2: 287–98.

Martin, Theodore Penny. 1987. *The Sound of Our Own Voices: Women's Study Clubs 1860–1910.* Boston: Beacon Press.

Matthews, V. H. 1973. "Adult Reading Studies: Their Implications for Private, Professional, and Public Policy." *Library Trends* 22, no. 2 (October): 149–76.

May, Elaine Tyler. 1999. *Homeward Bound: American Families in the Cold War Era.* Rev. and updated ed. New York: Basic Books.

McElroy, E. W. 1968a. "Subject Variety in Adult Reading: I. Factors Related to Variety in Reading." *Library Quarterly* 38, no. 1 (April): 164–66.

_____. 1968b. "Subject Variety in Adult Reading: II. Characteristics of Readers of Ten Categories of Books." *Library Quarterly* 38, no. 2 (July): 261–69.

McHenry, Elizabeth Ann. 1999. "Rereading Literary Legacy: New Considerations of the 19th-Century African-American Reader and Writer." *Callaloo* 22, no. 2: 477–95.

_____. 2002. *Forgotten Readers: Recovering the Lost History of African-American Literary Societies.* Durham, N.C.: Duke University Press.

McLuhan, Marshall. 1962. *The Gutenberg Galaxy: The Making of Typographic Man.* Toronto: University of Toronto Press.

McLuhan, Marshall, and Bruce R. Powers. 1989. *The Global Village: Transformations in World Life and Media in the 21st Century.* New York: Oxford University Press.

McNett, Gavin. 1999. "Preaching to the Converted." *Salon Books,* 12 November. www.salon.com/books/feature/1999/11/12/oprah.cpm/index/html.

Melich, Tanya. 1996. *The Republican War against Women: An Insider's Report from Behind the Lines.* New York: Bantam Books.

Messer-Davidow, Ellen. 1997. "Whither Cultural Studies?" In *From Sociology to Cultural Studies,* ed. Elizabeth Long, 489–522. Malden, Mass., and Oxford: Blackwell.

Metzger, Philip Allen. 1984. "Publishing and the Book Trade in Austin, Texas, 1870–1920." Ph.D. dissertation, University of Texas at Austin.

Meyerowitz, Joanne. 1994. *Not June Cleaver: Women and Gender in Postwar America, 1945– 1960.* Philadelphia: Temple University Press.

Mills, C. Wright. 1959. *The Sociological Imagination.* London, Oxford, and New York: Oxford University Press.

Newton, Adam Zachary. 1995. *Narrative Ethics.* Cambridge: Harvard University Press.

Newton, Judith, Mary Ryan, and Judith Walkowitz. 1983. *Sex and Class in Women's History.* London and Boston: Routledge and Kegan Paul.

The New Yorker Twenty-fifth Anniversary Album. 1950. New York: Harper.

Nussbaum, Martha. 1986. *The Fragility of Goodness: Luck and Ethics in Greek Tragedy and Philosophy.* Cambridge and New York: Cambridge University Press.

———. 1990. *Love's Knowledge: Essays on Philosophy and Literature.* Oxford: Oxford University Press.

———. 1995. *Poetic Justice: The Literary Imagination and Public Life.* Boston: Beacon Press.

Ohmann, Richard. 1976. *English in America: A Radical View of the Profession.* New York: Oxford University Press.

———. 1987. *Politics of Letters.* Middletown, Conn.: Wesleyan University Press.

Ong, Walter J. 1967. *The Presence of the Word: Some Prolegomena for Cultural and Religious History.* New Haven: Yale University Press.

———. 1982. *Orality and Literacy: The Technologizing of the Word.* London and New York: Methuen.

Pope, Alexander. 1711. *An Essay on Criticism.* London: Lewis. Facsimile edition at www.geocities.com/Athens/Trot/5201/Essay2.htm.

Porter, Dorothy B. 1936. "The Organized Educational Activities of Negro Literary Societies, 182–1846." *Journal of Negro Education* 5: 555–76.

Press, Andrea L. 1991. *Women Watching Television: Gender, Class, and Generation in the American Television Experience.* Philadelphia: University of Pennsylvania Press.

Putnam, Robert. 1993. *Making Democracy Work: Civic Traditions in Modern Italy.* Princeton: Princeton University Press.

———. 1995. "Bowling Alone: America's Declining Social Capital." *Journal of Democracy* 6, no. 1: 65–78.

———. 1996. "The Strange Disappearance of Civic America." *American Prospect* 24 (winter): 34–48.

———. 2000. *Bowling Alone: The Collapse and Revival of American Community.* New York: Simon and Schuster.

Radway, Janice. 1984. *Reading the Romance: Women, Patriarchy, and Popular Literature.* Chapel Hill: University of North Carolina Press.

———. 1997. *A Feeling for Books: The Book-of-the-Month Club, Literary Taste, and the Middle-Class Desire.* Chapel Hill: University of North Carolina Press.

———. 2001. "On the Sociability of Reading: Books, Self-fashioning, and the Creation of Communities." Manuscript.

Resnick, Daniel P., and Lauren B. Resnick. 1989. "Varieties of Literacy." In *Social History and Human Consciousness: Some Interdisciplinary Connections,* ed. Andrew E. Barnes and Peter N. Stearns, 171–96. New York and London: New York University Press.

Ring, Mrs. H. F. 1924. "A Paper Delivered by Mrs. H. F. Ring to the State Federation about 1924." Ladies Reading Club Collection, Houston Metropolitan Archives. Houston Public Library.

Rosaldo, Michelle. 1974. "Woman, Culture, and Society: A Theoretical Overview." In *Woman, Culture and Society,* ed. Michelle Rosaldo and Louise Lamphere, 43–66. Palo Alto, Calif.: Stanford University Press.

Rosaldo, Renato. 1988. "Ideology, Place and People without Culture." *Cultural Anthropology* 3, no. 1 (February): 77–87.

Rose, Jonathan. 2001. *The Intellectual Life of the British Working Class.* New Haven: Yale University Press.

Rosenberg, Rosalind. 1992. *Divided Lives: American Women in the Twentieth Century.* New York: Hill and Wang.

Rupp, Leila, and Verta Taylor. 1987. *Survival in the Doldrums: The American Women's Rights Movement, 1945 to the 1960s.* New York: Oxford University Press.

Ryan, Mary. 1990. *Women in Public: From Banners to Ballots, 1825–1880.* Baltimore: Johns Hopkins University Press.

Schudson, Michael. 1996. "What if Civic Life Didn't Die?" *American Prospect* 25 (March–April): 17–20.

———. 1998. *The Good Citizen: A History of American Civic Life.* New York: Martin Kessler Books.

Schutz, Alfred. 1964. *Collected Papers II: Studies in Social Theory.* The Hague: Martinus Nijhoff.

Scott, Anne Firor. 1984. *Making the Invisible woman Visible.* Urbana: University of Illinois Press.

———. 1991. *Natural Allies: Women's Associations in American History.* Urbana: University of Illinois Press.

Seaholm, Megan. 1988. "Earnest Women: The White Women's Movement in Progressive Era Texas, 1880–1920." Ph.D. dissertation, Rice University.

Sedo, DeNel. 2002. "Badges of Wisdom, Spaces for Being: A Social History of Women's Reading Groups." Ph.D. dissertation, University of British Columbia.

Sennett, Richard, and Jonathan Cobb. 1973. *The Hidden Injuries of Class.* New York: Knopf.

"She's All Chat." 1999. On Salon Brilliant Careers. http://www.salon.com/people/bc/1999/05/04/oprah/

Sicherman, Barbara. 1995. "Reading *Little Women:* The Many Lives of a Text." In *U.S. History as Women's History: New Feminist Essays,* ed. Linda K. Kerber, Alice Kessler-Harris, and Kathryn Klish Sklar, 245–66. Chapel Hill and London: University of North Carolina Press.

Skocpol, Theda. 1992. *Protecting Soldiers and Mothers: The Political Origins of Social Policy in the United States.* Cambridge: Harvard University Press.

———. 1996. "Unravelling from Above." *American Prospect* 25 (March–April): 20–25.

———. 1999. "Associations without Members." *American Prospect* 10, no. 45 (July–August): 66–73.

Skocpol, Theda, and Morris P. Fiorina, eds. 1999. *Civic Engagement in American Democracy.* Washington, D.C.: Brookings Institution Press; New York: Russell Sage Foundation.

Slezak, Ellen. 1995. *The Book Group Book: A Thoughtful Guide to Forming and Enjoying a Stimulating Book Discussion Group.* 2d ed. Chicago: Chicago Review Press.

Smith, Barbara Herrnstein. 1988. *Contingencies of Value: Alternative Perspectives for Critical Theory.* Cambridge: Harvard University Press.

Smith-Rosenberg, Carroll. 1985. "The Female World of Love and Ritual." In *Disorderly Conduct: Visions of Gender in Victorian America,"* 53–76. New York: Knopf.

Solinger, Rickie. 1992. *Wake Up Little Susie: Single Pregnancy and Race before Roe v. Wade.* New York: Routledge.

Stack, Carol B. 1974. *All Our Kin: Strategies for Survival in a Black Community.* New York: Harper and Row.

Stansell, Christine. 2000. *American Moderns: Bohemian New York and the Creation of a New Century.* New York: Metropolitan Books.

Stearns, Peter N. 1979. *Be a Man! Males in Modern Society.* New York: Holmes and Meier Publishers.

Stock, Brian. 1983. *The Implications of Literacy: Written Language and Models of Interpretation in the Eleventh and Twelfth Centuries.* Princeton: Princeton University Press.

Swidler, Anne. 1986. "Culture in Action: Symbols and Strategies." *American Sociological Review,* 273–86.

Tannen, Deborah. 1990. *You Just Don't Understand: Women and Men in Conversation.* New York: William Morrow and Company.

Terrell, Mrs. J. C. 1903. "Succinct History of the Women's Club Movement in Texas." *Dallas Morning News,* 22 November, 17.

Texas Federation of Women's Clubs. 1904–5. *Yearbook.* Dallas: M. P. Exline Co.

Thompson, E. P. 1972. *The Making of the English Working Class.* Harmondsworth, U.K.: Penguin.

Thorne, Barrie, and Nancy Henley, eds. 1975. *Language and Sex: Difference and Domination.* Rowley, Mass.: Newbury House.

Thorne, Barrie, Cheris Kramarae, and Nancy Henley, eds. 1983. *Language, Gender, and Society.* Rowley, Mass.: Newbury House.

Tolstoy, Leo N. 1964 [1857]. *Childhood, Boyhood, Youth.* Trans. Rosemary Edmonds. Harmondsworth, U.K.: Penguin.

Tompkins, Jane P. 1980. *Reader-Response Criticism: From Formalism to Post-Structuralism.* Baltimore: Johns Hopkins University Press.

———. 1985. *Sensational Designs: The Cultural Work of American Fiction, 1790–1860.* New York: Oxford University Press.

———. 1992. *West of Everything: The Inner Life of Westerns.* New York: Oxford University Press.

Tornius, Valerian. 1929. *Salons: Pictures of Society through Five Centuries.* Trans. Agnes Platt and Lilian Wonderley. New York: Cosmopolitan Book Corporation.

U.S. Department of Commerce. 2001. *Statistical Abstract of the United States.* Washington, D.C.: Government Printing Office.

U.S. Department of Labor. Bureau of Labor Statistics. 2001. *Current Population Survey.* Washington, D.C.: Government Printing Office.

Valelly, Richard. 1996. Couch-Potato Democracy? *American Prospect* 25 (March–April): 25–26.

Ware, Susan. 1993. *Still Missing: Amelia Earhart and the Search for Modern Feminism.* New York: W. W. Norton.

244

Welter, Barbara. 1966. "The Cult of True Womanhood: 1820–1860." *American Quarterly* 18 (summer): 151–74.

White, Allon. 1993. *Carnival, Hysteria, and Writing: Collected Essays and Autobiography.* Oxford: Clarendon Press.

White, Martha E. 1903. "The Work of the Woman's Club." *Atlantic Monthly* 93, no. 559.

Whyte, William Foote. 1943. *Street Corner Society: The Social Structure of an Italian Slum.* Chicago: University of Chicago Press.

Wiener, Lynn. 1985. *From Working Girl to Working Mother: The Female Labor Force in the United States, 1820–1980.* Chapel Hill: University of North Carolina Press.

Wilhelmy, Petra. 1989. *Der Berliner Salon im 19. Jahrhundert (1780–1914).* Berlin: Walter de Gruyter.

Williams, Raymond. 1973. *The Country and the City.* New York: Oxford University Press.

———. 1977. *Marxism and Literature.* Oxford: Oxford University Press.

———. 1983. *Writing in Society.* London: Verso.

Willis, Paul. 1977. *Learning to Labor: How Working Class Kids Get Working Class Jobs.* New York: Columbia University Press.

Winslow, Helen M. 1906. *The President of Quex: A Woman's Club Story.* Boston: Lathrop, Lee and Shepard.

———. 1908. "Story of the Women's Club Movement." *New England Magazine* 38 (July).

Wood, Mary I. 1910. "The Woman's Club Movement." *Chatauquan* 59, no. 1.

———. 1912. *History of the General Federation of Women's Club.* New York: Norwood Press.

Yankelovich, Skelly, and White, Inc. 1978. *Consumer Research Study in Reading and Book Purchasing.* BISG Report No. 6. Book Industry Study Group.

Zelizer, Viviana. 1985. *Pricing the Priceless Child: The Changing Social Value of Children.* New York: Basic Books.

Ziegler, Jesse A. N.d. "Looscan Home Was Reading Club's Birthplace." Ladies Reading Club Collection, box 11. Houston Metropolitan Archives. Houston Public Library.

INDEX

Academic Writing as Social Practice (Brodkey), 1

African American women's reading groups: in history of literary club movement, 228n.3; and Oprah's book club, 202, 225n.2; separation of book clubs along race, 49, 54, 229n.16. *See also* women's reading groups

Anderson, Benedict, 32

Barnes and Noble, 193–96. *See also* chain bookstores

Beecher, Catherine, 43, 229n.12

Bellah, Robert, 227n.9

Bernstein, Basil, 129

best-seller lists, 122

Blair, Karen J., 44, 45, 49, 229nn. 14, 16, 17

Bleich, David, 225n.1

book-centered model of reading: book's capacity to form character, 25–26; the ethical quality of narrative, 26, 27; ethical sensibility derived from reading, 24–25; missing consideration of the individual reader, 28, 29–30; reader as a witness to moral dilemmas of another person, 27; understood as a transfer of information, 21–22. *See also* reader-centered model of reading

book discussion: atmosphere of trust evident in, 187; avoidance of structured literary analysis, 147–48; cultural behavior of middlebrow readers with respect to values, 149; expanding of participants' ability to understand and empathize with different worlds, 152; focus on voluntary participation in an enjoyable leisure activity, 147–48;

group homogeneity and, 162–63; importance of sharing different perspectives, 146–47; individual's reliance on formative social experiences, 163; intimacy engendered by, 111; lack of formal structure as an aid to, 145–46; lack of requirement for closure or agreement, 146–47; literary value of a book tied to what readers can relate to, 147–48, 153; member departures due to quality of discussion, 137–39; organization of, 105–7; personal enrichment from process of, 110–11; readers' ideology of instruction and self-improvement, 152; realism as viewed and required by readers, 151–52; resistance to judging literature on formal aesthetic rather than personal value, 149–51; rules used or assumed, 107–8; social movements spurred by, 33–34; value of discussion itself to readers, 187, 188. *See also* characters in books and discussions; classics and book discussions; readers' subjective approach to books

book reviews, influence of on book selection, 122

book selection: and character of the group, 114, 125; for coed nights, 113; by consensus, 99–102, 104; in early clubs, 41–43; by formal methods, 97–99; groups' reframing of evaluative hierarchy, 127–28; importance from a scholarly view, 115; by individual choice, 103–4, 105; literary worth linked to worthwhile discussion, 126–27, 128–30; marketplace influences on, 116–17; as a process of self-definition or cultural